Praise for *No Hiding Place*

"*No Hiding Place* is a must-read. It is not just for people who are interested in drug use and abuse. It's a book for people who are interested in people. Through an honest presentation of self-evaluation and change in his life, Cecil Williams shows readers the path to change in their own lives. Cecil Williams could have remained an ordinary minister. Instead, he chose to reach out and make a difference. Glide Memorial Church and its programs are testimony to the greatness he had achieved—and we can achieve—through doing for others."

> —Mother Clara Hale, founder of Hale House
> Center in Harlem, NYC, and Dr. Lorraine
> Hale, her daughter

"*No Hiding Place* allows the reader to share Cecil's journey to claim his power, define his purpose, and harvest the fruit of a seed planted many years ago when his grandfather, Papa Jack, declared 'himself to a world that considered him beneath respect.' I recognize this journey. . . . This is a wonderful book."

> —Willie L. Brown, Jr., California
> Assemblyman, Speaker of the House

"Cecil Williams is an extraordinary man. He is leading the way for community transformation by recognizing the need for change and doing something about it. As the pastor of Glide Memorial Church in San Francisco, Williams has created something far greater than a church on the corner of Ellis and Taylor streets. He has created a community which lives up to the words emblazoned on Glide's walls: Justice, Dignity, Peace, and Self-Affirmation. Cecil Williams is a man who has made a real difference, and he serves as an inspiration to us all."

> —Dianne Feinstein, former mayor of
> San Francisco

"The church is a sleeping giant serving more as an escape than a meaningful response to the new slavery of addiction which is devastating our communities. Cecil Williams's recovery theology has helped awaken the church to its role and responsibility in the battle against addiction. *No Hiding Place* serves as both an inspiration and a guide for the church's response to addiction at the community level using culturally and racially relevant models of recovery. Based on the very successful program developed at Glide Church, this model can be used in every community in the United States faced with a drug problem."

> —David E. Smith, founder and medical
> director of the Haight Ashbury
> Free Clinics

No Hiding Place

▲ ▲ ▲

EMPOWERMENT AND RECOVERY
FOR OUR TROUBLED COMMUNITIES

Cecil Williams

WITH REBECCA LAIRD

HarperSanFrancisco
A Division of HarperCollins*Publishers*

FIRST EDITION

Library of Congress Cataloging-in-Publication Data

Williams, Cecil, 1929–
    No hiding place : empowerment and recovery for our troubled
communities / Cecil Williams with Rebecca Laird. — 1st ed.
      p. cm.
    ISBN 0-06-250967-5 (alk. paper)
    1. Church work with narcotic addicts—California—San Francisco.
2. Glide Memorial United Methodist Church (San Francisco, Calif.)
3. Williams, Cecil, 1929—   . I. Laird, Rebecca. II. Title.
BV4460.3.W55   1992
261.8'3229'0973—dc20   91-58987
                                                                CIP

92   93   94   95   96 ❖ HAD   10   9   8   7   6   5   4   3   2   1

This edition is printed on acid-free and recycled paper that meets the American National Standards Institute Z39.48 Standard.

▲ ▲ ▲

To my wife, Janice Mirikitani,
who would not let me hide

Contents

▲ ▲ ▲

(A section of photographs follows chapter 2.)

▲ ▲ ▲

Acknowledgments

Writing this book has been a communal act of mutuality. Many members of Glide's extended family have played active parts in this story of struggle, recovery, and empowerment.

We want especially to honor the New Generation of graduates from the Facts on Crack program. Their lives prove that telling the truth and living in the Spirit lead to freedom.

Throughout this book several individuals have dared to tell the hard truths about their lives. Those who are highlighted are representative of hundreds like them who have also experienced recovery and empowerment.

We are especially indebted to Edna, Janice, Janet, Eric, Janean, Jamal, and Mark. They are truly heroes for willingly declaring that there is no hiding place.

Other individuals provided additional background and details for this story as we retraced the progression of the recovery programs. We especially appreciate Tony, Carol, Charles, and Traci for freely offering their time and wisdom.

The staff at Glide willingly added the responsibilities of this book to an already heavy work load. The extra effort has not gone unnoticed.

A special word of gratitude is due to staff members Roscoe Allen, Leon Bacchues, Cleo Fast, Eddie Franks, Edward Jackson, Rosa Johnson, Jean Jackson, Jackie Keys, Etta Page, David Richmond, Allen White, and Glo Wright.

The publishing staff at Harper San Francisco pursued the vision of this book and put us together as a writing team. We thank Clayton Carlson, publisher, for his many years of professional support. Lonnie Hull, John Shopp, and Beth Weber served as the committed editorial team. To the many members of the production and marketing departments we also acknowledge your essential contributions.

Last, both of our families believed in this book and actively encouraged, contributed, edited, and cheered us on. To Cecil's immediate family, Janice Mirikitani, Tianne Miller, Albert Williams, and Kim Williams, and to Rebecca's next of kin, Michael Christensen and Rachel Laird Christensen, we acknowledge your unrelenting love with thanks.

Cecil Williams
Rebecca Laird
July 1992

▲　▲　▲

I went to the rock to hide my face.
The rock cried out, "No hidin' place."

It's Recovery Time

When I first planted my feet at the intersection of despair and hope, want and plenty in San Francisco nearly thirty years ago, I was already a minister in revolt. The complacency of the church, the passivity of the saints, and all those angelic smiles about the sweet by-and-by made me angry.

Long ago I decided I wanted my abundant life here, right here in this life. I looked in the Bible—I really did—and I found that the Jesus I know, the one who liberates oppressed people, is written about in those pages. The Jesus in Luke 4:11 says he came to preach the good news to the poor. The good news the poor want to hear is that they are free now. They are free from hunger, free from substandard housing, free from the need to use or sell drugs to survive. The Jesus I read about in Luke isn't going about saving folks for another life, by and by. Jesus liberates, here, now.

For decades, I have raised my voice against injustice and have shaken my fist at death. Sometimes I sound like a broken, soulful record that goes 'round and 'round singing and shouting through the urban wilderness, "Choose life. You have the power. Act like you are alive."

In 1969, after I had been four years at Glide Memorial United Methodist Church, I took down the huge white cross fastened to the white walls of our downtown sanctuary. Many of the members recoiled in fear. Was this a blasphemous action? Was I *craaaazy?*

That cross, a symbol of death, created a problem. The people were worshiping it, and they acted dead. Something was wrong. Jesus came to give us life, to bring us freedom, to empower us, and to bring us together. And most of those folks flocked in on Sundays to worship death, duty, security, and exclusivity.

Something had to be done. I changed my title to minister of liberation. I opened the doors and invited everyone of every color and creed to come inside. I was serious about bringing freedom and release to the church. I said then that if religion means anything at all, it means you put your life where you say you're going to put it and do what you have to do instead of just talking about it all the time. Because if your doing doesn't dance with your saying, you haven't chosen life.

This all happened in the 1960s while San Francisco was becoming a psychedelic, experimental city as it played host to swarms of beaded, beaten-down, and tie-dyed flower children. Hippies, drug addicts, those tripping on LSD and pot found their way to Glide Church. Our church was one of the few churches that had joined with them in the rebellion against the status quo. Some came to eat the daily meals Glide served and fewer to ask for help at the Crisis Center. Others were simply gathering one more experience to add to their bouquets of freaked-out happenings.

During that decade of revolution, I worked on the corner of Ellis and Taylor streets, where Glide stands. I played a part and touched lives with people of all colors, races, and perspectives.

I thought I had seen it all, but in the late 1980s, something toxic and lethal settled on the street. I began to smell death. The Tenderloin neighborhood looked much the same. Flophouses, dealers, pimps, and the refuse of humanity lined the streets—nothing new about that. The cops on the Tenderloin beat told me what I already knew. If I threw a stone from the side door of Glide across Boeddeker Park, it would land on the block that lays claim to the highest crime rate in the city. But it wasn't the spiraling crime rate that smelled so bad; something else was stinking up the neighborhood.

I began to see women, many young mothers, strung out on Crack cocaine, straggling through Boeddeker Park. They'd pull along their little children who were so dispirited they didn't even want to play in the concrete play yard. The mothers were holding the hands of their children as they all meandered down a path of despair. Crack cocaine was causing that stench of death.

Sometimes corporate leaders, civic achievers, and monied visitors would ask me to come to their banquets and conferences held at the upscale hotels nearby. Other times monied visitors invited me over when they were done shopping the boutiques on Union Square. When I walked past the slick doormen and into the posh lobbies, I hoped that I would find some life.

Yet even the smell of fresh floral arrangements and quarts of brass polish couldn't mask the smell of death that had infiltrated the whole neighborhood. We'd talk about the city, its problems, and what would fix all the trouble. But I have to tell you, when I looked at those leaders and achievers, I saw many whose eyes were bleary from alcohol. The rank odor of death clung to the white-collar people, too. Behind drawn blinds they were drinking too many nightcaps. The smell was the same. The death of addiction pervaded the halls of plenty, too.

I went to church functions and denominational meetings. People would smile and say, "Hi, Cecil. How you doin'?" Behind the friendly expressions, the smell of alcohol escaped from their breath. The smell of death was even at church with ministers all around.

During this time, my phone kept ringing. Ringing, ringing, ringing. I'd listen to the desperate voices as I surveyed the pictures of Martin Luther King, Jr., Malcolm X, Desmond Tutu, and Maya Angelou hung on the walls of my rose-toned office. I looked at the faces of those who fought for freedom and equality and shook my head in disbelief. Had our fighting been in vain?

All those phone calls were about a new slavery—the slavery of addiction. I took calls from friends in high places, benefactors of Glide, people who had the very best of everything. They asked, "Cecil, what should I do? My kids are strung out on cocaine." The smell of death even permeated the neighborhoods of plenty.

One phone call brought me some hope. William Bennett of the Bush administration invited me, some other community leaders, and drug treatment experts to Washington, D.C. As the newly appointed "drug czar," Bennett was soliciting input as he formulated a national drug policy.

Maybe the Feds were serious this time. Maybe they could smell the stench of death, too.

I flew to Washington, D.C. The Capitol building teemed with promises of increased resources and dedication to winning the war on drugs. How would this war be won? The Feds already had a plan. The Feds pounded their answers down on me and the others with a heavy-handed gavel. Enforcement was the only way.

There would be more money allocated for more jails, more cops, and more guns. That meant more black youth would sleep in concrete jail cells with bars for doors. Already one out of four black men in their twenties sits in prison or waits with his life in limbo on probation or parole. How many more did the Feds want to round up?

I knew the people that drug enforcement wanted to put behind bars were the children of poor black communities already burdened by the weight of despair. They wanted our children. They wanted to imprison our future.

Those of us who had lived in drug-ridden places awhile knew this New Generation of troubled young people needed a way out of poverty that promised more than the fool's-gold glitter of fast money skimmed from dealing drugs. The last thing this New Generation needed was more steel bars to cage them in like animals. All of the African American leaders gathered in Washington, D.C., knew that the kids from affluence who might get caught with Crack would find a way to buy their way out of prison. Statistics proved that those who do the most prison time are those with the least money.

Something quickened in me that day as I sat in William Bennett's office. The Feds, once again, would not provide the help desperately needed by the African American community. They were fighting a war on drugs. They had invited community leaders to come and talk, but they were really listening to the voters who were peeking out from their clean windows and looking at the world from across their mowed lawns. The Feds were writing a drug policy to pacify those afraid of losing their security. Those with money and influence had convinced the Feds that the evil lurks in the poor neighborhoods. Fight the battle there, they demanded; that is where the enemy lives.

This federal policy would be meted out in heavy blows on the backs of black youth. The war on drugs would be another way the folks in power would beat down and imprison the blacks and the poor.

Then and there in the Capitol building, I stood up. I couldn't help it. I raised my voice and shook my fist, "You are interested in a policy of enforcement. We are interested in a public health policy that puts priority on recovery and treatment programs."

I knew then that the black community had to face Crack on our own, using the tools of faith and resistance that broke down slavery and public racial discrimination in earlier generations. The Feds were not fighting our war.

We knew that drugs were not the new slave master. Drugs were not the real enemy; addiction was. The war to be won was against addiction. And the way to fight addiction was to offer recovery programs—offer support, jobs, and a new, empowered way of living.

I tried to tell the Feds that fighting drugs with force was like fighting slavery by sending the slave ships to another port. The ships would find a place to unload their profitable cargo. Force further punishes those who are field hands in the drug trade. Force doesn't touch the slave masters—the real drug traffickers. Force would do nothing to help the millions already enslaved, bent over in the urban drug fields, with no hope of freedom.

After I came home from Washington, I got together with my folks, the staff at Glide. We decided we'd call together a national network of black leaders. Nobody else could walk this road of fighting addiction with faith, resistance, and recovery for us. We would have to recruit and equip a nonviolent army of civic leaders, medical professionals, representatives from the criminal justice system, recovering addicts, ministers, and concerned citizens. On April 12–14, 1989, 1,100 people pushed through the doors of the newly refurbished Hilton Hotel across Taylor Street from Glide. They came to attend *The Death of a Race: The Black Family/Community and Crack Cocaine National Conference.* People flew in from everywhere. Coretta Scott King came from Atlanta. Mother Hale and her daughter, Dr. Lorraine Hale, traveled from Harlem. Willie Brown rushed in from Sacramento. Officials converged from New York City, Detroit, New Orleans, St. Louis, and Nashville. Others walked across Taylor Street from Glide. But it's funny—no one heeded the invitations we sent to Pennsylvania Avenue.

All of those gathered stood up together. The Glide staff, black community leaders, addicts, prostitutes, and grandmothers—poor and wealthy, illiterate and educated—we told our stories of recovery. We told our stories of faith and our stories of resistance.

Conferees studied models for recovery and shared the bits about recovery they knew with one another. As we put our heads together, we snapped a few corner pieces together in the puzzle of recovery.

As the conference ended, I declared, "We all came to a conference called *The Death of a Race.* Now we are going home to march for the life of a New Generation.

"Let's arrest drugs, not our kids. This is a war on addiction. Nobody ought to be looking for any quick fixes when it comes to this war that we are facing. It's going to take time. It's certainly going to take commitment. It's going to take us reclaiming our children, rejecting no one, and coming together to honestly tell the story of how it is for us."

The conference concluded and the folks scattered. We all began working on strategies to win back our own homes, our own neighborhoods, our own turf, and our own families. Having exchanged names and telephone numbers with others committed to the same cause, we kept the phone company busy.

Here at Glide we hung out a banner visible to all who pass by that declares *It's Recovery Time*. From the time of our first national conference we determined that everything we do, every program, and every Celebration service at Glide must live up to that banner.

Today the stench of death is not the most powerful scent around Glide. Those hardened by addiction, abuse, and despair are beginning to unearth, dig up, and plow through being honest and telling the hard truth about their lives. Even in this neighborhood of decay, it is springtime. There is a fresh smell of newly plowed soil. We're alive!

That's the story we have to tell. Since 1989 hundreds of Crack addicts have come to Glide to plant faith in themselves, sow belief in the Spirit, cultivate resistance to death and addiction, and celebrate recovery and life.

Choosing Recovery

Glide has two doorways that lead inside. The front entrance on Taylor Street leads directly to the sanctuary and is usually barred during the week. Monday through Friday we store donated bread, produce, and food staples in the church lobby.

Seven days a week the side entrance on Ellis Street serves as a universal gateway for three thousand people who come to Glide each day. Just inside the door, free meal tickets are handed out for breakfast, lunch, and dinner. An attendant just a few steps farther inside behind a counter points others to one of our six floors. People fan out throughout the building to recovery meetings, crisis care, social services, counseling, support groups, job training, computer classes, drug and pregnancy testing, HIV/AIDS information, child care, and church information.

To the right of the Ellis Street door is the Celebration office where three receptionists answer the constantly ringing phone and host those wishing to see me, or Janice Mirikitani, the director of programs and president of the Glide Foundation, or David Richmond, the deputy director of programs.

From the first floor to the sixth, each office and meeting room at Glide is inhabited by recovering people. They are dealing with some habit or substance they have used to block their feelings. People everywhere around Glide are talking about and living recovery one day at a time. Each day when folks walk through the door at Glide, they are choosing recovery; they are choosing life.

A Church in Recovery

On Sunday mornings more than fifteen hundred people enter the Glide sanctuary. People dressed well enough for lunch at the Hilton sit next to those who are wearing their only set of clothes and, by the smell of it, have been for days. A woman wearing a broad-brimmed hat with satin sash will be seated next to a woman wearing a low-backed sweater that reveals her black panther tattoo. The first woman drove from Marin County across the Golden Gate Bridge, while the second woman walked up the block from working one of the nearby hotels. Both are women in recovery, and both have found acceptance at Glide.

We estimate that 80 percent of the people who come to Glide are actively working on recovery of some kind. At Glide we've come to know recovery as a process in which everyone participates. We as a church have come to grips with the fact that we minister and live in a society of addicts.

When you become obsessed with anything to the extent that you rely on it for your grasp on reality, you are addicted. Some of us are addicted to substances like drugs, alcohol, cigarettes, or food. Some of us are addicted to relationships—we hang on when we should let go. Some of us are even addicted to religion—we crave being absolutely right about what we believe, and we think that everyone else has to become like us. Toxic relationships, toxic substances, and toxic faith are all addictions from which we need recovery in order to live fully.

I define recovery as the beginning of an experience by which we begin to discover the real meaning of our lives. Recovery is a process we have learned to live by at Glide. We discover that each moment is a choice between life and death. Everyone at Glide can tell you about his or her choices for life. Take a walk through Glide and keep your ears open. You will hear amazing things. Some would call them miracles.

Recovery Values

The recovery process at Glide is culturally based. Most of the Crack addicts who come to Glide are African Americans. As we've learned together over the years, we've found that recovery is both a miracle of healing and a movement for social change for our people.

One of the first things we learned about fighting the war on addiction was that traditional drug treatment programs didn't work for most African Americans. We needed something new. As a community we would honestly have to recognize our own problems and define our troubles in a way that took seriously our culture, our history, and our ways of relating to one another. This would be a new kind of drama—a drama of recovery written just for people like us.

Many people who came to Glide had tried and been helped to some degree by attending Twelve-Step groups that followed the principles first used by Alcoholics Anonymous. But the Twelve Steps didn't help many blacks. We wondered why. When people declared that the Twelve Steps were the only way to become drug-free, it sent a message to blacks: There is nothing missing from the Twelve Steps; something must be wrong with you.

We knew that as a race we weren't inherently incapable of recovery. Over time, as we talked we came to understand that while we could learn from the Twelve-Step program, some of its values contradicted African American values. That's why we didn't find the help we sought.

The Twelve Steps focus on individual recovery, as if independently getting clean and sober were the ultimate goal. But African Americans are a communal people—we fight for our freedom together. A recovery program that focuses mainly on the individual doesn't jibe to a people whose identity rests in belonging to an extended family and being a member of the black community.

And besides, when the Crack addicts attended Twelve-step meetings, they often were the only people of color. They felt isolated and alone. We must acknowledge our need for one another.

The people at Glide have observed that the Twelve-Step programs have been the most successful with middle- and working-class people. These programs teach people to get clean and sober and to go back out into mainstream society. Well, the only society many of our folks needing recovery know is the drug mix—they've never been in the mainstream. Many of our folks need to get clean and sober and to learn how to empower their lives and make their way in a world that is less than welcoming to many of us.

Also, the Twelve-Step programs honor anonymity as a means to protect people. To a black person who has felt invisible and unheard all of his or her life, being anonymous is already a familiar way of life. For many, protecting one's identity serves to cut the recovery meetings off from the rest of one's life. Many of those who come to Glide have no everyday lives. They don't have homes, jobs, or reputations to protect. For them, anonymity is one more way to remain faceless and hidden in society.

As long as blacks, women, and poor people remain anonymous, they remain invisible and unheard. When these same people speak the truth out loud, when they tell everyone who they are and what they have experienced, they reclaim their lives and a place in the world. They declare, "I am here. I am someone. My life matters." By telling their stories, they proclaim, "This is the truth about my life. My secrets and my addiction no longer have power over me. I am free."

What we need to recover is to speak up, to tell our stories, to claim the truth about our lives before anyone and everyone. We need to become faithful to our heritage as a race of storytellers. African Americans are oral people who pass on our history through stories. To us, anonymity feels like a place to hide. We believe there is no hiding place in recovery. We must open up and stand together.

Then there is the adage in the Twelve Steps that says "we must admit we are powerless." Well, people of color, women, and homeless folks have always known they were powerless. When some white person stands up and reads the first Step in a Twelve-Step meeting, a black person hears the call to powerlessness as one more command to lie down and take it.

At Glide we realized that together we would have to come up with a recovery program that worked for us. We told our stories to one another, and as the First Generation of folks in recovery began to reenact the scripts of their own lives, we noticed that each of us acted out four acts on the way to healing and freedom. Each person performed acts of recognition, self-definition, rebirth, and community. These four acts began to form the basis of our recovery program.

The Drama of Recovery

Recognition is the first act in the drama of recovery. Each of us must recognize the cunning characteristics of addiction, admit our true feelings, and face whatever pain we've tried to hide through our addictions. No secret is too terrible, no memory is too horrible, no rejection is too harsh. With courage, and in the company of others, we can tell the truth. There is nothing in any of our lives that others haven't faced in some way themselves. We share a common humanity and need for one another. We don't need drugs when we come to recognize ourselves and be honest with one another.

When we admit there is no hiding place, we walk back onto the open stage of life where we must stand up and tell the truth about our lives. We become the writers of our own scripts, the directors of our own dramas of recovery. We claim the power to change our own lives. Although we do have the power, we can't change ourselves all alone. We need one another and our faith.

Folks addicted to Crack start with so little self-esteem that success in most recovery programs seems impossible. At Glide we begin with the premise that because you are addicted doesn't mean you are a bad or worthless person. You've just got a problem and need some help and lots of support.

Self-definition is the second act in the drama of recovery. When each one of us begins to determine for ourselves who we are, then we are engaged in the act of self-definition. We must learn to name ourselves in the midst of the confusion of the world. When we each claim the responsibility for our own lives and the power that lies within each of us to determine how we will live, then we begin to name ourselves, no matter what is going on around us. No matter how heavy the drug culture may be in our neighborhood, no matter how many dealers wait in front of our apartment houses, no matter how many times they knock on our doors trying to sell us their deadly wares, by knowing who we are we can get beyond the confusion and the noise.

The names we call ourselves matter. People with drug problems must decide, "Am I an addict or a recovering person?" "Am I a helpless, weak-willed addict or a person who has anesthetized great inner pain with drugs?"

At Glide a strong sense of self-definition allows those in recovery to cry out to one another: "Don't buy their rocks. Don't listen to them when they call you by your false names: addict, basehead, toss up, whore. Stop buying their lies about you. Rename yourself. Be yourself. Be authentic and natural. Stop worrying about what others have to say about you. Listen to the voice inside of you that is telling you the truth. You have a void inside that needs to be filled. Now how are you going to fill it? With Crack or with community? With sex or with real intimacy? With lying or with honesty? With hustling or with authenticity? Only you can decide. What do you have to say about you? Who do you say that you are?" These are the questions of self-definition.

Rebirth is the third act in the drama of recovery. Rebirth happens when we go beyond wearing our real names like name tags and start living from the inside out. When we start facing the pain and telling the truth, the Spirit begins to flow again. We discover that we would rather shoot hope than dope into our veins. We want to breathe the air instead of taking a drag on a pipe smoldering with Crack. Rebirth happens when we stand up, tell our stories, and publicly say, "I am who I am, and I'm okay." Rebirth ushers us into a new way of living one day at a time, fully present to ourselves and the people around us. Rebirth is feeling good again.

Community is the fourth act in the drama of recovery. Once we recognize our problems, define ourselves, and start living again, we must move further into relationship with our brothers and sisters of all colors and all classes.

The other day I talked to a brother, a black lawyer, who is writing the drama of his life. After a decade of addiction, he has been drug-free for over a year. This brother told me that Glide Church has provided him with a "landscape" against which he could change and overcome his addiction to Crack cocaine. He was referring to Glide community, which is an extended spiritual family. And what a family we are! We've got black and white, gay and straight, upper class, lower class, and no class here at Glide!

This man has been through the Twelve-Step recovery programs, but he tells me that the Twelve Steps allow for small-group support and accountability for white people but not the kind of grass-roots community that blacks need. The church can be the group or community that breaks through exclusivity by making total unconditional acceptance of all people our main issue.

When you are in a community that won't let you lie—a community that allows you to express your anger and rage—a community that not only won't let you run away from what you are feeling and what you have been through but also encourages you to run into your anger, your pain, and your failures, then black folks, all kinds of folks can get healing. At Glide we encourage people to bring their rage in here and deal with it because we know if you try to ignore your rage, it will find a way to be expressed in violence, in denial, in abuse, in despair. We say bring all of your life in here and deal with it. That's what keeps us honest and steady on the stage of recovery.

The story of Glide is a drama of recovery. The many actors in this story, those who come to Glide, are actors on the stage of recovery. Together, the people in recovery and I will act out the drama of recovery.

Each chapter that follows will be played out in four acts. Each chapter will start with events that brought us to a point of *recognition* about what ails us as a community. As a minister, my best gift is taking the pulse of my people and then spinning my head, letting my imagination explore all the possibilities, to bring it all together. After the stage has been set, in the second act I will describe the process of *self-definition* that helps us discover who we are and what it means to be an African American, or a poor person, or a woman in recovery. What does it mean to be alive, free from drugs, free from the secrets of sexual or physical abuse, or free from the stigma of suffering with AIDS? Then in the third act of each chapter, a person who has experienced *rebirth* into freedom and empowerment will tell you his or her story. Finally, we will show how individual recovery relates to the life of our *community*—the extended family at Glide.

This drama is about to begin.

PART ONE

A Spirituality of Recovery

▲   ▲   ▲

CHAPTER ONE

There Is No Hiding Place

Recognition: A Community of the Rejected

When I came to Glide Church, I knew that this could never be a traditional church. The neighborhood, the environment, and those in the broader community all convinced me that there was a great unmet need. There were those who lived near Glide, mostly disillusioned people who had left the church, feeling angry and rejected. I picked up on the fact that a lot of people saw themselves as outsiders in society and strangers to the church.

Even I was among that number. I understood feeling like an outsider. I, too, had been rejected for being who and what I am.

I grew up in San Angelo, Texas, a segregated town prior to the civil rights movement. The buses, the drinking fountains, the railroad tracks, the rest rooms, everything in San Angelo constantly reminded me that I was colored, black, a nigger. The white people in power freely chose where they sat on the bus and from which drinking fountain they would sip. They could look at the rest rooms labeled men, women, and colored, and choose the door that provided privacy and dignity. I couldn't. I was not free. I was an outsider because of how the white folks defined me.

Outside our closely knit black community, I was not acceptable. It puzzled, angered, and frightened me. The white folks told me my life was meaningless, but if I wanted to live, I'd better go along with their rules. They told me I was powerless to change my life. I would always be a nigger, second-class. I was at their mercy.

As a boy I never understood segregation. I felt the message the whites sent to me, but it didn't jibe with what my family and the black community told me.

My mother, a woman who commanded respect by the way she lived, told me again and again, "You are going to be somebody." I believed her.

Early in my life, my family nicknamed me Rev, a shortened label of the ministry that was the highest praise and heaviest pressure that a churchgoing family could place on one of its sons. Growing up in the church, I was a bright and shining star. I was the up-and-coming one in the black Methodist conference. The saints in my church just knew I would become bishop one day. I believed them.

In my hometown I often stood on the boundaries between the races. I was the only black student to have a white voice teacher, and my brothers and I became quite famous in San Angelo singing to the Kiwanis and other service clubs. The white folks loved to hear me sing, but when the music stopped, I was shown to a chair in the back or quickly ushered out through the kitchen door before the meal began.

The contradiction between what I heard and what I experienced in the two worlds rattled my head. In the black community I was somebody. The white community said I was nobody. In fact, they said my mother, my father, my grandfather, my brothers and sisters were nobodies, too. When I raged against the pain, the injustices, the insults, my father told me, "Just let it go. It ain't our time yet." But Papa Jack, my maternal grandfather who was once a slave, never just let it go.

When times were hard, as they somehow often seemed to be, insurance men, bill collectors, and other agents of a white world I didn't even pretend to fully understand came by our house. They came in pairs and walked up the street as if they held its deed in their pockets.

"Auntie!" They belittled my mother, calling her by a racial title. Not bothering to call her by her proper name demeaned her presence. Mother, a woman who could balance ten of them on the scales of humanity, was being insulted once again. But I was only a small boy, so what could I do?"

As they badgered and threatened my mother for money she didn't have, Papa Jack, a black man so old he had to walk with a cane, would rise from his porch chair and march toward the white men. "Git outta here! We'll git you the damn money when we can! Now you git the hell outta this house! Git yo' ass offa this porch, git yo' ass away from here, or I'll beat the shit outta you with this cane! Now you git the hell outta this house!"

The white men always retreated. They looked astonished that Papa Jack would dare cuss out white folks, but they knew he wasn't playing. When Papa Jack declared himself to a world that considered him beneath respect, I watched with awe and was alive with something beyond pride.

Once a group of white students from the University of Texas sought out Papa Jack as part of a report on slavery. He had them sit on the porch with him, and all of us children gathered around his feet. The students asked Papa Jack about his experiences with slavery. The answers came slowly, as if he had to travel a long way down inside to collect them and bring them back again. Papa Jack spoke without pity or resignation. When all of the students' questions had been answered, he raised his right arm and in a broad sweep pointed to all of us children bundled around his feet. He spoke to us with a tight-jawed dignity. He said, "*Papa's an ex-slave. Now you all be ex-slaves, too.*"

Two months later Papa Jack died. The funeral was sad, proud, with lots of crying, singing, and testifying. Afterward someone drove us to the cemetery. I had never been there before. The grass was velvet; the graves neatly arranged and adorned with wreaths and bouquets. I was impressed and glad the cemetery looked as it did. If anybody deserved to rest this way, Papa Jack did. Lost in my observation, I heard a woman say, "We in the white section now."

The Negro section looked like a bumpy pasture. Uncut grass smothered the graves, and burial plots were marked by weathered two-by-fours. No tombstones memorialized the names of the dead; only a piece of plastic-covered notepaper attached to a metal stake honored our dead. Most of the papers, tattered by the wind and faded by the hot Texas sun, waved wordlessly. The names of our ancestors had disappeared, and our folks were as invisible in death as they had been in life. Even in death, Papa Jack and all of us were destined to be nameless and unremembered, while the white folks lay beneath manicured sod and marble memorials.

That summer I was ten. The rejection I felt, Papa Jack's death, the hopes I had for a better world, all caved in on me. The doctor diagnosed me with a nervous breakdown. A darkness overtook my world. I went crazy. I felt the darkness as a grave or hole with all of my family, all of my people at the bottom, as though we were buried.

Somewhere in the darkness I heard the long, sweet, mournful whistle of a train. That whistle blew like a slow funereal bell. Each night waking from sleep I screamed in the darkness. In my waking and sleeping dreams a train kept coming to take me farther into the darkness. Voices rippled and figures shimmered in the night as aliens came for me, bringing the promise of death. The voices beckoned me to give in, give up, accept the life of a nigger in the South. Stop the fighting. For several months my mind was engulfed in blackness, my emotions leapt and fell out of sync with reality.

In my paranoid state I feared that my family and the extended black community might shun me. They never did. They nurtured me as best they could, and not a day went by without a throng of people dropping by to see me. But they couldn't silence the voices or dispel the darkness, despite the love, caring, comfort, and prayer.

One night I didn't scream when two aliens came and stood by the foot of my bed. One was a little white boy, no more than ten or twelve, dressed up in his Sunday best. He had dark blond hair, a chubby—almost cherubic—face, and skin so fresh and pure it appeared polished. The other was an old white man in a somber black suit who held a candle in one hand and a revolver in the other.

In my mind I stood on the edge of a deep hole in the earth, peering down into its infinite blackness. The aliens came to convince me to leap into the abyss. If I would accept my station in life, give in to the white man's system, accept the crumbs life threw me, then my misery would stop.

That night I was alone with the aliens in the deepest recesses of my being. I had to decide. Was it worth doing something? Was I worth it? I had to decide. This could be the last time. Something in me quickened.

"No," I said. "No!" I screamed to the aliens who wanted to control me. "I will not go with you tonight. Not tonight, not any night." I didn't implore them; I told them. That night I began to feel my power.

It took all my strength to hurl my words of resistance at those mental aliens. It took everything I had to declare that I would fight for my life. In declaring myself, I found the power to resist that had been inside me all along. When I claimed my power to live, to choose, and to decide, then the aliens retreated and fled for good. My power returned with a jolt. For the very first time in my young life, I felt myself to be the master of my own destiny.

Who were the aliens? Who were they? I'd always seen them as creatures imposed on me by an outside force. Yet that night when I fought their attempts to control me, I was able to control them. The aliens were my feelings—my feelings of rejection by the whites who lived on the other side of the railroad track that sliced through San Angelo with the mute authority of an international border. Only when I confronted them face on and didn't run did I wrest control from them.

The morning after I resisted the voices in my head, I waited for sunrise. I sat motionless in bed, exhausted but alive with possibilities. Everything was changing, and I wanted to tell the family first and then the world.

"What happened to those people that was botherin' you, Rev? They gone now?" Bro asked.

"No, they was there. But I stopped them from botherin' me."

As the commotion gained momentum, Mother and Daddy burst into the room.

"Oh my God!" Mother shouted joyfully in a form of prayer. "My Lord, my Lord, my son is better!"

Throwing her arms around me, she kissed my cheeks and rocked me from side to side.

"Come on, Rev, I think it's all right if you get out of bed for a little while," Mother said, extending her arm to me. The others echoed her encouragement, and they led me to the living room, where an old upright piano that Daddy had somehow acquired stood propped against the wall. We gathered around the piano, and Titter began to play. Soon we were singing with an unchained abandon that recreated the old spiritual with every word.

There's no hidin' place down here.
There's no hidin' place down here.
Oh, I went to the rock to hide my face.
The rock cried out, "No hidin' place."
There's no hidin' place down here.

As I recovered from my breakdown, I knew that I would never accept anyone else's definition of me. I wouldn't live by the rules of segregation. I simply wouldn't.

I had come through the pain of mental torment and had survived for a reason. Rejection by whites had always been my greatest source of pain—great enough to drive me mad. The black church of my youth promised a certain relief from the pain but was never able to transcend the rejection.

There had to be another kind of church, another kind of society without borders. As I regained myself and claimed my power, I felt a new sense of power unleashed in my imagination. I imagined myself a minister before a huge group of all colors, ages, descriptions. Bright colors were everywhere, streaming down on the people. The whole place was loud, alive, unlike any church I'd ever experienced.

Daily when we kids got home from school, I tested out my dreams in a backyard sanctuary filled with my brothers and friends. But nobody ever wanted to play the white folks. I was not to be deterred. I wanted a church of all colors. The love and kinship in the Bible was going to be real in my church.

That was the vision. I held fast to it as I attended college, then seminary, but my early experience of ministry in the church didn't match even the shreds of my dreams. During my twenties I experienced another rejection. This time I was cast out by my own people. Something in me wouldn't be controlled, wouldn't accept serving the church as it was, black or white. I dreamed of more.

When I neared the end of seminary, the bishop called me in to say he was ready to assign me to a rather large church in El Paso. I was pleased and began preparing to go. Behind closed doors and unbeknownst to me, other black clergy in the conference lobbied against my appointment. My black brothers stopped me dead in my tracks.

I think they were threatened by my personality more than anything else. I have always been outspoken and often was the one seen when others went unseen. I've always had a way with folks. In undergraduate school I was the person who could make things happen, and later as a minister I was the one who could fix things. I would jump into any cause, any problem, with both feet at any given time. I was always out in the fore.

I have long been involved in social change. Even in undergraduate school I had demonstrated when the first black student tried to get admitted to University of Texas Law School. I acted as if my vision of a new church, a new society, were a coming reality. Why couldn't there be a world where black, white, yellow, red, and brown could live together with acceptance, tolerance, and love?

The bishop called me in again and told me he I was going to Hobbs, New Mexico, to start a church that had no members and no building. I later found out that the white minister of the First Methodist Church wanted me to come because his congregation didn't want blacks attending their church. He and his congregation wanted me to start a segregated church. I was appointed by the church to enable segregation—the social evil that had led to my breakdown. Wasn't the church to be about unconditional love, full acceptance, and being the extended family of God? I left Hobbs after one year, and my first ministerial job was a miserable failure.

I moved on to Huston-Tillotson College in Austin, Texas, as an instructor and dean of men. Three years later the bishop offered me the United Methodist Church near the campus, which was the church for the black middle class. But the bishop's cabinet intervened and refused me again. I left Texas as a rejected black clergy and a rejected black person. I never did pastor a church in Texas. Rootless and rejected, I came to the Bay Area to study and soon knew I would never go back.

In 1963 I came to Glide as director of community involvement at the Glide Foundation. Then in 1966 the bishop appointed me minister of Glide

Church, which at that time had a small, white, affluent congregation. The shock waves of my unlikely choice reverberated for years. Yet within a few years I found myself living out the vision that had captivated me as a boy. I was a minister standing before a huge group of all colors, ages, descriptions. Bright colorful banners were everywhere streaming down on the people. The whole place was loud, alive, unlike any church I'd ever experienced. I had found a new home.

Self-Definition: The Church as a Gathering Place for All People

Some visitors once tried to pay Glide a compliment by calling us a great melting pot where everyone melded together. But Glide isn't a soup pot where everyone is mixed and pureed until he or she blends in. No, it's not that way here.

Glide is more akin to a salad bowl filled with leafy greens, tart radishes, juicy tomatoes, and every other ripe, colorful, distinct, and hearty vegetable. When we come to Glide, we retain our color, our cultures, our tastes. Together we create something that we aren't when alone. The whole can't be what it is unless we are truly ourselves. Red tomatoes can't be like green peppers any more than African American women can be like Asian men. No one has to look, believe, or act like anyone else to be a part of the Glide family.

Glide is a microcosm of our larger community. The Tenderloin neighborhood, the city of San Francisco, the state of California, the United States of America, and the global community are all culturally and ethnically diverse. In the next decade diversity will become a reality for many people in this country. In California, for instance, everyone will be a member of a minority community. No longer will whites outnumber other ethnic groups. All of us will become minorities.

Diversity is a simple truth. We are all human, but we are not all the same. Our values and ways of thinking, praying, and living differ. Those differences help to define who we are; they are not to be ignored or forgotten.

At Glide when we talk about ethnicity, we don't use it as a weapon to exclude anyone else; rather ethnicity is a tool for self-definition. As a black man, I must claim my African heritage and my maleness. An Asian woman has to claim her Asian heritage and femaleness to be whole. Our actions and beliefs may differ as each of us seeks self-definition, but the end result will be inner wholeness. When I know who I am and she knows who she is, there will be acceptance and much joyful laughter.

What this society needs is a gathering place where we can come together, bringing all of our differences into the same room. That's what Glide is: a meeting place for all people. Essentially Glide or any community committed to healing must become a wailing wall or a screaming room. When we come together, we must understand that the welfare of the community depends on the welfare of the individual. If there is one individual in the community who is sick, the whole community is sick.

The church is a gathering of people of the truth, people of the exodus, people of justice, like those in the Old Testament. The church is the body that recognizes the intervention of the Spirit in concrete events, which brings about stories of deliverance, liberation, and salvation, just like those told in the New Testament.

The church is literally the extended family of humanity. The church is not just for believers. The church includes people who may not claim to be a part of the church, but they belong because they are part of the extended family of humanity. The church is the place where humans accept one another with all our differences.

When people come to Glide, we don't ask them if they are atheists, Methodists, or Buddhists. We ask them what their names are and how they are doing.

Rebirth: Cecil's Story

I HONESTLY DID START OFF here at Glide to make this a true, lively, inclusive church. I took down the cross so we'd stop focusing on death and put our energies into life. I never did put that cross back up. Instead, years ago we encircled the sanctuary with colorful cloth banners emblazoned with the words *justice*, *dignity*, *peace*, and *self-affirmation*. Up on the wall where that cross once hung we started projecting pictures of all of humanity. People, life, spirit—these are the focus of our weekly Celebration. Each Sunday the Glide Ensemble rocks the place with soulful songs while a light show flashes and vibrates with the sounds. For years Glide has been a weird, wonderful place.

Somewhere along the way our nontraditional ways made Glide famous. Stars and superstars began coming here. Shirley MacLaine,

Leonard Bernstein, Bill Cosby, Willie Mays, Sammy Davis, Jr., Roberta Flack, Maya Angelou, Quincy Jones, Steve Miller, the late Bill Graham, some members of the rock group The Who, Angela Davis, and others attended Glide while in town. Tourist guidebooks from around the world began listing Glide as one of the sights and sounds of San Francisco not to be missed. Each week representatives of the countries of the world occupied our pews. For a time, I think people came to Glide primarily to see the famous, the rich, and the different.

Along the way the fame got to me. I completely lost my priorities. The Celebration service often became a stage for the stars, a platform for the politically connected to use. Somewhere along the way I almost lost the vision of Glide. I felt barraged by questions. Who was Glide for anymore? Tourists? The famous who came and went? And who was I? A minister in and for those in the spotlight?

One Sunday in 1981 when I was preaching, the unplanned words "You are the answer to the question" found their way out of my mouth. Redefining and recovering myself was the answer to the questions. Something clicked. Janice Mirikitani, my longtime friend and colleague at Glide whom I was soon to marry, said to me after that service, "That is the best you have preached in years." I knew it was true.

Facing myself honestly was the answer to redefining myself as a minister and recapturing the vision for Glide Church. The priority of the church shifted when I began to face myself like I had never faced myself before.

As a minister I'd been good at fixing things for folks. For years people had come to me and said, "Pray for me, Cecil." As a clergyperson I let people hand over to me whatever ailed them and then I'd try to fix it. (People still try to give me the authority and power to make their lives better.) For years I took over other people's problems and, in so doing, short-circuited their power and tried to play God. I exhausted myself and lost myself trying to protect people from claiming the responsibility for their own lives. That delusion of being a healer allowed me to put all of my energy into someone else. I discovered I'd been a good codependent. I'd given everything to everyone else and kept nothing for me.

My inner alienation and loneliness forced me to raise the theological question of selfishness and selflessness. Most of us in the church have been taught to give and give and give. Conversely, we've learned that to affirm self is selfish, that to work on ourselves is narcissistic.

There had to be a way to care for myself while still being an agent for change in my community. I wasn't going to move from being overly other-directed to being completely self-directed. Trading one excess for another would be just another form of hiding.

I began to explore the idea of self-definition. Who was Cecil Williams now? I was no longer a young minister right out of seminary or the new, innovative minister at Glide. I'd been at Glide for decades; I was well known, some would say notorious, in San Francisco.

In my search for answers, I read widely, searching and seeking. As I read liberation theology, I found my theological home. In the late 1970s and early 1980s Third-World theologians, most from Central and South America, wrote about a new way of thinking about God and being the church. They wrote of the importance of taking "a preferential option for the poor," meaning that when God chooses sides in the struggle between the powerful and the powerless, the accepted and the rejected, God can always be found with the poor. No longer is theology the task of those cloistered in ivory-towered academia. Theology, or talking about and searching for God, is the job of those living in every ghetto and barrio in the world. As the poor and disenfranchised come together to tell their stories, reflect on God, and then take action in the struggle against injustice and oppression, truth would be found. Liberation theology is people-centered, not dogma-centered. It values both action and reflection, experience and theory.

I had embraced and acted upon the principles of liberation theology without knowing them, but reading the works of Ernesto Cardinal, Leonardo Boff, Jamis Cone, and Gustavo Guiterez moved me onward and gave me words for what I believed.

I began to see the issue of the outcast in a new way. I began to see that there would be no significant change in the lives of the outcasts unless they became empowered themselves. God wasn't somewhere out there waiting to be found. God was already among the poor. They had to take up their problems themselves. The people were the community of faith, and God would be found in their suffering lives. My role was not to be their powerful exalted leader. What I had to become, as a minister in a community of the poor, more than anything else, was one who stood with the rejected.

I could open the door and invite others in, but it was their power that would propel them toward healing and faith. As I read, I knew that the power had to come from them. I had watched Papa Jack claim his power and that is how he stood up to the white bill collectors. I remembered that marshaling my power during my breakdown had caused the aliens of rejection to flee. I knew I was on to something.

Again, this time as a seasoned minister, a man in my prime, I had to dig deep inside myself, honestly tell my story to trusted others, and then daily drink from my own well of spirituality.

In the last ten years, I've faced myself again. I learned to listen to the screaming loneliness that has always stood in my heart like a ravaged homeless urchin, wailing loud and long, begging to be cared for. I've learned to care for myself within the extended family of others who, too, feel fatherless and motherless.

Over the years I've learned that the act of self-definition is a spiritual act. Self-definition moves me and you toward authenticity and a new self. If we don't have a self, if the ontological being isn't there, we can't work through other problems or create community for ourselves. Self-definition is crucial to self-understanding and self-love. Truly defining myself allows me to open up to people in a new way. I no longer have to hustle, protect, or win with folks. I have to help me, work with me, and understand what it is that I am supposed to be doing.

People don't always like it now when I refuse to help them when they won't help themselves. They say, "But you're a minister." My typical response is "You are a minister, too. What are you going to do about you?"

I've got to make sure this minister is different. I'm not going to give and give and give myself out. I've found how fresh and exciting it is to also learn to love and care for me.

I can always tell when I've cared for myself when I walk into Glide on Sunday morning. If I have studied sufficiently, rested enough, exercised, laughed, and joked during the weekend, then I'm ready to preach and to celebrate. My energy is high, and I feel ready to risk whatever needs to be risked to honestly tell the truth.

I've learned to stay home on Mondays and not answer the phones. I'm giving up more responsibility to staff. I am giving up control. That for me is a recovery issue. If a program works, it works. If it doesn't, it doesn't.

My letting go of control, while being healthy and liberating, creates all kinds of problems. The staff and I have to constantly plow through issues of responsibility and leadership. Ten years ago I would have walked into a meeting regarding a church problem and said, "Stop everything. Here is the way you will proceed. If you can work with my plan, fine. If you can't, then leave." I took charge. Now I let the staff work it out.

Now I understand my task as a leader is to listen to all sides when conflicts arise, as they constantly do. So often, below the conflict the various sides are really talking about hurt and pain. If I can interpret that back to them, then each person begins to hear the other. They begin to understand and have compassion for one another.

I came home to myself in the 1980s. My home has always been with the outsiders; I just wandered for a while. No matter how much the glitter and gold of fame or acceptance beckon, I now know where I belong, where those like me belong. We belong at Glide. It is a home for outcasts.

At Glide the outsider is the one who is totally accepted. We give the outsider preference.

My own desire for acceptance and my knowledge of what rejection feels like allows me to offer unconditional acceptance and love. I won't reject people, whether or not they look like me, think like me, or act like me.

I always go to the outcast, the women, the minorities, the poor, the depressed, the mentally disturbed. I've got a real attitude about them. I may only see through a glass darkly about myself, but as I constantly work at defining myself, I can see where I need to go next to stay on the cutting edge. I could get comfortable, really comfortable, but that is not being who I am.

When I work on the issues in my own life, I'm a different person. When I drink from my own well, my commitment to the programs and people at Glide is clearer. I can tell a difference when I preach. My weekly sermon content becomes vital because it means something to my own life. If I don't drink from my own well how can I quench the thirst of others?

I drink from my own well by paying attention to what is going on inside me and honestly sharing the truth with the people of Glide. I have never been worried about what people would say. I've told the church everything. That's why I've been good for this church. Everybody at this church knows they can tell their whole story, with all the sordid details if needed, and they will not be judged. I've led the parade. I've led the march by telling my whole story, no matter how it made me look in anyone's eyes. Being seen as perfect, good, or respectable is not my concern. My concern is to create an open and honest community where it is safe to tell the truth. That is what people of all races and classes want today. Whether they're executives or homeless people, all people want to know, Who will care about me? Where can I go to tell my story and be myself?

Finding real meaning in life has to do with living with integrity and openness. Being fully alive happens by looking at yourself and looking at other folks honestly. And being fully alive is really the goal of recovery. Recovery happens by facing your attitudes and the way you live with other people, finding the Spirit and the destiny and commitment that you have. Big profits, money, or all that other stuff isn't going to work. Recovery really has to do with defining yourself, claiming your power, and learning to love yourself, your neighbors, and your enemies—whomever, whatever they are.

Community: Unrelenting Love

All of us in this extended family called Glide are fatherless and motherless. If this is a real community and if this is really the church, then none of us is father or mother. We are sisters and brothers in the sense that we become a support system of peers. No one takes the role of an authority figure who holds all the power. That kind of person impedes recovery by taking away the power and responsibility that belongs to each person.

What we do, especially on Sundays, is to shake folks up, to keep folks alive. We don't let folks settle down or settle in and begin to believe they have it made. That is where most churches seem to focus. Most church folks settle in, get comfortable, and build doctrinal walls to protect themselves from anyone who thinks or looks differently than they do. At Glide we believe that the true church stays on the edge of life, where the real moans and groans are.

As the minister of Glide, I keep my finger on the pulse of the present moment and the realities of the people's lives. When I first heard story after story from young black folks about their addiction to Crack, I knew I was hearing the story of a huge neglected crowd of people who were out there on the edge of society, out on the raw edge of life. They were moaning in pain out there. My own pain and need for acceptance allowed me to hear them. I was one with them.

A long time ago I committed myself to finding ways to take the church and the unconditional, unrelenting love it has to offer out to the people who live on the edge. Out there on the precipice of pain is where unconditional love and acceptance are needed most. The true church only exists on the edge, because that is where people become honest about their lives. Long ago I vowed never go to sleep on the future of the church by offering sure-fire programs and simple reassurances. No, I was going to give everything I had to keep the church out there where the people live. To do so, we as the church would go to the edge ourselves.

THE MARCH ON VALENCIA GARDENS

In the late 1980s, before Glide got serious about recovery and finding ways to unconditionally embrace those with raging addictions, we sent addicts who came to Glide to the Haight Ashbury Free Clinic. The professionals there have been dealing with each new crashing wave in the ocean-sized drug epidemic since the 1960s. The addicts we sent across the city kept saying to me, "To get to the Haight Ashbury, the bus goes through the Tenderloin and up through the housing projects in Hayes Valley. By the time I get to the clinic, I've jumped off the bus to shoot up, snort, or smoke something."

So I stopped sending them away. I knew Glide had to find a way to help these folks recover, but I knew little about recovery and less about Crack. I called together the real experts—the users themselves—and asked them to teach me what I needed to learn. I opened up Freedom Hall, our church social hall, and said, "Tell your story." They did.

Their stories put a human face on the hard, cold statistics. Over 65 percent of blacks in San Francisco lived in crime-ridden, boarded-up, graffiti-plastered projects like Hayes Valley. Folks on drugs, even if they managed to stay drug-free during the day, eventually had to go home to projects that had become havens for every imaginable habit.

I knew then what we had to do. Our folks were living in the projects, and so Glide had to go there, too.

One of the things I preach about is to "walk the walk that you talk." I try to help people understand it isn't so much what you say about Jesus and what the Bible says that matters; what is important is if you believe that the message of Jesus is addressed to you. Is it saying something about the kind of person you are? What does the story of Jesus say about the kind of attitude you have? How are you are going to live your life and take action? It's never good enough to say that "we have Jesus here in our church." The unconditional love and full acceptance Jesus talked about has got to show out there in the world, out there on the edge.

So we walked our talk. We decided to march on the most troubled housing projects in San Francisco. We checked the crime reports. Valencia Gardens was the project most out of control. So that's where we would start. We decided to march and call out the good news of recovery to our brothers and sisters.

We spent dozens of hours gathering together people from the community: the public housing tenants association, the mayor's office, and about six hundred people from Glide. We also decided not to be stupid with our faith. We took the police with us, too.

We created a human force to influence the people in the projects. Our goal was not to run the pushers, pimps, and users out of public housing. We came to embrace them with unconditional love and declare there was another way to live. We boarded buses, drove up Market Street, and turned on to Valencia Street singing songs of freedom. When we arrived, we unloaded and marched around the projects. Those in the front carried a streetwide banner that declared our nonviolent battle cry, *It's Recovery Time*. Others carried placards: *The User Needs Recovery* and *Welcome Home to Recovery*.

We marched as a posse of lovers. We marched to herald freedom from drugs, addiction, and despair. Jesus has said to each one of us, "I'm with you." Glide marched to say to our hurting extended family, "We are with you."

Each heart bore a commitment to accepting those we met. No one marched empty-handed either. Some carried paintbrushes and gallons of paint. Others bore heaping plates of fried chicken and potato salad. We marched to help. It does no good to go in shouting and screaming for change with your empty hands shaking in the air. You've got to have something to offer.

When the hundreds of marchers converged in the center of the four-sided square housing complex, I took a bullhorn and began to shout to those peeking out of the top-floor apartments. "C'mon down. Join us. It's recovery time. We know who you are. You're our sons and daughters. It's time for you to take control of your lives."

As people came down, some from apartments currently serving as Crack houses, we put them right up on stage and gave them a microphone. They talked. Then late in the day, one of my staff members came up to me and said a group of pushers wanted a tape played over our public address system. I said okay, and that was the opening to talking with the young men.

I walked up to the door where these young pushers were holed up. Someone from the crowd yelled to me, "You ought not do that Cecil," but I did it anyway. That's how we met Alex.

Earlier in the week Alex had begun to reflect on his life. Alex later told us, "I been taught by my father that if drugs and violence were the ways I was going to live then I was to be the best at whatever I was doin'. I took the bad road, being crooked, a criminal, and I was good at it. I had no mercy or concern for another's physical well-being. I did some time in jail. I was growing tired of the life.

"I kept thinking, I can get a job and if I don't make it, I can always turn back to what I was doin'—selling drugs. But the one who is always by my side, my baby's mother, said, 'Why turn back? You can make an honest living.' So I started thinking about it. That Saturday is when Cecil and all the people came in marching.

"I listened to Cecil, and what he was talking about was what I wanted to be about. After the walls at Valencia Gardens got painted, I realized that the march wasn't about covering up the dirty walls; it was about the people. There was a total change in the people who lived in the projects. People who didn't even talk to each other in the projects were now talking. There was so much bad around V.G., I wanted to help make some good."

Alex started coming to Glide. Many months later Alex spoke about the march on Valencia Gardens to some visitors who were interested in our recovery program. Alex said, "I remember my father telling me so many times that by being born in 1968 that I missed out on *everything:* Malcolm X, the Rev. Martin Luther King, Jr., Vietnam, the hippie movement, the Black Panthers, and the Zebra and Zodiac killers. But after I came to Glide I began to see that I'd been told a lie. I didn't miss everything. I've lived to see Glide and to know the Rev. Cecil Williams, who is not a killer but a saver. Glide saved me and my family from the madness. And one of the coolest things about finding myself is, I never had to go find Glide because Glide came to my home and found me.

"Coming to Glide was like facing a mountain where there weren't any stairs or a clear-cut path. Instead there were hands, all different colors of hands, reaching out to help me. All I had to do was hang on and keep climbing until I got to the top. When I reached the top, then I looked back and saw how far I'd come. It was and is a beautiful view—this is recovery." Alex now has a job; he's good at it. He's a new man.

Our message, the day we first marched on Valencia Gardens and every day, is a simple one: Recovery simply means to open the door to the possibilities. Life awaits.

CHAPTER TWO

In Spirit and in Truth

Recognition: Yearning for the Spirit

My office door was the first door at Glide to swing open to people dealing with Crack. Crack baffled me. What was it about this drug that made it so deadly addictive? Initially I invited some of the staff to tell me what they knew. At first we talked about the symptoms of Crack: instant euphoria, nervous twitching, grandiose feelings, constant talking, and hyperalertness. But when they talked about the paranoia that accompanies extended Crack use, it took me back to my own childhood battle with the aliens of death. I knew the terror they were talking about—the terror of being stalked by a mental enemy.

Little by little, the staff opened up. A couple admitted they knew about Crack from firsthand use. Then a few more users from the extended Glide family joined our talks. They heard we were talking about Crack and they had something to say. The group outgrew my office so we moved to Freedom Hall. We started with a small circle, and every day we added chairs until we encompassed the room.

No matter the topic with which we started our daily sessions, we ended up talking about pain and hopelessness. We talked about loss, rejection, abandonment, death, sex, and desire. We cried. I began to sense that Crack wasn't the ultimate enemy. Yes, we would have to battle it, but to win the war we would have to get at the root cause of the addiction, whatever that was.

One of the men gave words to what I was feeling: "Drugs just hide the hurt." The pain was deep and for most, lifelong. The folks kept saying they needed more than themselves to recover. They didn't believe they could make it alone.

At that time there were no programs for Crack addicts. The drug community thought Crack was a fad drug that would soon be replaced by something else.

Crack was no fad. The chemical grip it held on users was strangulating. These were ordinary people willing to do absolutely anything for a hit of Crack cocaine. They talked of stealing from the ones they loved most. I learned about toss ups, women and men prostituting themselves not for money but for another hit of Crack.

This drug war was being waged for life or death. These people were shot up, smoked out, and on the brink of losing their very lives and souls because of Crack. Some of them acted like corpses already fully prepared to be lowered six feet into the ground.

Some had tried Twelve-Step programs and found that adages like "Just leave it up to your higher power" were too simplistic when they struggled with survival issues of where to sleep that night and how to get their children back from foster-care homes.

The Twelve-Step programs were individualistic and prescriptive. These people had completely lost themselves. They had little self-esteem and less personal discipline to follow the Steps. Many couldn't read and felt intimidated when talking in their street vocabulary around white folks in Alcoholics Anonymous or Narcotics Anonymous groups. Then the call to become powerless nearly did in many of the black Crack users. They knew and had always known that as African Americans, they never had the power anyway. Powerlessness was not a choice they had to make; instead they needed to believe they had some power to work with. They needed the power of feeling like a worthy person and the power of a community that believed in them so that they could begin to believe in themselves. Most black folks don't have to be told they need a higher power; belief in God is a part of the black experience. The available recovery programs were missing a living, vital spirituality that could offer hope and freedom for African Americans.

If addicts needed a place to go to safely detox from initial withdrawal from Crack, the only places available to those without medical insurance were for alcoholics. Crack addicts told me of going out and getting drunk just so their blood alcohol count would be high enough to be considered for a bed in a detox center.

If Crack addicts got lucky and found an ongoing drug program willing to take them on as clients, they'd get twenty minutes of one-to-one counseling and be handed a list of local support groups they could attend around the city. That left twenty-three and a half hours of the day to fill without using drugs.

Being idle on the streets made the temptation too strong, and few succeeded. Occasionally one of the programs offered the addicts daily fixes of a substitute "nonaddictive" drug, but that did nothing to help the addicts deal with their habits and dependency on substances to get through the day.

Nowhere in San Francisco and, I learned as I researched, nowhere in the country was there a recovery program for Crack addicts that offered what they needed all in one place. To get clean they needed one to one counseling, support groups, social service advocacy, drug education, self-esteem workshops, and a clean and sober place to belong during the day.

Then the Crack users told me one more vital thing that they couldn't find in any program. They told me they needed spirituality. They longed for the Spirit and had tried pushing down that longing with every imaginable substance and habit. Still they yearned to feel the Spirit—the essence of life. The folks wanted the Spirit but didn't want the church they remembered from their childhoods. Most had felt rejected, unwanted, and shameful there. But they did want the Spirit; they craved it.

As I listened to their cries for the Spirit, I discovered in myself a "new" kind of spirituality that I had actually picked up from my mother and grandmother many years ago. When they took me to the little church in San Angelo, Texas, I saw the meaning of spirituality. The Spirit is the life-giving impulse. To have spirituality means you are alive. It means you have come out of the grave. It means you are victorious. You have overcome; you are free; you have gone over to life. A spiritual person knows there is ground underfoot. If you do go under and get swallowed up by pain and rejection, you'll find that the ground miraculously is solid even when you are farther down than ever before. You begin to get a firm footing and you start crawling back up again.

The spirituality I understand is rooted in faith and resistance; it is rooted in the experience of the black community. To resist slavery meant we had to laugh about some of the crazy things the white folks did to keep us down. We had to tell stories to one another about how our lives were developing. We gathered in the church because it was the only place we were free to be together; while we were there, we loved everybody else. We had to practice unconditional love when we came together because, God knows, we didn't experience full acceptance anywhere else outside those church doors.

My understanding of how spirituality and recovery go hand in hand came together for me one night in 1991 while my wife and co-worker, Janice Mirikitani, and I were having dinner with David Smith and Millicent Buckston, longtime friends and pioneers in the field of drug treatment from the

Haight Ashbury Free Clinic. We sat at a linen-covered table and I leaned against a marble-tiled wall designed to make us feel like we were in Italy, but our thoughts remained firmly planted in the Tenderloin. I was telling them what I was hearing from the folks on the street. Millicent, who is a strong proponent of the Twelve Steps of Alcoholics Anonymous, admitted from her experience that different approaches work for different groups of people.

"Why don't you develop a theology of recovery?" she asked.

Her question pierced through my mind like an hurtling arrow fired on target. Bull's-eye.

That is what the folks at Glide and I have been doing together for several years now. By our living, we've been putting together a spirituality of recovery. This is what we've come up with.

Self-Definition: A Spirituality of Recovery

Folks usually shy away from theology because the academic theologians have made us believe that theology is a formal structure of spiritual reflection. Somehow we've been duped into thinking that only intellectuals or ministers can really think about or know God.

I went to seminary and studied theology in the traditional ways. We turned to books to learn what others, wiser ones, had to tell us about God. I learned the right answers to the big questions of life: Who is God? Who is humanity? What is sin? What is salvation? What is the church? I learned what the masters of the ages thought, but when I got to the Tenderloin, none of the answers fit.

That's why liberation theology brought me home. Its approach matched my experience. I've always thought that believing has to do with living. None of us can *talk that talk* of what we believe until we *walk that walk* of experiencing our true selves and the Spirit. The experience of spirituality is found in the real flesh-and-blood world. Spirituality comes before theology. Living in the Spirit is essential. Live it now; talk about it later.

The best theology comes from listening to the poor, the outcast ones. Listen to those who suffer. God is the one who suffers with those who suffer. If God is found where the people live—out there on the edge of suffering—then the best theology is that which is lived and questioned in the midst of pain. *Theology is experiential.* The Spirit lives with us and is found in us.

At the root of every lived theology, or spirituality, there is a particular, specific experience of flesh-and-blood people who live in a particular time. The times and situations that we live in influence our experience of the Spirit.

The bodies of the First Generation of addicts at Glide had been eaten away by Crack. They had inhaled deeply of the paucity of inner-city life. These folks had come to accept a deadly belief system. They believed there was no hope, they were no good, and nobody cared. And like any deeply rooted belief system, these toxic tenets infused their lives with despair. Hopelessness covered their bodies, minds, and souls. They were spiritless corpses dragging through the door in shackles. We needed to recover the Spirit. We needed to find a way to be liberated. We had to start right where we found ourselves. *Theology is contextual.* God begins where we do.

And where were the First Generation at the beginning? They were in the tomb.

A theology of recovery starts with death, not life. It starts with those who hurt the most. It starts with those who suffer and with those who are slaves to drugs. It starts with battered women, women who have been raped, men who have been molested, and those who are slowly dying with AIDS. It starts there because the Spirit is with those who suffer most. And how do we find the Spirit in the pain? Just like the people of old, we gather to tell our stories, to tell it like it is. The Bible tells the story of the struggles of the people of God. The church today continues to tell of the struggle. *Theology is narrative.* The Spirit inhabits our stories.

A spirituality of recovery begins at the tomb, but it doesn't end there. When the spirit moves in, life moves in. When the spirit lifts, the people are lifted. Any spirituality that isn't about how you live every day isn't about the living Spirit. *Theology is living your spirituality.* The Spirit liberates us so that we can live now.

WHAT IT MEANS TO BE SPIRITUAL

To be spiritual, you've got to have the Spirit. What is it that you have when you've got the Spirit? The Spirit is the power of God that creates and liberates. When you are spiritual, you have the power to create and free yourself. The Spirit brings you back to life in the here and now.

Listening to church folks, you'd think that getting the Spirit makes you good, perfect, and holy. But read the Bible for yourself. The Bible is full of real, spiritual people who have messy, imperfect lives.

In the Old Testament Ezekiel talks about being in the valley of dry bones. He says the Spirit led him and told him to tell some old, dry bones to live.

Crazy stuff, but Ezekiel did it. And those bones started rattling. A host of dead folks stood up when Ezekiel passed on God's message to them: "I will put my Spirit within you, and you shall live."

The Spirit is always doing and saying things like that. The Spirit makes new creatures out of smelly, old, depressed folks. The Spirit makes cowards bold and honest about their lives. The Spirit frees us and moves us onward.

By reading through the Bible, you'd get the idea that the Spirit feels right at home here among us. We don't have to be perfect to have the Spirit.

To learn to live in the Spirit we begin at the tomb, the tomb of Lazarus, the tomb of Jesus, the tomb of those who are bound to their pasts. The tomb is where it looks like the suffering has won. The tomb is where it looks like there is no hope. That is where we admit we have hit the bottom.

There is no escaping the tomb. We have to accept that a large stone of addiction and despair blocks our way out of the darkness and despair. When we recognize that we need a miracle to live again, then a spirituality of recovery can be born in us. There is no resurrection or rebirth without death. There is no recovery without the Spirit.

To become spiritual we must stop being afraid of death. Instead of worrying about dying someday, we need to start living today. Many folks are afraid of dying and going to hell. But death isn't the greatest thing to be feared for it homogenizes everyone, makes us all equally dead. Fearing death, feeling despair, and giving in to hopelessness is easier that fighting for life.

More folks are afraid of living because abundant life requires risking everything to love, liberate, and accept yourself and others now. People are afraid of life for it creates diversity and requires commitment to action. To live is to struggle.

Jesus told a story about all this:

Lazarus, Jesus' good friend, got sick and looked likely to die. His two sisters got worried and sent word to Jesus asking him to hurry and come. The Bible says Jesus loved Lazarus and his sisters, but Jesus dawdled and Lazarus died. The sisters couldn't understand why Jesus let this happen.

When Jesus finally traveled to Bethany, Lazarus had been in the tomb for four days. Martha ran to meet Jesus and laid some guilt on him. "If you had been here, Lazarus wouldn't have died." Jesus promised Martha that Lazarus would live again, and Martha believed he meant in the sweet by-and-by. (People have been focusing on the hereafter rather than the present for a long, long while.)

Now Mary, the other sister, met Jesus at the tomb. She was bent over with disappointment and despair. Jesus saw her grief; he felt it. The Bible says he was moved in Spirit.

The Spirit moved Jesus to act, to do something. Jesus called for some helpers to roll away the rock sealing the tomb. (It's important to note that Jesus doesn't move that rock alone. People are always begging Jesus to fix their problems for them, but Jesus tells us to lend our own strength to the problem.)

But Mary didn't understand what Jesus was doing. She pleaded, "Don't go in there, Jesus. His body is stinky and dead." Jesus' actions made no sense. Mary advised Jesus to run away from the tomb toward life. But Jesus ran toward death (he always does).

Jesus knew the story of the dry bones in the Old Testament. He knew that dead bones, corpses, dead spirits could live again.

After the folks got busy and helped Jesus roll away the stone, Jesus went into the tomb and smelled the death. Lazarus was like all dead folks—smelly, rigid, unfeeling.

In the middle of that tomb of despair Jesus called out, "Lazarus, come on out of the tomb." Lazarus heard the call and stood up, still bound in the cloths of death, and struggled back into life.

Lazarus's story is the story of the First Generation of people in recovery at Glide. Jesus walked into their Crack houses, even though their families said, "Let 'em go, they're dead already." Jesus went in and called out to Edna, Jamal, and all the others, "Come on out." They came, still looking like corpses, dragging their pipes and addictions behind them.

Edna was one of them. When I first met Edna, she had been seriously deprived of all the human values that enable any of us to accept ourselves. I felt she was both wary of me as a man and somewhat awestruck by me as a minister.

Edna gave of herself all of the time; she felt comfortable on the giving end of things but never on the receiving. In the beginning Edna was a master at reversing the direction of any gift that came her way. She had so little self because she kept giving everything to anyone she met.

Many times I said to her, "Edna, stop trying to prove that you are someone by giving so much away. You are a wonderful, respected woman. Let something good come to you. Keep some of yourself for you."

Early on, when she came close to her pain, Edna said, "Praise the Lord" and "God will take care of everything." Her "Godtalk" became an excuse for not empowering herself.

I think it shocked her a bit when I said, "Seems to me you give more back to God than God has ever given you. You won't even receive the life God has already given you. Stop talking about God and start talking about yourself."

Edna took the risk and jumped into the movement of the Spirit by telling the truth.

Today if you walk into the Crisis Center, you will be greeted by a warm, loving woman with a heart-shaped face that matches her heart-shaped soul. Edna is a miracle; she's become Glide's very own Sojourner Truth, a black woman whose lips and life preach freedom wherever she goes. If I had been a pioneer preacher in the time of Frances Asbury, I would have taken Edna with me to preach on the frontier. She's a preacher—a powerful woman who overflows with Spirit.

Rebirth: Edna's Story

I CAME TO THE FOOD LINE at Glide about eight and a half years ago; I was new to San Francisco. My son was four years old, and my daughter was thirteen. We were living in a hotel room here in the Tenderloin, and I heard that Glide was a good place to eat. It had more of a family atmosphere and good meals. Glide lets families eat first with more privacy. That gave me a little pride about eating here. My daughter was ashamed to come. Had we really gotten down to this level?

We came to eat here as often or as seldom as we needed to. One day, in the middle of the week, a service going on up in the sanctuary was piped into the dining room over the speaker system. The Glide Ensemble sang, and I listened to Cecil preaching. I was trying to eat, but I couldn't. I loved the Lord, yet my Spirit was completely broken at that time. I've been through a lot in my life—childhood abuse, rape, domestic violence—a whole lot.

Cecil was talking about justice and freedom. As I ate, I was almost in tears. I wanted to find out, Where is he coming from? What is he about? Somebody announced in the dining room that anybody who wanted to could go upstairs to the sanctuary after eating.

I let my daughter take my little boy back to the hotel room, and I went upstairs. I wanted to look at this minister and deal with him. I sat in that sanctuary, and at one point Cecil said, "If there is anybody here who has something to tell me, then stand up and say it."

I got up and I told him that I had been trying to enjoy a meal but couldn't because the music and his preaching filled my soul. It had taken away my physical appetite. I let it go at that.

I heard about the Sunday services and began to come to the nine o'clock and stay for the eleven o'clock. I joined Glide about the third Sunday I was here. I listened for three or four months. Cecil made a lot of sense. I thought maybe he had a good cause, maybe he believed in what he was saying. But I thought he had no idea of the reality of pain, poverty. I felt a burning in my soul. I just wanted to talk to that man for five minutes to see if he was real.

I started volunteering. When Glide had special events, they would pay me to answer the phones in the Celebration office after hours. I'd work during the day when they were shorthanded. I'd sit in there, concentrate totally on my job, and still listen and watch everything that was going on around me. I wanted to find out if there was anything ugly about this place. I never found anything ugly.

I listened to everybody who worked here, from the kitchen to the business office. There were people of different colors, of different races; there were people with jobs who dealt with the money and so many things, but they never seemed above me. Never, not once, did anyone seem above me. That started a journey for me, as I took on respect for Cecil, Janice, Glide, and myself.

Little times when I talked to Cecil, I found him to be a real person. I'd throw questions at him, and sometimes he would ask me about something and listen, really listen to my opinion! I grew to love Glide.

I'd come to work on Saturday evenings and put out the little pamphlets and song sheets in the sanctuary. I'd take the gum off the pews. There would be no people in there, just me. I'd clean it from top to bottom and spend two or three hours just praising the Lord. I'd pray and thank God for Glide—whatever it was about.

Soon, I was hired part-time to work in the Crisis Center. At that time I was still tormented by my drug abuse that had been going on for four or five years. I had gotten away from injections. I stopped shooting all by myself by working here and hearing Cecil preach. I felt ugly about using needles. Just being here gave me that much more dignity, self-esteem. I stopped, but nobody knew because nobody knew I had been doing drugs in the first place.

I'd work here all day doing whatever needed to be done, cleaning the stove, it didn't matter. I just wanted to be here at Glide. I found myself going home and still wanting to get high. I was drinking a forty-ounce bottle of beer, smoking weed, and taking whatever pain pills I found. Crack was just peeking its head then.

When Crack cocaine came out, I was living in the projects, and one of my neighbors, with whom I often shared a joint, told me that she had something she wanted me to try. It was in the form of a joint, so I considered that okay since I didn't have to inject it. I was afraid to go back to any of that. I thought I was supposed to be getting further ahead in my life, and shooting would have been going back.

I had gotten off of welfare; I was working full-time. I loved Glide. I loved my kids. I loved my being. But nothing ever felt balanced inside me. Nothing.

I started smoking Crack.

Crack was the best high I thought I had ever had. I could simply smoke it, take a few hits, and I wouldn't have to think about the pain. I was always trying to balance my today's world with what my yesterday's world was like. The thought lurked in the back of my mind, "Nobody knows, nobody cares." If I thought that somebody might care about my pain, I wouldn't want to tell them about my abusive marriage because that would make me feel shame in front of them. How dare I tell them what had happened to me back then, because they were dealing with the me they thought they saw now. I didn't want my friends at Glide to know the real pain. That seemed to take away some of who I had become at Glide.

One day I was in the Crisis Center, and Cecil came in and said, "Edna, I want to see you and a couple more folks in my office. We gonna talk about something."

When Cecil says he wants to talk about something, I am always interested. What's he gonna do now? What's he gonna start now?

We got in his office; he said he wanted to know about drugs. He wanted to know about Crack cocaine. I was quiet at first. How could I tell him about it and not admit that I used it? How could I admit that I used it while I still worked here? That was a dilemma.

Praise God for the truth in me that day! I was the only woman there. We started telling Cecil the symptoms of Crack cocaine, what it makes you do. He was so amazed.

That day we gave Cecil just a glimpse of Crack cocaine. We didn't get too personal. We all admitted to trying it "once or twice." He told us that day that our information was considered private and that no one would be fired.

Cecil continued to meet with us over a period of weeks. We began to give him direct information about addiction in general. I could see Cecil get more involved every day. He got more intense. He got more quiet. He got looks in his eyes that I never saw before.

He started asking why we smoked Crack, and none of us seemed to really know why. Why? I always said I used so I didn't have to think. Then Cecil asked me, "What you got to think about that is so bad you gotta get high?" I was afraid that anything I said would sound like an excuse, so I didn't say anything.

But one day led to another. Cecil brought in experts. He brought in people from the Haight Ashbury Free Clinic to show us films. Before we knew it, we had more people involved in our talks, and we moved from his office to Freedom Hall.

We started out with a little circle. But each day as more people came, we added chairs. We simply added in chairs. No big deal.

One day Cecil came and said he wanted to meet with us in the sanctuary that evening. He told us he had found out something devastating. He said, "I don't know if it's completely true, because even the professionals don't know yet. I have heard some professionals say that if you have taken a hit of Crack cocaine, you may get addicted from the first hit and you will always be addicted."

Crack was no ordinary drug.* That was scary. Not only for me, but for everyone.

We all started to talk. Before Cecil or anyone else labeled us as hopeless because of our addictions, we wanted to tell him something about our lives. We wanted to show him the truth of our lives. We respected Cecil, so we said, "Here's the worst for me. Here it is."

---

*Crack cocaine is highly addictive, although a minority of users have been "casual" users and have managed to stop using Crack without joining an ongoing treatment program. Since Crack is smoked, it is immediately absorbed into the bloodstream through the lungs. The resulting high is intense and relatively short-lived. A sudden depression or "fall" follows the high, and users often smoke more Crack to delay the aftereffects. The physiological effect of Crack is serious. Crack disrupts more neurotransmitters in the brain than does heroin or LSD. Cocaine is a mighty chemical reinforcer—it creates a brief pleasurable sensation and chemically begs a user's body for more.

The simplicity of the truth changed the whole scope of where the recovery program is today. It moved from being about drugs to being about the pain of our lives. When we started growing, everybody started to talk. Whenever we started to talk about our mamas, our families, or somebody else, Cecil would say, "Now hold on, I want to know your story—only your story. It can involve anyone or anything it needs to, but don't put the responsibility anywhere else. Keep your story focused on yourself."

In the beginning of recovery nothing really mattered until we faced the hard truth of our individual lives. That is where the spiritual part of the program came in. The Spirit was found in the truth. In the truth, recovery for me and a lot of other folks was found. When I would stray from my truth, someone would say, "Edna, now back that up and say it again." I would say it again, and it would come out as ugly as it was. Bits of the truth about me came out.

Cecil came in one day and said, "I want to tell you all something. In order for you to gain recovery, in order to get from point *A* of addiction to point *B* of recovery, you got to go back to the beginning of your pain and come forward again. You gotta tell your *whole* story."

Well, all of the sudden I was ready to quit my job. No way was I going back to my past. I was angry. Where did he want me to go back to? To the man who first raped me when I was eleven? To the husband who beat me until I moved out here? How would I sit in front of him or anybody else and mentally go back? No, I wouldn't do it. It was the first time after all my years of coming into the building that I felt totally threatened.

I thought at that point maybe I didn't need recovery. I wasn't going back anywhere. But Cecil told us all we had to go back. I listened to one of the men go back. His mother had given him up as a baby. He waited twenty-five years to find her, and she told him, "I didn't want you then, and I don't want you now."

Women started coming just to see what was going on. I began to hear my story in other women. One time we broke up into small groups, and Janice had us enact each other's roles. I had to play the abandoned man's mother. He became my abusive husband. We reenacted the cycle of violence just as it had always happened. It was explosive, it was traumatic, and it worked.

Praise the Lord, it worked. I relived the pain, faced it, and let it go. Now I wake up in the morning and if I choose to think about any of the abuse in my life, I can think of it in the past tense. It's not in the present anymore.

The group of us that was here at the beginning started holding circle meetings at eleven o'clock, three o'clock, and five o'clock in the afternoon. Eleven o'clock was for those of us working to not be addicted. Three o'clock was for those who were interested in understanding the physical symptoms and mental effects of cocaine. Five o'clock was for anybody who wanted to come. We began to run those meetings, but we never separated ourselves from the group. We all sat together.

I would share with the five o'clock meeting. I based what I had to say on what my life was like, past and present. I would always remind them that, yes, this is me. This is the Glide child. This is the same Edna who works here. This is me.

I remember the day that we had the circle and I had used the night before. I was so angry with myself that I took it out on the group when they said that I had "slipped." I explained, "You slip on a banana peel; what I did was sabotage my own recovery." I was so tired of no one, especially my children, recognizing my recovery. My children couldn't believe that recovery was possible. They didn't believe I wouldn't smoke another chewy. They wouldn't believe that I wouldn't go in my room and close the door with a forty-ounce bottle and let the smoke roll. I had to deal with my anger as another part of my recovery. I had to accept my children's attitudes. Of course, they didn't believe me; they didn't trust me.

I'd gone home talking recovery, and I hadn't smoked. But then my daughter wouldn't do the dishes, and I'd get mad. I'd say, "Now listen, I'm in recovery. Don't do stuff like that." I was really asking them to be perfect children.

I had to deal with the truth that things were going to make me upset. Nothing would ever change that. As I kept talking in the circle and broke it down until I understood why I had smoked the night before, I saw how I had sabotaged myself and set up my children.

I had to deal with issues and accept myself and decide that, no matter what happened, I wasn't going to use no dope. I had to decide that I wouldn't stay in recovery for Cecil, Janice, or the children. Recovery was for me.

I have a right to live, to breathe, and to think clearly. I have a right to be the best that I can be. I can expect life to allow me the best that it has to offer. The dark days are going to come, but that doesn't mean I gotta run, I gotta hide. And it certainly doesn't mean that I can cop out, smoke Crack, and not think.

I was hesitant to give up all my pain and let it go. I thought, "If I give up my pain, what else do I have to hold on to?" Being human, there is something scary about the emptiness inside us. To me, emptiness now means having space.

I gave up all of my life, which has been full of so much darkness. Now I have a space, not a void. It's like I had a house with lots of rooms full of secondhand stuff that other people made me put in there. Then one day, I moved all that stuff out. My house is empty. Now, all I got to do is to spend my time very wisely, like money, and put in my house only that which fits and I want to be there. If someone wants to give me a brand new piano to fill up my empty living room but I don't play the piano, I gotta be careful. For whatever you take from other people, you someday gonna get stuck with and have to do something about all by yourself. You got to find a way to move it out at your own expense.

My emptiness sometimes tells me: "Don't you want to date? You know you getting older. You forty-five. Honey, when you gonna stop wearing tennis shoes and a ponytail?" I hear all of the supposed to's. But I don't have to do anything but live every second, every hour of each and every day. I have to live it in accordance with my Spirit, with my chosen way of life, which is very simple. I have to remain the way I am, so that my truth will always be the truth. Then I will always be free.

The day that Rev. Cecil Williams stuck his head in the Crisis Center and said he wanted to talk to me, I didn't know that what we would discover together would be so simple but so great. His approach, his attitude toward life and pain is so simple that it gets to the bottom of things that even psychiatrists can't get to. I know, I've had plenty of them. Never had I found freedom. Never had I been allowed the time, the space, and the people to experience recovery through them. I believe most of the brothers and sisters who come in to Glide and gain recovery do so because of what someone who sat next to them or across from them said. When they hear their own story being told by somebody else, each one comes to realize there are many me's. I lived my whole life feeling I was the only one who had this pain or coped with it like I did. But there are many me's.

In past years, especially since the recovery program started, I have listened to many women's stories and have shared prayers and tears and joy. I know what they are talking about. The victory is in the opening of the doors. Just open the doors and give everyone the same chance to tell the truth. Don't label what people bring in. Let them tell the truth.

At Glide we started with one thing in the drug program, and from that we stumbled upon many things—poverty, pain, abuse. Then we had to open more doors, to keep opening doors. That's what keeps Glide growing and turning over. We hold on to the basic foundation of life and let go of the ideas or programs that aren't bringing life.

I earned and learned a whole lot that new people coming through the doors don't know exists. I get to talk to some of them and tell the story. That helps; I enjoy that. I'm blessed. I never ever thought my life would be so good.

I often wonder what my life would have been like if I never had come to Glide. I am pretty sure that I would have been dead. I wanted to die. I thought it was much easier to be dead than to live. I struggled to die. I lived to die.

I never understood why God didn't let me die. Die, die, die. But then I came to Glide. I work here because all that is in me knows that it didn't have to be me that ended up here. There are so many me's out there.

Me and life, the good Lord and Glide, brought me as far as they could carry me. Now it's my time to carry myself using the tools they gave me. I use the tools of faith, Spirit, and everything I ever said or did to share with someone else. I can listen to someone else, and smile and hold them.

Recovery isn't something sacred for a chosen few. It's not a value like money that only those who have enough can use to enter society or own a condo. Recovery is something anybody can have. I wish everybody could know the joy that comes from a "freed me."

The spiritual part of the recovery program is found in the truth—telling your own story, setting your own stage, as Cecil calls it. I learned that to give others my truth and my pain is to free me from it. It's the secret part of our lives that destroys. If you don't have a secret in your heart or in your mind, then you don't care what the world knows about you. What can the world say that I haven't already said about me first?

That's recovery. Recovery gave me the right to finally speak the truth, be heard, take my pain off the shelf, get it out of the closet, and let it go. Then life came rushing in.

Community: A Spirituality of Community

Growing up in the church in Texas I heard a lot about those who had the Spirit, but those described as spirit-filled seemed to be elevated out of their bodies somehow. They were holier than life, better, above the rest of the community. Getting filled with the Spirit seemed to me more like an escape from loving, from risk, from commitment to real people in the real world.

That's not what it means to be spiritual. The Spirit comes to make us free and fully alive. Any church that teaches that the Spirit makes us dull, dead, at rest, removed from the pains and struggles of life isn't talking about the true Spirit. The Spirit lifts us but not off the earth or out of the community. The Spirit lifts us so that we can live right here and now.

THE PLACENTA GROUP

It wasn't long after the First Generation started to take shape and form that the press began to show up at Glide. Funny how the media thinks it is newsworthy when a black minister and a group of African American addicts claim they are doing something for themselves. Much of the initial coverage was negative or skeptical.

Some of the articles presented some widely held assumptions as if they were facts: Crack addicts don't recover. Everybody knows Crack addicts are the lowest rung of users. Forget them, they'll go away. What is a church doing messing with recovery? Doesn't Glide know the only role the church has to play in recovery is to rent out its basements for AA meetings after hours?

The Twelve Steps had become the new holy writ for secular America. The principles of the Big Book were infallible, inerrant, and complete.

Underneath the media skepticism lay the disbelief that black folks could solve their own problems without the experts, without the federal government, and without much money.

Every day more addicts came to Glide. More than a hundred had come, some choosing to stay, others returning to the drug mix. We needed people to get involved as counselors and as support people. I could no longer lead all the meetings or keep up with all the stories.

I didn't know how the people would come on board, but I knew we were on to something. So I did what I always do when I'm not sure of the next step. I start spreading the word about the need. I took the First Generation everywhere. Some told their stories on television. A group testified before the Department of Health. Every Sunday they were on the platform telling it all.

Some of them revolted. Like Jamal. He told me, "I'm tired of standing in front of all these people—especially the rich white folks from Marin County—and telling them I'm homeless, been on drugs, and have nowhere to go."

But I kept taking him and the others places and putting them up to talk. A few weeks later Jamal came back and said, "I see what you're doin'. By keeping us up front you are saying, 'Look here, these folk are right here in front of your face every day, every Sunday. These are the people on Crack; some are sitting next to you. Some of them are your kids. Here they are.'"

Jamal had me; he understood. By keeping the First Generation up front, I was issuing a challenge to the community, the congregation, and the broader community. I was asking them, What are you going to do about this problem?

In September of 1988, some months after I started meeting with the First Generation, I figured out what to do. It was time to do or die.

One Sunday I brought the First Generation up to the platform. I looked out at the congregation and said without much fanfare, "I need some people who will embrace these folks. I want to form a Placenta group around these people who are almost ready to be reborn in recovery. Y'all know a placenta is what feeds a fetus in the womb before it is self-sufficient. That's what I'm talking about. Do you hear what I'm saying?"

There was a silence that day, and that's unusual for Glide. "I need some folks willing to be vulnerable, to face this problem, and to help these folks help themselves. C'mon up, y'all."

A pause, yes, a pregnant one, hung in the air for a moment. No one moved. I didn't say anything. I waited.

I could tell people were counting the cost. It was one thing to clap and cheer on those in recovery. It was another one to make a commitment of time. And what about the risk? Who knew if any of the First Generation would make it and stay clean for the long haul?

I knew that some who came to Glide were glad to sit, sing, and celebrate next to an addict. They were even willing to come on Thanksgiving and Christmas and serve food and feel good about doing something for humanity. But this was risky.

The silence hung heavy, laborious. One white man stood first and walked up the aisle to join us on the platform. One after another slowly unfurled from the pews and stood up.

After the service all who had volunteered, and a few more who were curious, joined the First Generation in Freedom Hall. I told the volunteers that I needed the Placenta to listen to and support the First Generation. Together they could figure out ways to help. I told those gathered that I didn't want anyone slicking the Generation. No one could use the recovering people to perform free labor or anything like that. Then I left it alone. The group was on its own. Ideas started clicking. The Generation said it needed transportation help, doctors, dentists, and support from nonaddicts.

When the meeting ended, a schedule of future meetings was set. Twenty-five people, mostly white and black women and a couple of white men, showed up the following night. I slipped into the background.

There was little trust at first. Early on Jamal had a bellyful of anger and he dumped it. "I'm not here to tell a bunch of white folks what you can do for me. You can't do shit for me. You never did nothing for me before." Years of anger boiled over. "Why you here? Is this a hobby for you? You a bored housewife with nothing better to do? Why you turned on by helping me make it?"

He was trying their commitments and testing one of his theories previously tried only while dealing on the streets of Manhattan. In his earlier days he found a black man could easily intimidate a white person. He gave it his best shot.

One of the women shot back at him. She showed spunk. Jamal told me later, "Damn! These some bold white people." They were serious. Their spunk made Jamal decide to be vulnerable and give it a try.

Slowly the group overcame barriers. That was good. Some of the members were of a social status that they had never really talked to a person plagued by poverty, let alone a poor black person. As the walls came tumbling down, the members from the congregation discovered how coming outside of themselves actually helped them open up, too. Stories of alcoholism, incest, all sorts of problems got shared from both sides.

Then deeper motives began to show. Some weren't so good. A couple of the white women were from the South and carried loads of guilt over growing up in a culture that had benefited from slavery. A few wanted to help someone else as a way of running from their own pain. Looking on, I realized there is a fine line between encouraging growth in another and enabling bad behavior. I saw codependency at work. A warning went off in my head, but I knew that people learned best from experience. Time would clarify a lot of things. I also had to trust that the Spirit had moved me and the congregation thus far; the Spirit would continue to take us deeper into the issue of recovery as we were ready.

One of the women in the group purchased theater tickets for any who wanted to go. Potlucks at different people's homes followed. Relationships were formed; that was good. Some of the Generation leaned too heavily on the Placenta; that wasn't good.

On graduation day, the First Generation and the Placenta group crowded the platform. There was lots of crying. We learned a spiritual principle that day: If there is not healing on both sides, then there is no healing.

A few weeks later a second group of Crack addicts joined our recovery program. A Placenta group formed around this Second Generation. We marched on, struggling to walk the thin line that separates helping that leads to healing and helping that pushes people further into denial. I began to think more about the function of a placenta—the unborn feed off it. Some of the recovering addicts seemed to be more than feeding off the Placenta group; they seemed to be preying on its riches. Some of the members of the Placenta were hiding their own pain behind the guise of helping. It was time to try something else.

By the time the Third Generation formed, we waited to encourage interaction with the broader community until the Generation graduated from the seventeen-week program we'd developed by then.* After several months of intensive recovery work, the Third Generation was "born," graduated into the extended family. We no longer formed Placenta groups. Instead we began to understand the church initially acts more like the womb, the holding place, for those struggling toward new life.

After graduating or being "rebirthed," the members of each New Generation became a full, growing part of the extended family. Generation by Generation they keep pushing into the church, bringing with them the power of new life, the power of the Spirit.

---

*Our culturally specific drug education program, called Facts on Crack, evolved from the initial informal circle meetings. Facts on Crack is explained in more detail in chapter 5.

Cecil challenges the
Commonwealth Club
wih a rousing speech
on "The Liberation
of Poverty and Power"
in 1990.

Cecil and some of Glide's
program participants stand
on the corner of Taylor and
Ellis streets.

An army composed of the
Glide family, civil leaders,
and concerned neighbors
declare the war on addiction
in the troubled Tenderloin
area.

Cecil calls out to some dealers and users inside a Crack apartment in the project at Valencia Gardens in early 1989.

Addicts join Cecil in the Glide Sanctuary to smash their Crack pipes to symbolize the choice for life after death.

Cecil and members of the Thirteenth Generation review the Ten Terms of Resistance.

Marchers rally at Boeddeker Park to declare "The Tenderloin needs Recovery!"

Cecil listens to neighborhood residents during the March on the Tenderloin in September, 1990.

Eddie Lee Franks, III, Director of Facts on Crack, proudly graduates the Thirteenth Generation into Glide's extended family in the spring of 1992.

Cecil begins a Sunday Glide Celebration
service.

The soulful, spirited
Glide Ensemble.

The Glide family is a rainbow of races,
classes and sexes.

One million meals are served annually in Glide's two dining rooms.

Cecil, Mo Bernstein (center), and Fred Furth (center, second row), major benefactors of Glide's food program, pose with kitchen staff in 1990.

A peer tutor assists one of the five hundred children who participate in Computers and You, a literacy and academic skill-building program begun in 1988.

Janice Mirikitani, Oprah Winfrey, Cecil, and Maya Angelou offer Easter smiles after the Sunrise Celebration service in 1989.

Mother Clara Hale, heroine of Harlem for her work with Crack-addicted children proudly holds the first baby born drug-free to a Glide participant in the First Generation during the Death of a Race Conference.

Then mayor of San Francisco, Dianne Feinstein, and Edna Watts, Director of Glide's Crisis Care, join the festivities honoring the work of Mo's kitchen in 1987.

Leroy Looper, a Tenderloin community leader, joins forces with Frank Jordan, then San Francisco Police Chief (who later became mayor), in planning the march on the Tenderloin in September 1990.

Cecil extends an open mike to the crowd of concerned leaders and citizens from around the country at a televised Town Meeting during the Rebirth of a Race Conference, Glide's second national conference, in April 1990.

Coretta Scott King greets some of Glide's young people at the Rebirth of a Race Conference.

Eddie Franks, Jamal Leech, and Ed Jackson show their appreciation for Coretta Scott King's speech at the Death of a Race Conference.

Cecil and Janice, as
Minister of Liberation
and Director of
Programs, husband
and wife, fulfill various
roles for the Glide
extended family.

A warm hug is shared between
Janice and Tony during the march
on the Tenderloin.

Three Cambodian children march
carrying signs written for the many
Southeast Asian immigrant families
who live in the Tenderloin.

CHAPTER THREE

The Death of a Race

Recognition: A New Agent of Genocide

There is no stopping a group of people marching forward armed with the Spirit and girded with the truth. By 1989 the Third Generation started surging forward and a Fourth Generation was forming; many from the early Placenta groups had recognized their own needs for recovery and linked arms with those in the march toward freedom. The cry *It's Recovery Time* echoed throughout Glide and moved through extended families and into the black community.

People not associated with Glide wanted to know what was going on. Small groups traveled at their own expense from far and wide to come and see, to listen and learn.

Soon the plans for a national conference emerged. We'd do what we did on a small scale with the First Generation—we'd open the doors to people from around the country and let them have their say. We'd provide the gathering place and the open microphone.

A committee soon circled my office—folks from the New Generation joined with members of the congregation, ministers, substance abuse professionals, medical people, and black leaders. We brainstormed, asking one another, What issues are essential to recovery? Our scribe, Dave Richmond, the deputy director of programs, scribbled furiously, quickly filling the large sheets of paper taped to the wall. He wrote: The Medical Aspects of Crack; Models for Recovery from Addiction; Crack, AIDS, and Sexually Transmitted Diseases; Crack, Homelessness, and Poverty; Codependency in the Black Family; The Economics of Crack Cocaine; Crack and the Criminal Justice System; Women and Crack; Youth and Crack; The Role of the

Church in Fighting Crack; The Future of the Black Family and Community; Racism and Crack.

When our ideas ran dry, we sat silently, studying the list. Up until now we had thought that the goal of recovery was sobriety and getting off drugs. This list proved sobriety was but an important short-term goal—a step on the way to another destination. Addiction was but a symptom of a much greater problem.

What did all these issues, topics, and concerns add up to? A word sprang to my mind; it ambushed me: *Genocide*.

The very existence of African Americans was at stake. The battle against Crack was but the most recent skirmish in the long war fought by black Americans for the freedom to exist and the right to participate fully in society.

Now I knew why seeing the women strung out on Crack wandering through Boeddeker Park had made me smell death. I was smelling the death of a race, the African American community, my people. Crack dealers had told me that their primary targeted customers were black women. If you get them, you get to their children and their men. While the dealers had their minds on selling drugs to gain money and power, they were really selling away the future of our race.

Genocide is a loaded word. But genocide is not only the extermination of a people through systematic mass murder. What I began to think about and talk about was genocide, 1990s style: when the spirit of a people is destroyed, when the culture of a people is eradicated, when basic human relationships are ripped apart, when large numbers of people are killed because of drug-related crimes and overdoses. This amounts to modern genocide— the spiritual and physical death of a people, my people.

African Americans have faced many attempts to destroy us. Two hundred years of slavery tried to break the Spirit and culture of our people. For more than half of this century, economic oppression, legalized segregation, and lynch mobs were set against us. During the sixties and early seventies, the American intelligence community engaged in a systematic effort to discredit and destroy individuals and programs in the black community. The seventies and eighties saw the erosion of the social and economic gains of the black community. This was accompanied by a general acceptance of the attitude that blacks were, at best, expendable.

Somehow, some way, through it all, African Americans survived. Our people's Spirit flourished with courage and creativity. A special human relationship had ensured our survival: The extended black family had always sustained us. Even if you had no mother or father, you had "mother" and "father" in the community.

Slavery held power for so long because it tore apart the black family. Each new generation was sold away before it could put down roots. The stories of strength and survival that had passed from one generation to the next were silenced. Children were taken away from their parents at birth. The new slavery of Crack results in a similar family disintegration. In the 1990s babies are taken from their mothers by the Department of Social Services, often without any effort to connect the children with a healthy extended-family member, and placed in foster care. This methodology has proven effective before. Destroy the extended family and black will turn against black.

Another similarity between slavery and the cocaine epidemic became starkly clear. Both are firmly grounded in economics—at the expense of a race of people. There was, and is, money to be made.

Cocaine, like cotton, is foreign to the African American culture. We did not create it; we did not produce it; we did not ask for it. Crack is an import, and while members of other races use Crack, its full destructive fury was unleashed in the black community.

People asked me during that conference planning meeting, "If there is genocide, who is behind it?" As the weeks went on, I was asked that question again and again.

I didn't have a pat answer. Every time someone raised that question, I got irritated. The questions implicitly assumed that somewhere there is a lone individual responsible. If we could just capture that person, the problem would be solved.

That assumption, that naive hope, that there is one culprit on the loose allows all of us, black and white alike, to escape responsibility. I have long believed that the only way to solve any social problem is for each segment of society to assume some blame for creating the problem and to grab hands with others in the community and work together to make things better.

There are many active agents of genocide: those who are allowed to continue importing drugs and those in our government who have winked and nodded at drug trafficking in the name of "national security." The agents of genocide are the dealers—white, black, brown, and yellow, who stand on the corner and sell drugs to our young. The police officers who let them deal freely are to blame. There are those in the "justice" department who hustle Crack addicts into jail, with no thought or care given to their recovery.

Just as significant are the passive agents of genocide—the millions of Americans who are indifferent, afraid, or don't want to get involved. Those who don't do what they can to solve the problem of Crack support genocide.

With such a huge sleeping army behind the drug trade, how could genocide be stopped? I asked myself that question and knew that the answer would be found, once again, by looking at the tools and power that African Americans have used before. We would have to use them again. I looked back at our history as a people and my history as an African American. Where had our power to survive, resist, and overcome come from? Where did it originate? How could we become empowered to overcome *again?*

FAITH AND RESISTANCE

I thought back over the many examples of faith and resistance that were told to me as a young boy. Most of the New Generation didn't know these stories. My peers had failed to fully pass on our heritage to the New Generation.

Those coming up in the black community needed to hear that before the Civil War, Harriet Tubman, born into slavery, escaped, but she wasn't satisfied that she herself was free. Again and again she walked south and stood on the edge of a plantation singing:

Steal away, steal away,
Steal away to Jesus.
Steal away, steal away home,
I ain't got long to stay here.

Harriet sang, not to soothe those still enslaved. No, she sang to call out to those willing to risk everything for freedom. She sang to signal them to join her in the flight northward. Many did, and their flight to freedom was hard. No one could tell mother, father, sister, or brother of the plans to leave. Each one had to follow Harriet's every word and command. No matter what happened or what lay ahead, there would be no turning back.

When the New Generation heard the stories of faith and resistance, they began to realize they were not alone. I told them more.

A century later, on December 1, 1955, Rosa Parks, a volunteer secretary for the local NAACP, pushed toward freedom simply by boarding a bus after a long day working as a tailor's assistant in a Montgomery, Alabama, department store. She sat in the back, taking a seat in the black section, but as the white section filled up, she was asked, as blacks often were, to vacate her seat for a white man. An entire row was told to move; a white man couldn't be expected to sit next to a black woman. Others moved, but Rosa refused. When the bus driver asked a second time if she was going to move, Rosa replied, "No, I'm not." She resisted.

Rosa was arrested. By refusing to move, Rosa proved she, and thousands like her, weren't going to take it anymore. Blacks in Montgomery boycotted the buses. They walked to work. They began to march toward freedom.

I told the New Generation of my own experiences of racism.

I remembered riding the train as a young boy prior to the civil rights movement. My mother put my brothers and me on the train and handed us brown bags full of fried chicken. The conductors escorted us to the dirty, shabby Jim Crow car reserved for blacks like us. The conductor sneered as he pulled the curtain separating white from black, as if he had power over us.

I'll never forget that my brothers and I started laughing. We laughed until we cried. We laughed at that man because he thought he had put us in our place. We laughed because we knew he would be the one chastised. Someday we would be free.

Harriet Tubman had started the Freedom Train on the Underground Railroad. Rosa Parks refused to give up her seat for a white man, and she started our people marching. That white conductor thought he had power over us because he knew the rules and laws were in his favor. What he didn't know was that the power of the Spirit and the truth were on our side. We had the power of knowing who we were and that someday we would be free. We had a power born of the Spirit. That Spirit was alive in the souls of our people.

Liberation had come for us before because we gathered at night on our front porches and told stories of our ancestors, of their struggle, and of ours. We sang spirituals, moaning out the truth of our troubles and soaring high on the freeing, unshakable hope rooted in our souls. Then when our stories were told and our songs sung, we discussed strategy late into the night as to how we could get beyond being enslaved in body, mind, and Spirit.

We spent a lot of time on our front porches figuring out how the white man thinks. We surely knew more about him than he ever took the time to learn about us. My friend Maya Angelou and I compared notes on how we and our forebears had studied our oppressors. Maya read from one of her books in her throaty, powerful voice:

For centuries we had proved their faces, the angles of their bodies, the sounds of their voices and even their odors. Often our survival had depended upon the accurate reading of a white man's chuckle or the disdainful wave of a white *woman's hand. . . . Oh, but we knew them with the intimacy of a surgeon's scalpel.* *

We studied and learned well. We discovered the white man's strengths and weaknesses. There was one clear conclusion to make: The true love of our oppressors was money. They wanted us to make it our true love, too. If we did, then they would have us. We would start to mimic them, to use their ways, and they would be able to stay several steps in front of us. We would always remain in their debt.

During the days of the civil rights movement we all knew that money would never be the source of black power. Somehow some of those in the following generation of African Americans had come to crave the power of money. To get it, they were selling Crack and preying off their brothers and sisters.

Black power is rooted in Spirit, in truth, and in the extended family. We can overcome any ill as long as we march and move forward together.

When the extended family gathers and by so doing answers the question of who we are as a people, incredible power is unleashed. That's the kind of power that stops genocide in its tracks and turns around those who have been holding us enslaved to drugs. The power of a committed, marching army makes those whose power is found in money run for their lives.

Then and now, the only way to stop genocide is for those who are being enslaved to be empowered. It's time to claim the power to change ourselves and make our lives better. God placed the strongest power in the world inside us at creation. Like a diamond crystallized from ordinary coal, the power to choose, to be, to change, to risk is buried inside each of us. God gives us the task of mining, honing, and polishing this mighty gift of power. What lies within us is pure Spirit: unbeatable strength, undescribable beauty—a prism able to reflect the burning light of truth. We are the answer to the problem of genocide.

As the New Generation at Glide gathered in Freedom Hall and as we retold the stories of our people, we understood ourselves anew as people of faith and resistance—people of the Spirit. Edna, Jamal, and a host of others had joined me and the extended family of Glide. Together we were marching toward freedom. By April 1989 when the Death of a Race Conference convened, I was euphoric. Knowing that the 1,100 people were thirsting for freedom filled me with hope. Admittedly, a few hundred folks, mostly

---

*Maya Angelou, *The Heart of a Woman* (New York: Bantam, 1981), pp. 179–80.

black folks, were a small army to fight the most potent drug of the century and the social and political structures that benefited from drug trafficking. We were a small army, yes, but an empowered, unstoppable one, marching for freedom.

Self-Definition: The Inner Source of Power

When my family gathered on the front porch during my childhood, we let loose. We were ourselves. Sometimes we were sad, silly, or silent. Other times we danced, screamed, or acted up. On that porch we found the acceptance that allowed us to be real. We were authentic, natural. On that porch we found our individual and collective power by being ourselves and being together.

I learned there that *empowerment begins with authenticity.* Each of us has a wellspring of spirituality, our own inner source of power. That power can be tapped, drawn up only when we are authentically who God created us to be. The Spirit wants Cecil Williams to act like Cecil Williams, not like anybody else. Whenever I lie, cheat, put on airs, pretend I'm something I'm not, or run from my pain, then I'm not being authentic. I'm being toxic, impure, powerless.

When, as a race, African Americans accept the definition of others, we are accepting a false definition of ourselves. When one of us believes that getting rich is the key to power, even if it means selling Crack to our younger black sisters and brothers, then that one is believing a lie, living a lie.

The truth is that it is not black to smoke Crack. Crack is someone else's crop that we are selling. Someone else is getting really rich, and we are the ones who are falling over in the fields with lungs full of poison and bullet wounds in our chests. That's toxic living for African Americans.

Accepting another's means of power leads only to ultimate powerlessness. It's time for African Americans, for every person caught in unauthentic living, to define ourselves. It's time to be natural and authentic.

To act authentically, we must write our own lines for the drama of our lives. No one can say other people's lines. I can't live out someone else's story. We must write and act out our own life stories. Each of us has a story to tell and a life to live. The diamond inside—the Spirit—must be uncovered, carried with pride; its beauty and strength must be shared with the extended family. It is our source of power.

Jesus shows us what it means to be an empowered and liberated person. In the Book of John in the Bible, Jesus declares himself by a series of statements that all begin with the words "I am." He says, "I am the Good Shepherd." "I am he." "I am here." Jesus declares himself and takes a stand.

We, too, have to learn to declare ourselves, to say, "I am someone. I am here. I am important. I am taking a stand."

Jesus was a very special person who came with self-declaration, with self-affirmation, with self-recognition. He came acknowledging who he was. He was saying, "I know something about me."

In the Bible Jesus admits, commits, asserts, protests, and says, "I am the way. I am the one who brings living water." Jesus witnessed to who he was. He asserted what I call his I am–ness. Jesus was an "I am" person. He had the audacity to make a self-declaration. He exposed his being.

We must acknowledge, claim, and assert our personhood, our deepest identity, too. We are called to witness to who we are.

By declaring who he was, Jesus required a response from those who heard him. When we hear who Jesus is, we must say something in return. Essentially Jesus says, "Here's who I am. Who are you?"

I must say and believe completely that "I, Cecil Williams, am created and loved by God. I am African American. I am a man. I am a minister. I am a member of the human family."

When Jesus, or anybody else, fully and authentically declares himself or herself, we can't just sit there. We have to acknowledge who we are. We have to say out loud who we are.

Empowerment requires claiming ownership of your culture and your life. An empowered person is one who knows where he or she has come from. An empowered person has found his or her dependable cultural, ancestral, and spiritual roots.

Jesus had a special way of articulating and living his identity. Jesus claimed his relationship to God, his Jewishness, his humanness, his roots in the small town of Nazareth. Then he built upon these declarations of his identity and lived out his world-changing mission.

So, too, with us. All of our "I am" statements converge into a cosmic and cultural sense of identity that helps us find a sense of destiny.

Jesus didn't have a problem dealing with identity. Some folks in recovery have said to me that declaring my I am–ness is being selfish or conceited. But I always say in return, "How can I ever become somebody if I never discover my I am–ness? How can I ever love you if I never learn to love me? How can I ever stand my ground if I'm not firmly planted somewhere, with my roots pushing down deep, nourishing me and holding me upright? My ancestors have plowed the ground before me. They pushed down roots that hold me up."

Self-declaration is hardly selfish. It is acknowledging that each of us is a full, important member of the human family.

Empowerment comes in knowing that you have power but you are not the ultimate power. We each must claim every bit of power that we have. We must tap into the deeply flowing wells of our own lives. But someday, when the well runs dry, and it will, we can be sure that there is another source of power, a greater source that is found in God.

When I was a boy in San Angelo, we had a garden, a small plot of property. Every year we would plant beans, corn, potatoes, black-eyed peas, and mustard greens. We had a few peach and apple trees. Each year my mother and grandmother would can and preserve the harvest for the winter. More than once, inclement weather or invading hordes of grasshoppers destroyed our garden. Then we didn't have provisions; our cupboard was bare.

As I remember, somehow, during those lean years, there was always food on the table when we children came home from school. Through the care of the extended family, through unexpected but much prayed-for miracles of an unexpected day job or gift of a few dollars at just the right moment, we survived. Those early experiences taught me that no matter how you till your soil or try to make things work, there will come a day when something happens and everything underneath you crumbles. You feel like there is nothing left.

It is those times that help us understand that the meaning of life is not found in always having enough food; it is not found in having plenty of money; it is not found in being in control in every arena of life. Meaning in life is found in knowing that we have the power to plant the seeds, to water, to watch for the harvest. We have the power to work and to make choices that will keep us healthy and alive.

When we have done all we can to care for ourselves and to till the ground of our lives and, despite our best efforts, one day there is no crop and no clear way to survive the winter, then God will provide. A way will be found.

When we come to the end of ourselves, then we are confronted with the truth that our power is not the ultimate power. The fact that my family somehow survived those winters without provisions taught me that when I have worked hard and still we don't have what we need, then I can point my finger beyond myself. Ultimate power is beyond me. While I till my own garden, I am assured that God is planting an unseen garden that will fill my cupboard even if my garden fails.

But most years, for most problems, God's provision is found in us. God has given us our lives; they are ours to live. When we begin to understand that we have ownership in this world, that we have an identity and something important to say about ourselves, then we begin to claim our power. We have been given the authority to name our names, to discover who we are, to till and plow the soil of our lives.

We must take ownership. When you are the owner, you have to do the work, and you alone must decide which tasks are meaningful to do. It's time to declare: "This ground belongs to me. This life belongs to me. My roots nourish me. The survival of my race, the quality of my life have something to do with me. My life, my actions, and claiming my power matter."

Those of us who have had our cultures snatched from us must be re-rooted. Those who have never learned about the courageous ones who came before us need to be nourished by hearing about their lives. Our roots are reestablished through storytelling, through spirituality, through sitting on a front porch with others who are like us. The best nourishment comes from solid, deep roots that know where the water, where the power is found.

True empowerment can be measured by the good it offers to the extended family. Each of us is empowered so that the community, our race, and all of humanity can be empowered, too.

When each person brings his or her I am–ness together with others, we create a new community that can say, "We are a force, a group that is taking a stand." Whenever we say who we are, we open up and a new community is formed. Men, women, and children who declare "I am" become a part of a greater "we are." Every time I say "I am" I step into a new community. We each take a step or two by the way we live every day.

We observed at Glide that when some people discover their power for the first time, they may be tempted to think that their power is for their use alone. It is easy for one who is oppressed to use newly found power just as the oppressor wielded power. How often does a man resist a deal for a day and yet go home and pridefully smack his woman when she fails to do his bidding? It is easy to do, but it is never right.

If we treat our families like they are nobodies, if we treat our neighbors like they are nothing, we are misusing our power. People who think they are better than anybody else are living a lie.

As a new community of people committed to Spirit and truth, we cannot misuse or neglect our brothers and our sisters. We cannot oppress one another or ignore one another. How can we ignore the addicts still smoking their brains out in our neighborhoods? How can we neglect the women who stand on the street corners in the Tenderloin every day, filling their sex with the leftovers, hoping to make ends meet? Shall we hate our oppressors and in so doing become just like them—wrapped up in greed and selfishness?

No. That is not the way.

Power that oppresses, that puts down, that enslaves is never the power of the Spirit. Power that empowers is good, spiritual, and from within. We are empowered when we begin to accept the fact that we are more than our brother's keeper or our sister's keeper; we are our brother's brother and our sister's sister. We are kinfolk.

Becoming authentic, claiming one's power, and living in an extended family is never easy. But authenticity is the most powerful thing we can embrace. I preach authenticity and self-definition every week, in many ways. But I have to live it, too. That's my challenge.

No one has called me to authenticity the way Janice, my wife, has. Not only are we married to each other, but we have worked together daily at Glide for more than twenty-five years. She was my colleague and my friend before she became my wife. She has helped me to confront mutuality and equity in power at work and at home.

We are partners. I am the minister of Glide. She is the president of the Glide Foundation, the director of all our programs. To work together so closely, I have had to confront my male biases, sexist feelings, competitive urges, and autocratic ways.

Janice has had to come to grips with who she is as an Asian American woman. She has learned to stand her ground. She has reclaimed spirituality, and despite cultural taboos, she has told her story, a horrifying, painful story. Telling her story has freed her, and it has freed the women at Glide to keep telling their stories until they are heard, until they are believed, and until they are empowered.

On Sundays Janice stands near the platform, often wearing a wide-brimmed hat and flashing a wide, laughing smile, as she directs the flow of the service. Janice makes sure that people are recognized and information is accessed. She's not invisible or unheard, although that is how she felt for many years of her life. Janice has reclaimed herself. She's one of the most empowered persons at Glide.

Janice is a poet, and a couple of lines from one of her poems tells all:

Who is singing this song?
I am. *

Years ago Janice and I decided not to hide the truth about our lives from the congregation. It's been hard but good because the church knows we are human, struggling to make it just like they are. We're in this together.

Sometimes I'm the one standing at the platform's edge. When it's Janice's turn at the microphone, I just applaud and whisper, "Sing your song, Janice; tell it all."

Rebirth: Janice's Story

I WAS BORN IN Stockton, California, and immediately after my birth my family was sent to a concentration camp, as were 110,000 other Japanese Americans. My family spent three years incarcerated in an internment camp in Rohwer, Arkansas. That event was formative for my life and for my family's understanding of ourselves as Americans. Our incarceration was such a blatant act of racism, unconstitutional and unjustified. When we were released, the country as a whole tried to sweep our experience under America's vast rug of hostility and indifference toward people of color. History was written to minimize both our losses and the great courage Japanese Americans showed by rebuilding our lives. The experience of incarceration served to intensify our self-hatred and internalize our alienation from society. That experience of isolation, of being labeled because of our ancestry, skin color, and the shape of our eyes caused great shame and humiliation when indeed we were American citizens. The particular circumstances of my family, of my own experience in the camp are so much a part of who I am that it shaped my soul.

The camp experience of Japanese Americans has become my metaphor in many of my poems for the ongoing struggle against

---

*"Who Is Singing this Song?" *Shedding Silence:* Poetry and Prose by Janice Mirikitani, Berkeley: Celestial Arts, 1987, pp. 102–9.

racism. I keep a perpetual vigil within myself against complacency and the false sense of having somehow "made it" in American society.

Our extended family, like many Japanese-American families, was separated in the different camps. When we were released, the family didn't all regather in rural California; we didn't all return to the chicken farms where we had formerly scratched out a living. The camps served to break up the extended family and our means of community support.

When my family got out of the camp, my mother, father, and I moved to Chicago. Later, I was told, we moved there to escape racism. We escaped nothing. My parents, the products of an arranged marriage, divorced soon after our arrival.

The separation and divorce of my parents had a great impact on me because I felt that my father really didn't love me. I felt responsible for his leaving. I felt an inexpressible, profound loss. I was almost five years old.

Chicago with all of its extreme weather provided a metaphor for my young life—the bitter cold, windswept winters, and stifling summers were all things I felt both on my skin and inside my heart. My mother and I were very, very poor. As a single parent she worked two, sometimes three, jobs so we could survive. I remember waking up in the middle of the night, and she would be making crepe-paper flowers for the American Legion for a penny a bloom.

Seeing my mother's struggle to survive made me feel her pain. I felt her anger at being left by my father. He was involved with another woman, and that made it that much more difficult for her to feel good about herself.

I think I became my own absent parent, the partner my mother no longer had. A part of me felt responsible for my father's leaving, and I took on the responsibility of not being a burden on my mother. I took it upon myself to be home alone, to take care of myself when I was sick, and to not make demands on her. I still believe that she was doing the best that she could.

When she left me alone as a small child, that was the choice she felt she had to make as a woman without extended family, friends, or money. I internalized her sense of powerlessness. I believe she really felt that we were not going to be all right until a man came into our lives. She seemed so vulnerable. I felt that pain.

Then my mother remarried. Relief—there was a man in her life again. For me, her remarriage brought more tumult, more isolation, and more pain.

When I was in grammar school, my mother, stepfather, and I moved to Petaluma, California, to be near my mother's family. Still poor, we built a house and several chicken houses with our own hands and the help of one carpenter.

Farm life was very isolated. A cluster of us—aunts, uncles, cousins, grandparents, and friends—lived near one another, but the closest neighbor was several miles down the road.

From the age of five to the age of sixteen, I experienced sexual abuse. I never felt that I had any option other than hiding in the attic or going to school. I felt the abuse was inevitable. I was convinced if I told my mother outright, I would be responsible for her being abandoned again. I was warned that there would be death if I told. I would rather have my own shame than to be the cause of another departure, another death, and more pain for my mother.

There was a tremendous amount of denial. I would go to my grandmother for comfort. She didn't speak English, and I didn't speak Japanese well. She understood the cruelty I suffered, though I'm not sure how specifically. But I knew she also felt she couldn't stop it. What she could do was give me love. It was her unconditional love, her acceptance of me, her feeding me from her plate, her stroking my head buried sobbing in her lap that saved me.

She gave me the clues and cues on how to survive. When the pain from her aching bones brought tears to her eyes, she would sit and rock for a moment, hum something, tell my mother or the chickens or the grandchildren who flocked around her a funny story (we only knew it was funny because she laughed), and she'd get up and continue her work.

She bore twelve children (I think three were born dead). Without a day's rest she would be back out in the fields or in the sugarcane or carrying fifty-pound sacks of grain on her back. I don't know how she and others like her came through it all—coming here to this country via Hawaii, working sugar plantations; saving enough to have their American-citizen children, the Nisei, buy land; clearing away rocks and tree stumps to create the farm in California that they were forced to abandon during World War II; being incarcerated in concentration camps. Now that's survival. That is woman power.

My mother and her sisters, like many Nisei women, had to give up careers, college, jobs, and relationships because of the camps. But life went on. They did not give in to the stench of injustice and the descending boot of racism.

But Grandmother was like that old magic pot in her kitchen. No matter how bad it got, no matter how poor and hungry we were, no matter the drought or the pox epidemics in our chicken flocks, no matter how deep the indebtedness or the humiliation of the dust swirling from the long white car of the bill collector, Grandma would have something in that pot. And it was always good, tasty, nutritious. We grew out of that pot.

Grandmother was the embodiment of compassion. The animals sensed it in her. The children clung to her. She waited on my grandfather every morning and night, fed him and massaged his feet, warmed his sake and his bed. There was no question of diversion, no change in the routine she kept. But always, like the turning of the earth, like the rising of the sun, she was to me the power of survival.

So perhaps because she was my lifeline during my childhood, I did not succumb to insanity or suicide. I was abused, fondled, and violated by several adult males including a family dentist, friends of the family, visiting "uncles"—close and distant relatives. I remember some of them sitting on top of me and rubbing against me, all in the name of playfulness. My mother would scold me and tell me that I should not allow those "things" to happen. She gave me, a young child, the responsibility to stop an adult male. I couldn't.

For eleven years, almost daily, I was stalked in the darkness of closets, the barn, in muffled bedrooms. I would not tell anyone; I remained silent.

I feel I grew up in a dome of silence. The silence about the concentration camp experience created in me a longing to know more as I grew older. When I would question my mother about the camps, she would simply change the subject. It was as if my mother had closed those doors and sealed them tightly. When she finally broke her silence of nearly forty years and testified before the Wartime Commission on Redress and Reparations, as did many Nisei, it was as if the walls had crumbled. The significance of the testimonies was tremendous. However, after her public testimony, my mother simply put the experience back into the folds of her memory and I could not get much more information from her.

I believe that the silence about the camps deepened our sense of alienation about ourselves. The testimonies became part of our self-definition, the reclamation of our lives, and the resurrection of justice.

The silence imposed upon and created by me regarding the incest is far deeper, more disempowering. The self-hate internalized because of my Asianness, unacceptableness, and ugliness, coupled with the powerlessness I felt because of the abuse, rendered me totally invisible. I did not exist. I fabricated myself by creating a fantasy world. I escaped through reading and writing, imagining myself in stories about snow-white princesses who were rescued by white heroes on white horses.

There were few stories, movies, or images of Asian women back then. (And certainly even now there are too few positive images of people of color in mass media.) We were always depicted as evil, emasculated, small, stupid, and uncaring of human life. Asian women were one-dimensional caricatures or exotic sex objects.

I fantasized that I was a cream-complected girl with long blond curls, the good but mistreated, beautiful stepchild who was a victim of jealousy and evil, rescued inevitably by the prince.

I escaped by studying all the time, by excelling in school. Education was my means of escape, from home, from the farm, and from the dreariness, but it was also a cultural demand. Asians are usually required to study hard, with the belief that education is the means to success. I was even more motivated to escape. I wanted out from that isolated and cruel farm.

My family relocated to Los Angeles after I graduated from high school. I attended UCLA and studied English and dance; I moved into my own apartment.

At first, I pursued being white and middle-class during college. I tried to be a beauty queen, a cheerleader, all the things that I thought were part of the American dream. I Scotch-taped my eyes so they would be rounded; I bleached my skin.

When I graduated, I moved to Berkeley to get my teaching credential at the University of California. Then I taught high school for two years. At one suburban school, I encouraged the students to talk about war, peace, abortion, and birth control. The principal started sitting in on the class, and I wasn't asked back the next year. I decided that if I couldn't liberate these kids' minds, there was no point in teaching at that level. So I decided to go back to school and get my master's degree at San Francisco State University.

The political changes of the 1960s reflected the internal changes I felt. The Vietnam War intensified. American soldiers were again waging war on Asian soil. The civil rights movement was at its height. The black power movement was really affecting all people of color. Radical events were happening.

The SFSU ethnic studies strikes occurred while I was a student. As we protested for the right to study our own cultures, I was transformed. I went through the fire of seeing myself for who I really was and was affirmed for being just that. As ethnic students, we championed yellow pride and black power. It was a time for us to define ourselves.

In 1965 I started working part-time at Glide transcribing tapes of interviews of people who had been harassed by the police. The church secretary went on vacation, and I was asked to fill in for her. When she returned, I was asked to stay on as her assistant in the church office.

I shall not forget the first time I met Cecil. Someone introduced me to him, and he asked, "Don't you know who I am?" He seemed shocked that someone working at Glide didn't recognize him. He asked again, "You don't know who *I* am?" I should have said, looking back at myself at that time, "Hell, I don't know who *I* am!"

I soon became Cecil's administrative assistant, a post I held until 1969. During this time I married my first husband. Cecil actually performed the ceremony. My daughter was born a year later.

Working at Glide turned me around. I had to become responsible for myself and for my power or else drown in my own cesspool of self-pity and narcissism.

Personally, and as a support system, the Glide staff got involved in the free speech movement and the antiwar protests. They also supported justice for political prisoners by aligning themselves with the Black Panther Party and Angela Davis, and they showed solidarity with Native Americans on Alcatraz and at Wounded Knee. When gay teenagers and runaways walked the streets, Glide started Hospitality House and Huckleberry House for Runaways, two programs that still exist independently today.

Through working together for social change, I began making friends who helped me to break through my own denial and despair. One such friend cared enough for me to intervene in my life when I tried to push away my pain by drinking myself to sleep at night.

He told me he wanted me to meet a friend of his. He and some of my other friends wanted to warn me, to wake me up to what I could become if I kept drowning my sorrows. The meeting shocked me into seeing the truth. As I often do when faced with the stark reality of life, I later wrote a poem about that day.

> *Lydia*
> *sat up from her bed*
> *long enough to vomit in the bucket*
> *and guzzle again from her bottle of fortified wine.*
> *They brought me to her, my friends did,*
> *because I was drinking,*
> *and they wanted me to see the room,*
> *her in bed, surrounded by photographs,*
> *her bucket and the sour smell of death.*
> *Her long, bone-thin finger*
> *curled into her palms,*
> *dragged across the sheets beckoning me closer.*
> *Lydia's flesh bloats around her eyes,*
> *her skin, dark red, rusting from throttled kidneys.*
> *Her hair is scant and patchy, and when she smiles,*
> *her gums reveal one loose tooth.*
> *She vomits again, blood this time.*
> *She points to a photo of a young woman*
> *who is smiling, cheeks smooth, her eyes shining*
> *and black as her thick braided hair.*
> *I have never seen such a beautiful woman.*
> *Lydia vomits once more and laughs.*
> *Her toothless grin sparks a moment.*
> *"That is me," she gulps, swallows wine, her throat*
> *bobbing up/down like a boat.*
> *"THAT IS ME," she says, pointing to the photo.*
> *And she says, pointing to herself,*
> *"THIS IS YOU."*

Lydia stopped me in my tracks. I came face-to-face with my responsibility and realized I had to choose between life and death.

In the late sixties and early seventies I became involved in Third World Communications, an arts and literary collective. I was the editor of the first Asian American magazine on the West Coast. Others quickly emerged. That was my way of being involved in creating a voice for those of us who had been silenced or excluded. Ethnic writers of color came together to create five anthologies. We wrote poetry, es-says, music, stories, and novels, and we supported one another on the journey of self-definition, empowerment, and liberation. We held ben-efits for every cause imaginable, many in Glide Church's sanctuary. We provided support, advocacy, and a platform for civil rights functions.

The poetry readings and meetings with Third-World women cre-ated a new community for me. Finding these women was like finding my family. We said to one another, "You do that to your hair, too?" "You bleached your skin, too?" "Yeah, my grandmother would dig up roots, cut up chicken feet, scrape the belly linings, boil up the cockscombs, pickle pigs' feet, save the pigs' blood, and eat the eye of the fish for good luck." And more, so much more.

Maya Angelou, who was a mentor and an inspiration, supported and encouraged us, lending her name, her advice, her empowering voice. We came together and gave amplification to the stories, to the affir-mation of who we are.

We revealed ourselves. Having other women echo my experience and my feelings was a miracle. Before, when I looked into the mirror, I was an ugly, worthless person, without definition. When I looked at these sisters, I saw beauty. And I saw the possibility of creating mine.

In this gathering of women, I experienced power—the power found in community. The power that changes society and changed me can only emerge through community. Because the extended family strengthened me, I could engage in a journey of self-discovery. I began to define myself, realizing I could not be white and did not want to be. I no longer wanted to be dependent on the man in my life. I was fully responsible for my choices, and I could not control anyone else's. My marriage, which had been woven from my desire to be white, un-raveled.

I had to accept the consequences for my choices and that made a great difference to me. I was breaking my "victim" cycle. In many ways I was learning to say to the people in my life, "My choices may not be acceptable to you, but all I can give you is who I really am."

My struggle to be more honest earned me friends who were willing to mirror back what they saw in me—both the beautiful and the dys-functional. I could see my life more clearly as a journey toward em-powerment.

Cecil was my friend for many years. It was hard for me to have a friend whom I didn't want to make into a father—someone who would take responsibility for my life. Cecil helped me to pull myself out of a pool of narcissism. He did not put up with my games of coyness or mysteriousness. He said in so many ways, "You are my friend and I have to be honest with you." He would tell me what he saw. "Innocence and naiveté don't work. Accept responsibility." Cecil treated me the way he treats everyone. He offered full acceptance and that pushed me to define who I am.

After Cecil got divorced, our friendship grew. I had been a single mother for almost eight years. It was very difficult for me to decide to get married again. Cecil's personality is such that it is easy to get enveloped by it. I was afraid I would not be able to maintain my own identity. He was raising his two kids as a single parent. Albert and Kim had much bigger, more assertive personalities than did I or my daughter Tianne. I thought we might be swept under the tide and never be heard from again. But I took the risk, and we were married in 1982.

As marriage partners Cecil and I worked incredibly hard. I had experienced so much sexual trauma that fully trusting any man was extremely difficult. I was filled with so much shame and guilt. I had learned early in my life how to separate my body sensations from my mind in order to survive. Relearning how to feel and enjoy sexual intimacy demanded from Cecil more compassion, patience, and sensitivity than most men are capable of bearing. It wasn't easy for either of us. Because of compassion, kindness, and the capacity for empathy, Cecil and I began our ongoing journey toward recovery as sexual beings and full partners.

Long before our marriage, in the work at Glide, it was necessary for me to evolve out of Cecil's shadow into my own light. When I was promoted to director of programs, it was a difficult period for both Cecil and me. He had to let go of his dependence upon my taking care of him as his assistant, and I had to give up the feeling of being in control of him through keeping his schedule, and managing his information as a secretary. I had to move into grappling with my power as a decision maker.

Cecil and I not only struggled with each other in defining our roles, but it was necessary to do so in the context of the institutional church. The walls of racism, sexism, classism, and all the other barriers that needed to crumble in society were in fact needing to crumble in the old order at Glide. I did battle with former staff and board members about "my place" in the church and claiming my voice as a woman with decision-making power.

Cecil was very supportive of me, but it was my struggle. I had to earn the respect and the power of my position for myself. As director of programs, I had to create from my own authenticity and style, yet never lose sight of the community, the "cause." It was uncomfortable, frightening, and demanding for me. I think it was also hard for Cecil because the changes forced us to engage in a journey of mutuality. No more lip service about women and equality—we had to *do* it.

When I was appointed president of the Glide Foundation in 1982, we had to further come to grips with the issues of women and power and what kind of leadership would emerge at Glide. Looking back, I think the health of this organization is enhanced by its willingness to constantly struggle, evaluate, and make radical changes when necessary.

I continue to battle not being distracted by other people's image and definition of me. I love the challenge and the privilege of my relationship to Cecil, but being wife/co-worker/partner to him is, to put it mildly, never easy.

When the recovery programs started at Glide, I thought they were great. I was behind them fully. But inside I thought, *"I don't do Crack. I don't use drugs. I'm okay. This doesn't apply to me."* I decided to sit in on some of the group sessions. I would observe, help if I could.

The women in recovery started talking about their histories, their experiences with abuse, with rape, with physical and emotional battering. They told of destructive relationships that they perpetuated because they thought they deserved no better. They honestly admitted what had happened to their children as a result of their addictions. When they started revealing their stories in such honest ways, I cracked open. I fell apart. I crumbled. I had to admit to myself and to them, "Here I am. I'm one of you, too."

Even though I had been through years of therapy, I never really felt the long-term effects of my childhood abuse until I started to deal with recovery. The victim in me made my abuse so exclusive, so precious, so mine, that it solidified inside me and became a rock. I built layers around that rock until I could carry it around, pretending it wasn't there.

When I cracked open and that rock split, it wasn't rock-solid inside after all. It was lava—hot, molten, uncontrollable emotion that poured out of me. I had denied my spirituality, and I had denied God. I was furious at God. Years before, I had rejected God because I felt that God had rejected me. I went back over my life and asked for the first time,

What has kept me alive? Why am I still here? Why are these other women still here? Their stories were so extreme. *What had kept us from going under into the depths of insanity, of death?*

I heard the women in recovery say that there was someone who pulled them out of the deep on their third time going down. I began to understand the journey of life as a rocky one for each of us. We are always in danger of going down. Therefore, we must always be open to the stranger who offers a hand or throws us a rope just in time to save us from drowning.

I was taken by surprise. I didn't know until I saw myself in someone else's life that I was still here because of something greater than I.

I have an extended family whose members—in addition to Cecil, my daughter, my literary Third-World sisters, and the women in recovery—at the most critical moments in my life have told me the truth and reassured me of the garden within my soul. I cannot minimize their lifesaving gifts. Without the community, I could not have faced the liberating fact that I am indeed a motherless child. I have had to let go of my longing for mother, father, the biological family that never was what I wanted it to be. The dysfunctional cycle of abuse that is perpetuated generation to generation had to be broken. And I had to start with me, and for my daughter's sake, I had to create a new family from whom I could receive love and acceptance. Therein lies true empowerment. In our shared stories, in affirming our common bond, struggle, and pain, the Spirit comes alive.

When I listen to Cecil in Celebration, as he verbally dances with some phenomenal unknown force, in his strange rush of words like a speeding train, a phrase catches my breath or cuts my heart. The Spirit's presence is undeniable.

As I sat with women in recovery, weeping at their indomitable will to survive the most atrocious circumstances, I realized that God was present for me in my grandmother, who through her unconditional love caused me to choose to live. I began to believe that the Spirit was and is present in the most awful and the most authentic moments, nudging me to continue to recover, to find my power, and to claim my faith.

My struggle with God is uneasy and unsettled. The intensity of my fight is perhaps the greatest affirmation of my belief.

In the spring of 1989, a few months after the recovery program started, Cecil talked about incest in a Sunday Celebration. He had known my history and had struggled alongside me for a long time.

He has been incredibly supportive, sensitive, and caring through some very difficult times.

That Sunday Cecil opened up the issue to the congregation. He said if anyone wanted to talk about it to come on up. Neither he nor I expected much of a response, but ten or fifteen people stood up.

Up to this point, the stories of abuse had been talked about in the privacy and confidentiality of the recovery groups. They hadn't been made public. When these women and a couple of men stood up, I was blown away. Everybody was.

Shortly after that experience, Cecil told me that he wanted to be able to talk publicly about his experience as the partner of an incest survivor. How would I feel about that?

I asked him before my fear could stop me, "Would it be helpful if I talked about it?" He said that would be very freeing.

That next Sunday I stood up and spoke briefly in both services. My statement that Sunday began, "I am a survivor of incest. I've experienced incest by a number of adult males in my family for over eleven years of my childhood." I told them that the incest made me feel like an insect impaled by a pin. I had felt that all my limbs were wriggling in the air. I longed for a quick death, but death never came. I had to do the deed myself. I had to kill my feelings.

After I spoke in Celebration, I couldn't hide anymore, hide behind the rock in my heart, hide behind the exclusiveness of my abuse, hide behind my Asian American mysteriousness, hide behind being a minister's wife. I couldn't hide. I was naked.

A few weeks later I spoke to an Asian American conference on recovery. Instead of talking about the issue of recovery as an observer, for the first time I talked about my own recovery from abuse and about my near bout with alcoholism. I talked about my daughter and having to face her alienation from me. Revealing my own hell—and climbing out of my own hell—gripped me and, I'm told, gripped the audience.

Typically, Asian Americans don't "air their laundry" in public. The cultural pose of "saving face" is very real to us. To reveal things about your family is to disgrace more than yourself. You disgrace your mother, your father, all immediate relatives, your ancestors. You are made to feel responsible for the loss of reputation, humiliation, divorce, famine, and other catastrophes. That cultural taboo deepens the suffering, the isolation, the need to hide the dark, the bad, the ugly.

I took the risk to reveal it all and to let it go without trying to control the response. I stepped into myself.

I believe that telling it all allowed me to step over the line of defining myself either as a victim or a survivor. I engage in my journey each day to define myself as an Asian American woman who is striving to attain wholeness. In community, I must continually reveal the secrets that isolate me, empower my daughter by telling my stories, and shatter the prisons of guilt and shame.

Shedding the silence is the key to unleashing power.

No, I am not invisible. I am here.

Who is singing this song?
I am.

Community: Telling Our Stories

My African ancestors who endured slavery and deprivation carried with them across the Atlantic an oral tradition, a way of communicating that remains solidly rooted in African American culture today. At Glide, we most often speak in our mother tongue, which is a language of passing on truth through storytelling, of engaging one another through dialogue, and of immersing ourselves in the Spirit.

For us, the Bible is a record of the life of the Spirit—it reminds us that we stand in a long line of people of the Spirit. The church is the place where we gather together.

In the "spokenness" of the African culture each person has the freedom to tell his or her real story the way it really is. You don't have to hold back. Our tongues become the weapon that cuts through the chains of isolation. When we tell our stories and when we hear the echoes of our own stories in the words of others, we begin to see there is a cousin, an uncle, a sister, a brother, a son, and a daughter out there in the world. We begin to see the commonality, the likeness of God that we share. We understand that we are kin.

EASTER SUNDAY

This all came true for Glide on Easter Sunday 1989. The sanctuary became a front porch where the extended family gathered to sing and tell our stories.

On the day that we gathered to celebrate Jesus' coming out of the tomb to reclaim his life, I retold the Easter story in my own words:

On that long-ago Sunday Mary Magdalene, Salome, and another woman named Mary went to the tomb where Jesus lay buried. The three women went to weep and embalm Jesus. The women's traditional role was to weep and to mourn, to soothe the horror of Jesus' death. When they approached the tomb, an angel appeared and said, "I'm going to roll away the stone, and you are going to be surprised." As the tomb was opened, the angel said, "Look in there, look in the tomb." They did. There was no body in there. The tomb was empty. The women wondered where Jesus was.

The angel whispered to them, "Listen, you have seen what no one else in the world has seen. The tomb is empty. Jesus is raised from the dead. He is gone. Now go back and tell everyone what you have seen."

I stopped telling the story right there and declared to the people of Glide, "It's resurrection time! Telling Jesus' story asks for us to tell our own stories. Just like those two women we have become witnesses of the empty tomb. It isn't like it used to be. The old has gone away and the new has come.

"The past is over. That's why Jesus died on Calvary's cross. He died to eliminate the past's hold over us so that we can live for the future.

"I want you who have witnessed your resurrection or the resurrection of some of your friends to come on up to the front and tell your story. There is an empty tomb somewhere in this room this morning. I invite you to come now."

Like an army of the Spirit the witnesses started marching forward.

David* stood first and took the microphone. "Two days from now I will celebrate nine months clean and sober. I never had an Easter like this. I've been on drugs for the last ten years. My life has been out of control for many years. My life is in control now, thanks to the program here. I thank the Lord. I know where I've been. I know where I am. I know where I want to go."

Amanda, a recovering alcoholic and addict, followed. "I remember nine years ago when I didn't know how to wake up; I just sort of came to. This morning even before the alarm went off I was awake, standing in my kitchen dyeing Easter eggs for the children. Nine years ago I hadn't driven across the Golden Gate Bridge. I was afraid to go anywhere alone. This morning I walked across the bridge looking at all the lights. Today, I live in the light."

---

*The names and some identifying details of the following witnesses have been changed, with the exception of Jamal, Magnolia, and Eddie Franks.

Lisel came next. "This is a beginning for me. I came from New York City about a year ago. I escaped from madness. I was married to a man who was in the Mafia and heavily into Crack cocaine use. I came to Glide three weeks ago and things started happening for me. I think I can stop running and start to live again."

A man who didn't give his name took Lisel's place on the platform. "I keep thinking about that song we sang earlier, 'When I Laid My Burdens Down.' When I came in here, I had lots of burdens—addictions. I didn't know where I was going, where I was coming from. I stopped into Glide for a bite to eat, and I've been here every since.

"This man here, Cecil Williams, saved my life. He taught me the respect of a family; I didn't have a family. When I came here I was shot to the curb.* I had nothing. He was the only one who believed in me. He took the time to talk to me, to find out what was bothering me.

"Twenty-two months ago I was an addict. Today I'm working on myself. I'm blessed. Twenty-two months ago I didn't believe in God. Today I say, 'Thank you, Jesus, for the strength to stand up here this morning.'"

Carletto marched up next. "Two and a half years ago I was diagnosed with AIDS. I kept hearing Cecil's words in my head, 'Don't get depressed, get angry.' 'Feel your true feelings.' 'Deal with the truth.' I also stayed in touch with the fact that we all suffer. Whether it's Vietnamese children who are displaced or Native Americans, we all suffer. But as long as we keep looking to the light, we can get through. Happy Easter."

Eddie, a tall, powerfully built man with chin-length braids, took his place in line. Within weeks he would become the director of our Facts on Crack program. That Sunday Eddie was a witness.

"Hi. My name is Eddie Franks, and I'm a recovering alcoholic and addict. Nine months ago, as a substance abuse counselor, I saw that Crack cocaine had reached astronomical proportions and none of the agencies in San Francisco were addressing the problem. I take my job very seriously, and my heart went out to those who were hurting and needing some help. I said a little prayer: 'Lord, we got to do something.' Then I started seeing all these flyers that told about a Facts on Crack program. I started coming to the meetings to see what the program was about. I found that something was really going on here. The program started out as a little spark and now it is a great big blaze."

---

* *Shot to the curb* is a phrase used by addicts to describe a person who has lost everything to Crack.

Then Magnolia stepped forward. "I'm a recovering alcoholic, addict, and incest survivor. On March 23 I turned twenty-one years old. Also on March 23 I had thirteen months of being clean and sober. It was a great day for me."

Magnolia, who is a published author and a powerful poet, brought the house down with a rap song she wrote the day before. The congregation went wild.

Then a man stepped awkwardly forward. The skittish look in his eyes told me he was still in the tomb. His thoughts were still tied up in the grave clothes of Crack cocaine. He told us that every time he came to a Crack meeting, it took him two days to get back to his drug use because he was so inspired. He was honest: "I've got a little Crack in my system right now, but I wasn't going to miss this!" His honesty counted for something.

Tyrone strode to the front next, and with a buoyant voice he said, "On the second of next month I'll have six months clean. It's going to be a big month for me. I'm flying home to Pittsburgh. It will be the first time in a long time that my family has seen me sober. I'm really excited, and they are really looking forward to it. I can't even say how happy I am about it."

Jamal strutted up behind him. "Cecil said tell your story. I've been out of control all my life. Here at Glide I learned how to gain control over my life. I know that my mother is locked up in a mental institution this morning, my grandmother is dying. And I got to stand up here because I got to be strong for everybody. I can't afford to go out of my mind or go out of control again. Last Easter I was sitting at home with a base pipe in my mouth and some cocaine. I was too tweaked out to know it was Easter or what it meant. Today I'm here to affirm myself. I'm here to be authentic. I thank Cecil, Janice, my brothers and my sisters in the New Generation, and my *shero** Maya Angelou, who is visiting us this morning. Every day, I remember something Maya said: 'Ain't nobody gonna turn me around.'"

Trisha, one of the first foot soldiers in the Crack program, was next. "I'm a recovering Crack cocaine, marijuana, alcohol addict. For ten years I had a good job. I was diagnosed as a manic-depressive in 1981. I was smoking a lot of marijuana. When I turned thirty-three, I turned to Crack cocaine because I wanted a bigger high. After a year, I didn't know where to turn. I was based out on that pipe. I came here. I was shot to the curb. I said to Cecil, 'What can you do for me?' He said, 'Sister, we are going to work

---

* *Shero* is the word used at Glide to describe a female hero—someone who has shown the way for African Americans to live with faith and resistance.

with you.' I got 139 days clean last year, then I went out and used the pipe. Then I got 90 days clean; then I went back out and used the pipe. Now I have another 90 days clean, and I didn't go out and use the pipe." The congregation stomped their feet and cheered for Trisha.

The last woman to share didn't give her name. "I'm originally from Arkansas, and I've been here in San Francisco for about a year. I'm not an addict. I've never tried drugs. Before I came here I was attending church every Sunday with my parents. Then I moved to the big city and stopped. I thought that I was well on my way, grown up, and didn't need anything. Then as I rode my scooter through the Tenderloin on my way to work, this awareness came over me that what is happening in this neighborhood isn't just Cecil's problem; it is all of our problem. I came to Glide to volunteer. I'm going to help, however I can, and not overlook the problems."

"Right on, sister. Right on," I affirmed her words. She was beginning to understand the meaning of being a part of a community.

Then I took the privilege of introducing Maya Angelou, a woman who has been my sister in the struggle. Maya, ever radiant and robust, came to the platform while members of the New Generation chanted, "Shero, Shero, Shero."

I said to Maya, "Tell your story. Witness."

Maya commanded our attention. "It is true. In those years, in those centuries, in those mean and humbling times when black people recognized themselves by the sounds of the chains they wore, they stood up somehow in the coffles, on the auction blocks, on back porches. Somehow they stood up in the cane fields, in the cotton fields, and sang:

> *Don't let nobody turn you 'round,*
> *Turn you 'round, turn you 'round.*
> *Don't let nobody turn you 'round.*
> *Keep on walking, keep on talking,*
> *Marching to freedom land.*

Maya moved from talking to singing to talking, as she often does. Then she said she had three sisters, witnesses of her own, to introduce:

Beverly Coleman from Chicago.

Betty Young from Dallas.

Oprah Winfrey from the world. The congregation hooted and clapped as the warm and funny talk-show host came forth. Maya handed Oprah the microphone.

Oprah smiled widely and told us, "This is the best Easter I have ever had. I wasn't expecting a church like this. When I got up at four thirty this morning, I thought Glide was going to be one of those organ-music churches. I just want to praise the Lord Jesus Christ for the resurrection. I pray daily to resurrect in my own life. I pray for the light. I strive to save the world from its own darkness. I am filled, so moved. I haven't seen a church like this. I haven't seen a church that is really racially mixed and where the white folks can sing! Glide is what church is supposed to be. I am thankful that I have had the opportunity to see it for myself, to feel it for myself. The love that I feel today makes me feel resurrected myself." Maya's other friends, the other sisters, spoke similar words.

That Easter Sunday Glide understood the resurrection. People reclaimed their lives. On that first Easter Sunday three sisters went to the tomb. They led us, and now centuries later we, too, have seen and witnessed a resurrection. Recovery is resurrection. The tomb is empty. We are standing up, marching to freedom land.

CHAPTER FOUR

The River of Recovery

Recognition: Wade in the Water

Telling our stories as an act of faith resistance brought recovery to every corner of Glide. Recovery was no longer a program at Glide—it was a process that swept us all up and moved us onward.

The Sunday I preached on incest and broke the conspiracy of silence, I felt like the prophet Ezekiel in the Old Testament. Like Ezekiel I was lead forward from standing ankle-deep in the river of recovery, until I was knee-deep, and then waist-deep. When Ezekiel got out into the middle of the river, he began to see where this river was going. I saw it, too. Wherever this river of recovery flows, it brings freedom to every living creature.

When I said the final "Amen" to my sermon and moved down from the platform, I was wading waist-deep into the powerful flow of the Spirit. A stream of people heeded my invitation to come and confront the silences in their own lives. They joined me on the platform and together we trusted that this movement of the Spirit would take us to where there was more life, more power, and more freedom.

Many people, mostly women, were coming forward to tell of the horrifying abuse they had experienced. They described the parched, barren places incest left in their hearts. Silence fled. We cried, and the incest survivors began the long trek back to health and trust.

As more people told their stories, it became clear that Crack and incest were but two of the blighted patches on the banks of our homeland. We were beginning to see other bleak places where people were struggling to survive. All sorts of people needed recovery from all types of privation.

Facing Crack had brought us into the river of recovery in the first place. Incest, physical abuse—What else would force us deeper? What other privations of the Spirit would we see from our vantage point in the river of recovery?

The specter of HIV/AIDS soon beckoned. HIV/AIDS goes hand in glove with drug use, drug addiction, and the drug life. Even in a city like San Francisco that is renowned for the very best in AIDS services, the specific needs of the black population with AIDS remained unserved.

Men, women, and children in our midst carry the virus, spread through sex or needles, or passed on in utero. People living with HIV/AIDS need the refreshment of the Spirit, the love and acceptance of the community.

As the adults came to Glide looking for freedom from addiction and long-hidden pain, they brought hordes of children with them. The children needed food, fun, family, and facts about drugs and recovery. Most of all they needed constant, honest affirmation, which is the very best form of prevention.

Recovering people—female and male, old and young, folks of all kinds—kept wading out to join those of us who stood waist-deep in the river. Soon there were hundreds of us.

We told the truth and bathed in the Spirit. We began to wade deeper in the river, believing that the river of recovery would lead to freedom.

THE PROCESS OF RECOVERY

There is an old spiritual we like to sing at Glide:

Wade in the water,
Wade in the water, children.
Wade in the water,
God's goin' trouble the waters.

As we broke the conspiracy of silence at Glide, we essentially invited everyone to wade in the river of recovery with us. We risked believing that the Spirit would lead each of us into the deep waters, through the pain, and back to solid ground. But before we risked everything, I took stock and concluded that I had prepared myself. What we'd already been through had made us ready to take the next step.

The process of recovery begins with personal and community preparation. My years of struggling alongside my wife Janice had taught me a lot. I knew she, an expert on incest from her own experience, stood with me. The women in recovery who had already told their stories had become a stronghold of support, and we had lists of professional therapists to call upon. Most of all, we knew we had a community of honesty around us. We also trusted that it was the Spirit that was calling us into the deep waters.

The process of recovery is dangerous. When a mass of people wade into the river of recovery, it is risky. Daring to break through denial and face addiction without lies or excuses is dangerous. Recovery demands living without illusions, and that is painful.

Everyone doesn't make it. Everyone doesn't recover. Some go under and go back to drugs and despair. Some try to recover without support. At Glide we committed ourselves to be in recovery together. No one should be swimming in this river alone for no one recovers alone. We believed that as long as we waded into recovery together, we could keep an eye on one another and offer a hand when necessary.

We soon discovered other dangers.

There is the danger of holding back, of trying to prescribe how healing should happen for people. Recovery, like a river, is unpredictable. It is fluid, moving, unstoppable. It ebbs and flows. At Glide we didn't have a rigid program as much as we had people and a process.

There is the danger of going the wrong direction, trying to swim upstream. For me, I discovered this danger in the early years at Glide when my desire for fame nearly took me under. I was moving toward the rich and the famous, and that was the wrong direction. The Spirit flows downstream. When I took a look around, I realized that it was the rejected and the poor who were in the river with me.

There is the danger of not knowing who you are and whose you are. Self-definition is an ongoing process. We change and so does our self-definition. We constantly must reclaim ownership of our lives, hone our skills, and trust that the Spirit will be with us when the powerful pull of addiction threatens to once again overtake us.

There is the danger of looking for a map, a fixed way to recovery. Following twelve set steps or reading a self-help book that helped a friend may be like following an outdated map—the general direction of recovery may be the same, but we may still find ourselves swirling in the currents. All of us in recovery must keep alert, be watchful, and lean on our brothers and sisters every day, or we will drown.

There is the danger of wanting to turn back. The only real hope any of us has is found in our willingness to go in the river together. When we commit to go all the way in the company of our brothers and sisters, we increase the chances of lasting recovery. When we agree to stay together, we can offer a hand of help, a cheer of encouragement, or a bit of wisdom along the way.

The process of recovery requires wading in the water, but there are some lifelines that we can carry with us that safeguard our journey.

Self-Definition: Terms of Resistance

Over time the people in recovery at Glide identified some lifelines that have helped us stand firm in recovery against the currents that would take us under. Together we came up with these lifelines, which we call Terms of Resistance. The First Generation sat with me and we listed the things that seemed common to our experience. We lived our list for a while and later regrouped to revise the Terms of Resistance.

Now Generation after Generation regularly repeats the Terms of Resistance. They are reminders of the process we have begun. They are the ways we say to ourselves and one another, "Hold on," "Stand firm," "Never turn back," "Keep your head above water."

TERMS OF RESISTANCE

1. I will **gain control over my life.**
2. I will **stop lying.**
3. I will **be honest with myself.**
4. I will **accept who I am.**
5. I will **feel my real feelings.**
6. I will **feel my pain.**
7. I will **forgive myself and forgive others.**
8. I will **rebirth a new life.**
9. I will **live my spirituality.**
10. I will **support and love my brothers and sisters.**

These ten terms are not steps to follow one right after the other. They are not a new set of commandments. They are the lifelines that keep us afloat as we risk recovery and have faith that day by day we will live into our freedom.

Recovery is a daily process. Self-definition, recovery, and spirituality are life processes. Programs help, but they don't cure. The support of other people helps, but it comes and goes. What we always have is our lives and the power to choose to live in the Spirit and tell the truth.

Let me illustrate what I mean.

When I was growing up, years ago in Texas, we didn't have electric lights in our house. We had two oil lamps with wicks that had to be lit daily. Once they were lit, a glass shade fit over the flame and they glowed.

My mother kept telling us, "Y'all clean the shade before you put it over the lamp. If you don't, you won't get as much light."

I didn't like cleaning the shades. It took a long time and lots of elbow grease to scour off the sticky, gray soot. But when the shade was clean, one lamp would be bright enough to light up the whole living room.

Back then, cleaning the lamp shades was my job. I couldn't ask my brother or my sister to do my job for me. If I took a day off, everybody could tell. The light would be dim.

I've discovered that what was true back then about lamp cleaning is also true about life cleaning. Neither you nor I can ask anybody else to clean up our lives. My life belongs to me, and your life belongs to you. I have to clean my life daily or my light won't shine; so do you.

When you start to clean your lamp, after years of letting the grime build up, you might find some distortion in the beginning. Each of our lamps is distorted some way; it may just be that the soot is heavier on one side of your shade than another. We might have been through something that makes it harder to clean. The soot in our lives is heavy, but we have to clean it anyway.

When people first begin the process of recovery, the job is hard. The inner light, the Spirit, seems almost extinguished. The soot of addiction, the grime of dishonesty, the toxicity of hustling others and pretending we are okay when we are not is lethal and life-threatening.

There is no one cleaning solution that cleans out our lives once and for all. It's a daily task. Each of us must find what gets at the grime, the distortion of our lives.

It just so happens that I've found that the church, the community, is what helps me clean my life. With love, faith, compassion, courage, fellowship, and honesty, the church helps me clean my shade and recognize when my light is dim. If I ignore dealing with my life, the church calls me back to the task, just like my mother always reminded me to clean those shades.

Those who recognize that their inner shades are dirty are the ones who begin to understand that facing the truth and living in the Spirit is the solution to the distortions in our lives.

THE WOMAN AT THE WELL

In the weeks and months following the Sunday that I first preached on incest, many "Sunday people," those who come to Celebration services but who aren't actively involved in the daily recovery programs at Glide, began to admit their pain, their bondage, their addictions. I knew then that a similar process was occurring in the second-floor sanctuary that had been unfolding on the ground floor of Glide for several months.

Downstairs the Terms of Resistance, the affirmations many of our recovery groups used, gave the generations some lifelines they could live by. I began to wonder what would help the Sunday people understand what it would mean to wade fully in the waters of recovery. For months this question swam around in my mind like a piranha that kept attacking, reminding me of the difficulty I faced in articulating what made Glide such a successful recovery station for so many different kinds of people.

Since my preaching always arises out of my own life-cleaning process and the interaction of the community, I worked at articulating the process of recovery at Glide. I told stories, had others stand up and witness to the truth of their lives, and relayed kernels of truth that I had read in many books that dealt with recovery and liberation.

Then one week, preparing for Sunday, I reread a story in the Gospel of John. This familiar story jumped off the page at me. I had found the words to describe what was happening for so many people at Glide.

In this Bible story Jesus traveled through the hot, dusty land of Samaria, and he sat down to rest by an old well in a field. A woman from a nearby town came to the well to draw water with her empty jug . She, too, was hot and parched. Jesus asked her for a drink, and his request startled her. She replied, "Why are you asking me for a drink? Don't you know I'm not your kind? Why would you talk to me?"

Jesus was a Jew, and Jews usually had no tolerance for Samaritans and even less time for women. These two were of different ethnic groups, different genders, different classes. That well was a gathering place where two who were very diverse in their lives and values came together.

Jesus broke through the barriers. He reached out to a burdened, rejected woman. The woman Jesus met was heavy-laden with pain. She was not unlike many of the women at Glide who had streamed forward to break through their own conspiracy of silence. Jesus stretched beyond himself. He opened up to become a brother to his Samaritan sister that day.

Jesus and the woman began to talk about water, the woman talking literally about her need for a drink. The woman, like most of us, came looking for a fix, an easy solution to her sad life, but Jesus offered her something else, something more.

Jesus knew that water wasn't enough for that woman. Neither is a recovery program that only offers clean and sober living enough for addicts; we all need more. We need the empowerment of the Spirit.

Jesus talked the language of the Spirit. "Whoever drinks the water I give will never thirst again. Yes, the water I have will become a spring of water welling up inside of you."

Jesus was talking about the Spirit that lies within us, the image of the divine that we carry in our humanness. He was talking about the Spirit that we touch through being authentic and truthful. Jesus was talking the language of true, lived spirituality.

The Samaritan woman had heard men make incredible promises before. Could this man be any different from the rest?

But she wanted what he promised. She didn't want to keep making the long, dusty walk to the well for water that only temporarily satisfied. Just think of what she could do with her life if she wasn't always dragging through the desert for a drink.

Jesus told her, "Go get your husband."

"I don't have a husband," she replied, covering up the truth just a little bit.

"Yes, I know you don't have a husband. You've had five husbands already, and the man you live with isn't your husband. What you say is quite true."

Jesus was saying "I know you" and was asking her, "Do you know you?" Jesus was challenging her to tell the truth.

The woman met an authentic man, a person who saw through her denial. She didn't need to hide from him. This man saw her true condition. He saw beyond her pain and called out to the divine likeness, the authenticity deep inside her. Jesus was telling her that the well was inside her.

She wanted what he offered, but could she trust him? Who was he? The woman had to know. Would he really accept her just as she was? Or was he one of those religious types who offered acceptance and then would tell her how to feel and how to behave?

So the woman tested Jesus. "I can see you are a prophet. My people worship here on the mountain. Your people tell us we are wrong, worthless. Only those who worship in your churches, singing your songs, are worshiping correctly."

Maybe her tone was sarcastic. She had been told and shown she was worthless, wrong, and powerless all her life.

Jesus cut through her pain, her barriers with an answer so clear and so different that it sent her scurrying back to her village to tell the others: "Those who worship in Spirit and in truth are the true worshipers God seeks. God is Spirit, and true worshipers worship in Spirit and in truth."

Jesus was on to something.

The woman said, "I hear someone is coming that one day will explain everything to us."

Jesus answered her with an "I am" statement. "I am the one."

When Jesus declared himself, he showed the woman how to get living water. He showed her it was found in defining who she was—in Spirit and in truth. The woman found the well inside her, and she couldn't wait to tell her friends.

IN SPIRIT AND IN TRUTH

What happened to the Samaritan woman is what happens to all who recover at Glide. Each person is welcomed into a diverse, extended family as a brother or a sister. That requires an attitude of acceptance.

When our extended family gathers, we celebrate; that is how we worship. We come together to wade in the waters of the Spirit. The Spirit is both the river, the context of recovery, and the propulsion, the force greater than we that moves us to action.

While we are together, we tell the truth. Together we practice loving one another and we practice what it means to stop lying. We worship by being authentic with one another. We each tell of our pain. We each tell of our dreams, our values, our beliefs. By telling the truth, we offer lifelines to one another. We repeat the Terms of Resistance.

Through acts of self-definition and daily attention to our lives, we learn to drink from our inner wells. We learn to take responsibility for our own lives. We stop waiting for someone else to live our lives for us. We are empowered to live in the Spirit.

Then, just as the woman at the well ran to bring her friends to the well, the people at Glide who have tasted the waters of freedom walk out of Glide and walk back in bringing their friends.

Recovering people become what I call worldly people, meaning those who are able to drink from their own wells and live in the present in this world. Worldly people want to make a difference each day. They want their abundant life now. They want abundant life for their brothers and sisters; consequently, they bring others to the waters.

Thus people are always coming and going, wading in and calling back to beckon to those who haven't yet begun to recover. That is the process of recovery at Glide.

Janet, a tall, graceful, and articulate woman who has a strength of presence about her, waded into the waters of recovery by joining the Placenta group that formed around the First Generation. When Janet first came to Glide, she would slip quietly into the sanctuary. She came every Sunday and cried through the Celebrations. After a few months, she began to volunteer. When she joined the Placenta, she got her toes wet in the recovery process.

After coming to Glide for more than three years, something visible has happened to Janet. One Sunday, a few minutes after the nine o'clock Celebration began, Janet came in the back door. Her face was alive with anticipation. I had just said to those gathered, "Turn around and embrace each other." Janet literally ran down the aisle with childlike abandon. An unashamed, expectant smile glowed on her face. After the service when Janet descended the back stairs, I reached out to greet her. I said, "Janet, do you realize that you ran into church today?"

"I didn't want to miss the hugs from my friends who were sitting up front. I guess I did run down the aisle. I really felt free."

Janet has been led through the deep, troubled water of recovery. Now she is standing firm.

Rebirth: Janet's Story

A VERY GOOD FRIEND who was aware that my life wasn't exactly smooth brought me to Glide. She said, "Why don't you come to church with me? Glide is different; it isn't like other churches."

I grew up in this very fundamentalist, structured, and strict environment, and I let all of that go long ago. I didn't use the word *God*. I believed in the power of the universe, the energy that is in every plant and in every little toe of every person on the planet. I didn't attend church for years.

I came to San Francisco as a junior in college. One of the things I loved from the moment I arrived here was the diversity. I grew up where there were no blacks or Jews. There was no stricture here that said, "This is what you need to be to be okay."

The first Sunday I came to Glide, I started crying for no discernible reason seconds after arriving. I didn't even make it through the songs.

One of the few things I had loved as a child in church was hearing the choir sing. I went to the "big church," the largest and most influential church in my hometown. The choir was made up of over a hundred strong, amazing voices. I loved singing and joined a trio in the fifth grade.

When I sat in the sanctuary at Glide and the Glide Ensemble sang, many of them waved their hands and really danced in celebration. I felt deep inside that they were defining what it meant to "make a joyful noise."

I didn't miss a Sunday Celebration for a long time. I carried lots of tissue with me for over a year. There were always tears, rivers of tears, from the moment I sat down in the sanctuary.

I hadn't been attending Glide all that long when the idea of the Placenta group came up, but I had been there long enough to know that I really wanted to do something in the way of service. I had volunteered before, helping with the children's Halloween party, giving away the Thanksgiving turkeys, and putting together Christmas bags.

Cecil started talking about this Placenta group he wanted to form. Now I grew up on a farm so I've seen animals born, and the placenta was not something appealing to look at. Still the idea behind the Placenta group intrigued me.

The idea of joining kept going 'round and 'round in my head. I didn't know what I could give to the people recovering from Crack as that was a world far removed from my world. I've never been a Crack addict. I'm educated, a longtime career woman. And most of the First Generation was black. I'm white. What could I offer?

Cecil said that we would be the placenta around the newly forming recovering persons. The Crack addicts were about to be born into a new life, and we were simply to be supporters. We were there to give them "food" by osmosis, through the process of being present. We were to let them know that there were people in the world who looked like we did—mostly white, mostly middle-class—who would be available to them.

The Placenta started meeting after Sunday Celebrations. When we first gathered in Freedom Hall, we made a large circle. I never knew for sure how many there were in the First Generation and how many there were in the Placenta. The group was in flux at first.

We continued to meet on Sundays, and I would guess that there were more Placenta than Generation in attendance. When we added meetings on Wednesday nights, there were often more Generation than Placenta present.

We ended up using a format that was very much like that used in the Twelve-Step groups,* yet we never read the steps or referred to them. One of the Glide staff who worked with the New Generation would get us started. Then there was a lot of individual sharing. The person would talk about what was up for them without a lot of cross talk or overtalk.

Early on, the Placenta members had signed up, listing practical help we could contribute to the Generation members, such as resumé writing and job interview practice. When the Generation members didn't focus on job skills and weren't taking us up on our offers of help, some of us began to get frustrated. Those of us with control issues wanted to make lists and timetables for what "should" happen for the New Generation members.

Looking back, I can tell that it was too soon for those in the Generation to deal with job-specific tasks. They were so newborn that they needed to be dealing with entry-level issues that those of us who had been in the work force take for granted. Self-esteem, self-discipline, and self-confidence were all important issues they were ready to address. Going out and passing out resumés was not yet a reality they needed or could effectively deal with.

Those of us in the Placenta who were frustrated wanted to have things happen on our timetable. When things didn't happen, the frustration erupted with people saying, "I don't know what is happening here," "I don't know what I'm supposed to be doing." Some of us got uncomfortable without the trappings of a sign-up sheet and an outline to follow.

Things stayed pretty calm, but sometimes people would be waving their hands, waiting for a turn to talk, wanting to be directive with those who had just shared.

---

* Groups using the Twelve Steps allow each participant to share whatever he or she wishes. Often the Twelve Steps are read at the beginning of a meeting, and one of the Steps becomes the focal point for sharing. Cross talk is a term that refers to one group member commenting or giving feedback about what another shares. Overtalk refers to interrupting another who is speaking.

The codependency of the congregation was beginning to show as well. The Placenta made that plain.

I remember times when members of the First Generation ranted and raved about their anger toward the white community. But more than that, they were remarkably able to talk about the specifics of their childhood wounds. I was at a very vulnerable place myself, and I didn't get through a meeting without crying.

I thought "God bless them," when they got angry. I thought that it was healthy for them to get it out.

When I joined the Placenta, I didn't know what "it" was that I needed recovery from. I did know there was something. I rarely raised my hand to talk, but near the end of our meetings together, with tears in my eyes, I spoke up: "I know I need recovery but the only thing I know to call my problem is spiritual laziness."

Some of the Generation members looked at me as if I had rocks in my head. I'll never forget Jamal's face. It seemed to ask, "What in the world is that woman talking about?"

The term *spiritual laziness* really stuck with me. I had spent a lot of energy looking at myself as a spiritual person while I was in college. But that was a long time ago. I hadn't looked at the issue of spirituality for years and had been fairly content with the philosophy of the universe I had worked out. During those Placenta meetings I started feeling the stirrings of something going on. In fact, I was very depressed, and I didn't understand it.

About the time that a Placenta group started forming around the Second Generation, Cecil said that he was going to have a Bible study that initially met earlier on the same night as the Placenta. In one of the first nights of the Bible study, I was one of maybe two of the Placenta members who attended. It was almost all First Generation members. Cecil read about the children of Israel on their way to the Promised Land. Then he asked everyone to talk about his or her wilderness experience.

I got hysterical. The wilderness that overwhelmed me was my upbringing. I was emotionally beaten up with the Bible. Once I could accept that I had been an emotionally and spiritually abused child, it wasn't long before I began suspecting that I had also been sexually abused.

I certainly did need recovery, but until then I didn't have any idea what I was getting myself into.

During this time I was living in the Haight with a friend and her daughter, and there had been incest in their family. I remember going to a bookstore and seeing a book entitled *Father/Daughter Incest.* Standing up in the bookstore, I read two chapters; then I went home and told my friend she should buy the book to better understand what had happened in *her* family. She did that very day, and I went out of town for the weekend.

When I got back, we sat down at the dining room table to catch up. The book was sitting on the table, and my friend looked at me and said, "Janet, I'm really concerned about you."

She had read enough of the book, recalled enough of my life history, and remembered what had happened to her daughter to recognize the danger signs in me.

Right then, I began to become a little girl again. I felt incredible pain in my neck and shoulders. I shook with terror and had to wrap a blanket around me. My body began to remember.

By early March of 1989 I knew that incest was my problem. Later in the month is when Cecil preached on incest. It was an amazing, wonderful day. That Sunday I didn't go forward to tell my story, but I remember feeling like I was a part of the group, an insider. No one would choose to be a member of this club of incest survivors, but when I saw that some of the women could smile, that joy was on their faces, I knew that life was possible after the pain.

Immediately after the terror of the incest began to resurface after being submerged and unremembered for decades, I started going to Incest Survivors Anonymous meetings. Soon I had attended every meeting in San Francisco. Sometimes I went to a meeting every day. All I felt was terror.

I didn't have specific memories of incest until August. After trying a couple of therapists who seemed incapable of dealing with such an emotional issue, I found a primal therapist who specialized in holotropic breathing, a process that allows so much oxygen into the body that it somehow liberates the subconscious. The process of breathing deeply to rhythmic music was done in pairs. While I lay on a mat with my eyes closed, a support person sat alongside me to care for my needs, whether I needed a sip of water or a tissue.

Early on in one session I found that I had put my index finger into my mouth sideways. Emotionally the process had taken me back to when I was an infant. I tried to get my hand to go away. I tried to imagine that it was a nipple, everything that I could think of. But then I saw the truth. My finger represented a penis. My body was remembering how my father put his penis in my mouth sideways when I was teething. He used his penis like a teething ring, ostensibly to "help" me. At that time, I was still hoping that maybe my father had abused me only one time.

As time progressed, one of the other members of the Placenta, Ian, often went to my therapy sessions as my support person. He was there to wipe my face when I lay flat on my back and the tears dripped into my ears. I gasped for breath as if I were choking.

My body remembered those sensations, too. I relived the terror of many nights of childhood tears that dripped in my ears while I thought would die. I couldn't breathe when my father thrust his penis in my mouth repeatedly when I was very small.

I had colds all through childhood and couldn't breathe through my nose. Having my mouth full was truly life-threatening. Later when I was in the fifth grade, I had an operation to open up my nasal passages. But during the years that my father abused me, I could not breathe and tears dripped down my face as I lay there terrorized, afraid to move. No one had been there to dry my childhood tears.

The remembering process unlocked all the physical memories stored in my body. I reexperienced the abuse that started when I was six months old and stopped about the time that I was five. My father probably stopped because he thought I might talk.

My therapy sessions were on Wednesdays. The Wednesdays were hard but the weeks got better. My depression started lifting. I started crying less at church because I had another outlet for my tears. I also had discovered what I was crying about.

Today I have recovered enough to have some historical perspective. I can see the progression, the process that opened me up and made me willing to see the painful truth. I now understand that my downward spiral into depression was so painful that it forced me to let go of my control enough to see the cause of my deep depression.

For me, there is no question that the Placenta functioned as a place of healing. I joined the group to help others and ended up helping myself. Listening to others talk about their pain opened me up.

Early on in my recovery, when anybody said how courageous it was of me to do the work around remembering the incest, I thought, "Why is it so courageous to choose freedom?" Inside I knew, really knew, that the truth would set me free. And as my recovery has progressed, I've come to know that, yes, freedom does require courage.

The freedom of knowing what happened allowed me to stop being one who reacted to life because of some unknown event. The denial and hidden nature of the abuse was a filter distorting everything. I had never seen life without that filter.

The filter of mistrust and terror isn't completely gone, but I can now more easily recognize it when I begin to look through it. I can understand and choose to act differently, especially in relationships with other people.

I now have the option to adjust my vision, to look through another lens. I now know where the shame I've felt for so long comes from. For years, I thought it was absolutely silly that I felt great fear at speaking in front of large crowds. Although I was confident in my intelligence and knew I was articulate, still my face would burn with embarrassment. I felt like I had something to hide.

By being truthful, I now feel I can be the honest person that I always intended to be. Being raised as a good little Christian, I had put a high priority on honesty. But the abuse kept me in a fog. Today I can cut through the fog and see my life more clearly.

It is worth the work to become unblocked because it brings freedom. There is no comparison to the freedom I now feel in the world.

People who have known me all of my life would tell you that I have been a happy, positive, cheerful person who had a good time. Some would say that I was happy-go-lucky until I got depressed.

I can't overstate how unburdening the truth is. A literal weight left my body.

My chiropractor tells me that my body is different. She watched as I went through therapy, and she told me how amazing it is that I have so much more movement in my neck. I have had a stiff neck and bad back all my life. Now I'm freer in body and in Spirit. Telling the truth permeates all of life.

Growing up, I didn't want to be on the planet. Now I'm learning to be present in the moment. I'm seeing the benefits of being here on earth.

Growing up in a fundamentalist home taught me that the wonderful time would be heaven—"pie in the sky, by and by." Even after I rejected the fundamentalist ideas, I see now that I bought into the same thing when I believed in reincarnation. I thought I would be happy in my next life. Although my picture of the next life wasn't streets of gold like my father's, I still was waiting for the answer to be out there in the future sometime.

Today there is not a moment that I doubt the efficacy of dealing with the pain and growing.

My spirituality is very important to me. It is an everyday reality and part of my existence. Spirituality is tied into learning through the pain, being in the present moment, and being connected with a greater community. It means being available to do whatever I can for someone else when it is healthy and right.

When I was a child the phrase "Here I am, Lord, send me" scared me to death. I had a picture that the Lord would want me to be a missionary in Africa. I would have to be a dowdy woman with no figure, no form, only frumpy clothes. Now, "Here I am, Lord, send me" means being present in the moment and available to talk with whoever is in my world at that time.

Just last week I was talking with a woman I have been working with as her realtor. We really like each other, and we're an odd pair for friends. She's much younger than I am, married right out of high school, and has two kids. She's now divorced. I'm single, a professional woman who doesn't have kids.

Just after we closed the transaction on her house, I was standing outside the window as she sat in her car. Somehow in the flow of the conversation, I said the words "As an incest survivor I learned. . . ."

She stopped me and said, "It's interesting that you say that. I was just telling a friend of mine the other day that I don't know why, but I think I may have been sexually abused as a child."

I got shivers up and down my arms and legs. That moment was like a confirmation that there was a bigger reason for her to be in my life than for me to sell her a house.

I'm beginning to see that it is very, very possible for the Lord to send you to exactly where you already are to be available for others. Whether I'm at Glide, involved in Incest Survivors Anonymous, or working at the real estate office, my spirituality is a reality.

Going to Glide touches the core of me. It is a place of measuring growth. Glide helps me tune into the truth of my life so that I can hear what the Spirit says: "Do."

For me, Glide is community. I defined community before I came to Glide as the neighborhood in which I lived. Community has come to truly include everyone in the world community. I can never again be content to think of myself as separate from any other person or group.

Community: A Community on the Move

Every day at Glide people are wading in, recovering, and moving on in their lives. Every day new people step into recovery. They test the waters by wading in ankle-deep. Others who have been around a while move in knee-deep by beginning to deal with the cause of the pain that led them to addiction. Some surge forward until they are in over their heads, baptized into an empowered life. When they are rebirthed and firmly replanted on solid ground, they are the ones who return and point the way to others who still stand thirsty, addicted, and powerless. Those who have been in the waters can best point the way for others to follow.

Glide is a diverse, recovering community in motion.

THE "CLEAN AND SOBER" FAMILY PICNIC

Monday through Saturday the first floor of Glide serves as a recovery station for people in need of food, support groups, peer counseling, drug testing, housing referrals, and an available extended family. On Sundays the sanctuary becomes a second recovery station—a place to tell the truth and feel the Spirit with others. Both are points from which people step into the river for the first time. Several times a year, Glide brings together the people who only frequent one or the other of the recovery stations.

Every September after a Sunday Celebration, Glide has a "Clean and Sober" Family Picnic. In 1991, more than a thousand people descended on Glen Park, a eucalyptus-lined hollow located only a few miles from downtown. The grassy ball field felt a world away from the concrete squares and asphalt roads that pave every inch of the Tenderloin. Several footballs were tossed around, while the beat from different ghetto blasters vied for the airwaves.

A fleet of yellow buses carried hundreds of people who, on a normal Sunday, would have lined up along Ellis Street and entered the side door to eat lunch. Hundreds of other people came out of the front door from the sanctuary after the Celebration service. Both groups of people belong to the Glide family.

Some of the Sunday people had never seen many of those who came to Glide daily to eat or participate in the recovery programs. Some of those who came on the buses hardly knew it was Sunday or that Glide had just held services. How in the world did these vastly different groups of people come together?

I heard one church member say, with disapproval in her voice, "I've never seen most of these people at church."

Another one answered before I could pipe in. "One of the beautiful things about Glide is that these people aren't held hostage to some kind of service. They don't have to earn the food. They don't have to worship our way or any way."

The first member checked her attitude, nodded, and agreed with the other, but their conversation pointed out that it is a continual struggle to find ways to break down barriers and help all of the Glide family to understand themselves as sisters and brothers.

No one group solely owns the responsibility to bridge the distance between the diverse groups. As each person tells the truth and steps into river of the Spirit, each begins to understand that we all stand together.

At the picnic we all were fed from the same tables laden with fried chicken, ribs, baked beans, pasta salad, and fruit turnovers. There was only one line. Thirsty and hungry, we all stood together talking.

Our goal at Glide is for every day to be a clean and sober family picnic. Every day when we wade in the river and realize others are in the waters, too, we all have a chance of recovering our lives.

▲   ▲   ▲

PART TWO

The Practice of Recovery

CHAPTER FIVE

Facts on Crack

Recognition: Face-to-Face with Myself in Africa

In 1987 I made my second trip to Africa. My brothers, Reedy and Claudius, and I traveled to Abidjan, Ivory Coast, at the request of Dianne Feinstein, then mayor of San Francisco. Abidjan and San Francisco were discussing becoming sister cities.

While in Africa my brothers and I took a side trip to Dakar, Senegal; I wanted my brothers to see the slave castles of Gorée Island. I had seen them the decade before when I had traveled to Africa with a group of Bay Area students. I remembered that the castles had been eerie, dead, like a museum of hardship.

On this second trip, when my brothers and I boarded the afternoon boat to Gorée Island, we sat among a group of school children returning home to the island after finishing classes. The children were animated, full of themselves. They pointed to me and my brothers and called us Afros; they could tell we were Afro-American. As they teased us with a playful banter, I saw an unusual spark of life in their eyes.

Tourists from the far corners of the earth filled the rest of the boat's benches. Everyone's attention focused on the children's antics. Then one of them yelled to me, "Hey, Afro, let's sing!"

So I started in.

O Freedom! O Freedom!
O Freedom over me!
And before I'd be a slave,
I'd be buried in my grave
And go home to my Lord and be free.

I sang a phrase and expected the children to echo it back, but the children already knew the song. They joined in and sang, breaking into a tight harmony. We laughed and sang freedom songs for the next half hour until we docked at Gorée Island.

We disembarked and as we were being herded into a restaurant with the other tourists, some of the children gathered around us. The leader of the pack said to me, "Afro, we want to take you around the island after you eat."

Sure enough, when we came out an hour later, half a dozen children were waiting. They had gone home and left their books and school clothes.

The children took us to places on the island my tour hadn't shown me during my first visit. The children added tidbits about famous people and courageous exploits of our ancestors. They kept saying "our ancestors." Those words got to me. These children understood that we all came from the same people, the same island of slavery; we were just born centuries and a world apart.

As we walked the island, I saw things that I had only seen before in the heart of the black community in San Angelo. An old woman swept her hard-dirt front yard with a homemade straw broom that looked exactly like the ones my grandmother made and used when I was a boy. An old man whittled a stick that he used to pick his teeth; my grandfather had used the very same technique. And everywhere around us, people shuffled along, walking with a dancelike gait. I felt like I was back home. When no outsiders were around demanding that they march like slaves, the elders in my community had walked the same way.

The children led us to an open courtyard where 150 drummers pounded out powerful rhythms for a foreign movie company that was in town filming. Off to the side of the courtyard local women, men, and children began to dance. The children pulled us to the group, and we joined in the dancing. I felt the rhythm of those drums in my bones. As I moved and swayed next to my African kin, I felt like a new spark was being fanned to flame. This was a Spirit-filled place, a Spirit world. I had never felt so close to home before.

All too soon we had to move on to see what we had come for, before our boat returned to the mainland. When we got to the slave castle, the attendant at the door looked up and said with both a question and a declaration in his voice, "You are African Americans?" We nodded.

He motioned us aside. "You are my brothers. *You already paid.*" Those in line behind us were required to hand over their money.

We waited until the attendant was free so we could thank him. He brushed aside our thanks by saying, "We have not been destroyed, have we?"

His question moved something deep inside me. Something in my self-understanding shifted. "No," I answered. "We are still here, and we've come back to sense what our people have experienced." The slave traders had taken away our land, our religion, our customs, and our freedom, but we had not lost our souls.

The curator of the castle soon joined us and showed us the rooms that are so tiny that many of our great-great-grandparents, aunts, uncles, and cousins who were held there had no room to even sit down. For days they stood in agony, but they stood together.

The curator also showed us the larger rooms where our beautiful ancestral mothers had been taken to be raped and beaten at the whims of the slave masters. I shuddered as my imagination put images to the stories the curator told.

Then we traveled down to the bowels of the castle and walked through a tunnel to a tiny courtyard at the ocean's edge. The curator wordlessly pointed back toward the tunnel gate. Overhead these words were etched: *Door of No Return.*

The curator told us that once the slaves stood where we stood, they were pushed, one by one, onto a gangplank and weighed. Those who weighed enough and were deemed strong enough to survive the long, horrible middle passage across the Atlantic were pushed along the plank into the slave ships. Those who were youthful but small, or emaciated by the long suffering in the castle, were pushed off the plank and left to drown.

I was reeling with the horror. How many mothers and fathers had stood by helplessly while their child was pushed off and left for dead? How many tears had been cried in the smelly holds of those ships as family members yearned for those left behind?

We got back to the boat with only minutes to spare. We said good-bye to the children and handed them some money as a gift of gratitude for all they had opened up to us.

We boarded the boat and stood at the rail, trying to take in all the events of the day. Before we left, one of the children's mothers hollered up to me, waving the money we had given her child. "Why did you give the children money? They just wanted to share what they have here with you."

We told her the money was just a way of saying thank-you. Finally she accepted the money. The island people were hardly well-off. But she kept saying, "Come again. We will share with you what we have."

Her words stayed with me all the way home to San Francisco. Everywhere my brothers and I traveled in Africa the people we met shared what they had with us. And what they had was a deeply rooted sense of who they were.

When I came home, that's when I began to notice the Crack addicts dragging through the Tenderloin. The children didn't have the same spark as those children on Gorée Island. The African children were like flowers thriving from their deep roots of heritage and history. The children in the Tenderloin were rooted in poverty, drugs, and self-hatred.

I knew then that there had to be a way to pass on what I had seen and felt in Africa to my African American brothers and sisters.

In the 1960s and 1970s we fought for civil rights; we fought for our lives as a people. But when would we start fighting the battle for self-definition? When would we confront our heritage as Africans and not only as slaves?

Before our ancestors were slaves, they were like the people I met on Gorée Island. In Africa I had found something that I had been looking for all my life. I had found my missing family and my home.

There I met my extended family—people who extended themselves on behalf of their brothers and sisters. I had been in a place where everyone understood themselves to be a brother or a sister.

By God, I knew that Glide could become such a place. With my renewed understanding of the importance of self-definition for African Americans, I knew that we must add more afrocentric elements to our recovery program. The spark that had once shined bright in us could be uncovered, given air, and again it would flame in us and give us renewed life.

Self-Definition: The Facts on Crack Program

At Glide we have extended ourselves to help liberate others. The "proof" or effectiveness of our programs over the years has always been best found by watching those who are *doing* the programs on any given day. Are the people involved becoming more free, more empowered, more aware of who they are?

All our programs are process-oriented. We prepare, act, then reflect, and then act some more. Glide's programs evolve as the people at Glide take control of their lives, become empowered, and move out to offer the same to their brothers and their sisters.

Glide is an active place. People are always coming and going, moving and changing. Likewise, our programs are updated and improved as we learn through experience. Nothing is forever set in concrete or hammered out on stone tablets, unchangeable or undebatable. Our programs are people-centered, and as people change so will the programs.

The only real way to understand the recovery programs at Glide is to experience them. Most who come in to explore our recovery programs simply walk through the door one day. Appointments aren't required.

Depending on each person's most pressing need, those who come to Glide for the first time are directed by one of the door monitors downstairs to Mo's dining room for a meal, to room 101 for a talk with Edna Watts in Crisis Care, or to Freedom Hall for a Facts on Crack circle meeting.

I still long for the day when there will be no need for the Facts on Crack program, but that day is far off. When there are no longer people dragging through the Tenderloin with their minds buzzed from a recent hit of Crack, then we will close down the program and redirect our energies where most needed. Until then, we open our doors, tell our stories, talk about our experience and history as African Americans, and remain open to new directions as we honestly learn together.

As it nears eleven o'clock each weekday morning, most of those who come through the doors will head toward the first of two Facts on Crack circle meetings that are offered each day. Twice daily anywhere from a couple of dozen to fifty people gather. Some will be entering Freedom Hall for the first time, some for the umpteenth.

They come to the circle because they know it is a place where they can tell the truth about their pain. The circle is a safe, trustworthy place where anyone can honestly admit failures and the lies told to others. The circle is where any who wish can speak aloud their intentions for recovery and be assured that they will find affirmation and wisdom daily to steer their lives in the direction of clean and sober living.

Freedom Hall is only a few steps from my office. In fact, only a thin wall separates my desk and the circle of metal chairs. Even when I don't attend the meetings, I can hear through the wall when a pained or angry voice is raised. Without hearing the exact words, I can sense what is happening in the circle meetings. The sounds of people struggling, giving voice to their recovery, remind me why Glide exists.

THE RECOVERY CIRCLE

One recent Tuesday as I walked into Freedom Hall a bit after the daily eleven o'clock Facts on Crack meeting had begun, Eddie Franks, director of Facts on Crack, was reminding those who sat in the circle that Glide's program is a spiritual recovery program. Eddie was telling the folks, "We all have a light inside us, but when we are strung out, that light goes way down; it almost goes out. When we recover, we discover that light again. It wants to burn, to shine. It will if we are honest with ourselves and live our spirituality."

Eddie was getting at one of the main reasons the circle meetings work. By coming to the circle, each person makes time to get in touch with what is really going on inside. Recovery demands honesty—and one of the best ways to be honest is to tell the truth to a group of people who have the same troubles that you have. One addict can't get away with lying to another addict. They all know the excuses and the mind games.

I listened for a while as several in the group talked about the paranoia they experienced after freebasing Crack. One spoke of sitting in a dark room on the top floor of an apartment building believing someone was trying to get in the window.

Eddie joked, "Who did you think was out there? Spiderman?"

"Yeah, I know what it means to be tripping," a woman chimed in. "I went to the Bahamas every other day without leaving my couch." The group began to roll with laughter as several others tossed in their experiences of peeking through keyholes, busting through closet doors, and falling out of a second-story window, all because of smoking Crack.

They could laugh now. Looking back in their right minds, they could see how outrageously they had behaved. But one man set the record straight. "We can laugh now 'cause if we don't, we'll start crying."

This man's comments took me back to my own childhood breakdown. Even fifty years after my experience of paranoia and craziness, I could still identify with the heaviness these folks were feeling. I've moved on, found health, but I won't ever forget what fear can do.

My paranoia arose from my running away from my feelings of rejection and alienation. The paranoia described by those in the circle is induced by smoking Crack, but as one of the men in the circle said, "Drugs are only the surface problem. And yes, we got to deal with that, but the issues down deep are the true problem. Drugs just hide the hurt." Hurt and pain are the core issues of addiction.

The man continued, "This is the first time I've ever started to open up. I'm a recovering addict and dealer. I went through another recovery program and had ninety days clean. But I was the only black man in that group; the others weren't like me. I was always afraid they were going to kick me out for something I said wrong. They wouldn't let me talk about my experience of racism or my pain around losing my family. They kept reminding me I was there to deal with my addiction, not anything else.

"So when I would share, I'd say something trivial. I minimized my addiction and hid my pain. I knew I had to find a place where I could deal with the deeper issues. I'm just starting to be able to say out loud that inside I feel despised, rejected, and abandoned.

"I had parents, yeah, but I had to raise myself up. My dad was a single man in the sixties. My mother was white, and she left us. My grandmother loved us, and I remember when she begged me to come and do something about it if she ever got sick and was put in a nursing home. She did get sick and go to a home. I remember standing there—I was about eight—holding her hand with one of mine and clutching her arm with the other.

"I wanted to do something, to take her home. But someone came and pulled me away. Emotionally from that day on, I was on my own.

"God, I got pains to deal with. Whenever I feel like I'm no good, that I don't belong, that's when I want a hit of Crack. That's when I don't want to feel anymore.

"But I'm learning to feel my real feelings, pain and all."

The man fell silent and the others in the circle clapped in affirmation of his honesty, in acknowledgment of his pain.

The woman sitting next to him leaned forward, ready to talk. "I was raped and molested when I was young. Everyone in my family was on some drug or another. I've been drinking or doing drugs since I was nine years old. I didn't come on to the pipe until I was twenty-nine. And that pipe really messed me up.

"I lost my marriage of thirteen years, my two kids, and a beautiful house. I smoked them all away. Now I have a chance to get my two-year-old back, and that's all I really want.

"I remember when I was pregnant and went in for my six-week checkup, I saw this little boy in the doctor's office. I said 'God, that is what I want. I want a baby boy.'

"God gave me my son, and look what I have done. My son is in child protective services, almost like a jail, because he's away from all his family. Look what I have done.

"Today, I want my recovery. I got some pictures here. Anyone want to see my boys? I want my baby back. Today, I'm sixty days clean."

A big cheer, applause, and the stomping of many feet resounded in the room. We all joined to celebrate her miracle of sixty days of drug-free living.

I had taken the seat next to the woman working to reclaim her children. It was my turn. I knew that the circle was the place I needed to speak out loud about something new I had been seeing in myself.

"I've been talking on Sundays about 'toxic hustling.' Toxic hustling is trying to sell others the lies we have told ourselves. Toxic hustling is the opposite of living by the Spirit and the truth. Toxic hustling is pretending, denying, and conning.

"I realized this week that I've been hustling some of y'all by asking 'How are you doing?' when I see you around here. I've been pretending to listen to your answers. I've nodded and smiled, but my mind has been on other things. That's hustling. I want to tell the truth. I'm not all that good either. I'm still working on me. Always will be. I'm going to work to be honest when I meet you day by day. If I don't have time to talk, I'm going to say hello and go on my way. Y'all help me now. If you hear me ask you 'How are you?' and then I act faraway, you call me on it. Say, 'Cecil, are you listening to me?' I'm always calling you folks on your hustling; I need you to do the same for me. I'm recovering, too."

The circle clapped for me; I needed their affirmation and encouragement to stay honest with myself.

Jamal was sitting next to me. He was next to check in. "I don't know if it's okay to say this, but since the circle is about being honest, I'm going to mention something that happened yesterday.

"Eddie and I went down to city hall for a reception the mayor had for all the drug programs. They handed out certificates left and right, and every time someone went up to receive one, everyone raised a glass and sipped some champagne.

"Now we were in the library and when the mayor walked over past the window and then turned his back to it, I couldn't help but think that outside that window in the park, not five hundred feet from the mayor, there were brothers and sisters blowing the pipe that very minute.

"The mayor handed the city housing folks an award for fighting drugs when we know that more people have been evicted and more units boarded up under this administration than have been admitted to treatment programs. Then awards were given to the person in charge of all the city's drug programs. I remember a few years ago when no one wanted to talk about Crack. Remember when all the drug programs were asking people who wanted in if they drank alcohol. If they didn't, they couldn't qualify for the program, so there were people going out and getting drunk, just so they could get some help with their Crack addiction! It was so bad.

"Then the mayor called Eddie and me up to the front of the room and thanked Glide for being on his task force on Crack.

"Cecil, I could smell the alcohol in the room. They were drinking glass after glass and getting wasted all the while we were praising one another for having succeeded in the war on drugs.

"It felt like a toxic hustle going on, Cecil. Those folks seemed tired, really tired from dealing with all the problems, but they couldn't say it out loud. They couldn't admit that after all the money and time, there were folks smoking Crack only a few feet away on the other side of the window. The city officials were trying to sell the lie of success rather than admit the truth. They were quenching the Spirit of truth with champagne.

"Who did they think they were kidding? I'm a recovering addict. I can recognize a toxic hustle when I see one. I remember telling myself not so long ago that I wasn't addicted, that I really didn't have a problem. I remember feeling so tired, that there wasn't any way out of all the pain, so I masked it with the pipe. I thought it made me feel good for a while. I sold myself a lie; then I tried to sell it to others. That's what I saw yesterday at city hall."

The circle members applauded. We were all practicing how to recognize a toxic hustle wherever one is found. It's not just the down-and-out who are hustling in this world. All sectors of society need recovery. We need to tell the truth.

The circle closed; we all stood and joined hands. Eddie read each of the Terms of Resistance and we echoed after him. Together, we voiced our litany of recovery.

As I walked down the hall away from the circle that Tuesday, I was humming an old, old spiritual. It was the same one my family, all eight of us, gathered around the piano to sing many years ago, the morning after I said no to my fears and yes to my power to face my feelings. That was the day my own miracle of healing began.

The words, then and now, rang in my Spirit with unchained abandon.

There's no hidin' place down here.
There's no hidin' place down here.
Oh, I went to the rock to hide my face.
The rock cried out, "No hidin' place."
There's no hidin' place down here.

THE GENERATION ADDICTION EDUCATION CLASSES

Recovery from Crack cocaine begins in the circle meeting. The circle provides a place for people to tell the truth and start to recognize the habits and lies that are toxic to our lives. Some people come to the circle for weeks before the truth comes out. Others seem ready to move forward from the first day.

The timetable of recovery differs for each person. At Glide whenever people get serious, ready to dig in their heels and stand firm in their commitment to recovery, they eventually decide to join the Generation program. For seventeen weeks, each New Generation meets in classroom 618 on the top floor of Glide.

The day the Twelfth Generation began, sixteen recovering addicts who had attended the circle meetings for a while were seated around a horseshoe-shaped table. Eddie Franks led the class session, and I joined them to help launch the newest Generation on its journey.

Eddie started the class session. "Over the years at Glide we have learned to listen to what you people in recovery have to say. This program is designed to deal with the hurts and needs the recovering people who have come before you have declared that they have. We believe it is imperative to address felt needs. You know what your problems are better than any expert.

"Given time, a safe place, and the support of your brothers and sisters who will encourage and challenge you, each of you will be able to figure out what it is that you really need to do to recover. Your recovery is your job. We are here to assist, but your success depends on you.

"I've asked Cecil to join us today. I've asked him to tell you why we have the Generation classes."

I pulled my chair into the center of the group. My hopes were high for those seated in the room. I knew this day could be a landmark day in their journey toward empowering their lives.

"Today is an important day. I want you to know three things about this program. One: The Facts on Crack program is fully a part of everything we do. Two: Your recovery is essential to the black community and to your extended kinfolk. Three: Your recovery is important if we are going to have African Americans alive in twenty years.

"Lots of folks have said that your generation is killing itself. They think you don't care and that you'll just destroy yourselves. Many government officials, community leaders, and even some of your families have given up hope that you will recover.

"We haven't given up on you. We want you here. Glide is your home. Like in any good home, you won't be abused or misused here. Neither can you abuse or misuse Glide.

"I trust you. I want you to trust me. If at any time I misuse the trust you have in me, let me know. If you misuse the trust I have in you, I'll let you know. When we make mistakes at Glide, we say we are sorry. Let's be honest with one another."

"Glide is your new family. I can guarantee that you aren't going to love everybody here, but we are going to make sure we get along. The strong person around here is not the one who is the toughest, the meanest, or the last one to give in. The strongest person at Glide is the one who has a new spiritual attitude and admits his or her problems. The strong person is the one who can declare he or she has a new mission in life. That new mission is *you*. God wants you to accept your power and make your life work for you. Don't wait for God to fix you up. You have the Spirit already; tell the truth and you'll find the power to change."

One of the members of the Twelfth Generation, a tall, very volatile young man with a poet's soul who had been around Glide awhile, raised his hand. I nodded at him to go ahead and speak.

"I feel like I have a home at Glide. The other day someone on the street said to me, 'I got a gun.' The first thing I thought of was, 'Let's go rob someone and get some rock.' But then I thought of my friends at Glide. I want to change my attitude. I want to be able to hear people say they have some money without trying to figure out how I can get it from them. That's a dangerous attitude."

"Right on, my man," I said. "You are moving in the right direction."

"There is no amount of money and nothing that you can smoke, sniff, pop, snort, or drink that can make you feel the way you will as you move further into recovery. Being honest with yourself and feeling the Spirit is better than any high."

Eric, a statuesque, quiet, and dependable man and a regular volunteer at Glide, was another of the members of this Generation. He waved his hand and said, "I really appreciate Glide being an extended family. You know that I was a member of the Eleventh Generation, but I went out and used Crack while I was in the program. You knew that, Cecil, and still you took me with you to Texas to speak to a bunch of people about Crack. You told me to tell them the truth that I'd relapsed. Now, I'm learning to open up and be honest, no matter what the truth is. When I was honest in front of all those people, it was like a light went on inside of me. I learned I don't need to be ashamed. I can be honest when I need help."

I smiled at Eric and affirmed him. "Eric, I'm proud of you for being honest. That's what counts."

Traci, a vivacious Generation member who was several months pregnant, wanted to talk when Eric had finished. "I was in the Eleventh Generation and now I'm in the Twelfth, not because I have dirty urine tests, but because I've still got an attitude. I've got to put patience in my toolbox.

"I gotta be here this time around to open up and say things I've never said before. There is a lot of scar tissue built up to cover my pain.

"I started using drugs because of a man who used to abuse me when I was a kid. Before he came demanding that I pay him with my body, I went and paid the dope man. Then I became the dope man."

Traci's honesty moved me. She's one of those people who just draw people to them. I'd heard her talk many times before, but she had just voiced the core of her pain for the very first time.

"Traci, you don't have to pay anybody anymore. Your freedom has been paid for. Claim it, sister, for you and for that baby you are carrying.

"I'm going to tell y'all one of my dreams. I'd love to find a lump of money somewhere and take some of the graduates of the Generation program to Africa. There just isn't any way you could go to Africa and come back with a desire to do drugs.

"The last time I was in Senegal, I took a tour of the slave castles. When I got up to the ticket booth, the attendant looked at me and my brothers and said, 'You are African Americans?' We nodded. 'You already paid.'

"Our great-great-great ancestors already paid for themselves and for us. Did you hear that? Your admission to freedom has been paid for; now it's up to you to walk on in with your heads held high."

I handed the meeting back to Eddie. Now Eddie used to be in the military. Sometimes he drills the Generations like a sergeant. That first day he took the Generation through an overview of the Generation program just like it was boot camp.

Some experts from other drug programs have come to Glide with an attitude that seems to ask, "How dare you challenge the Twelve-Step model? How dare you bring the issue of drug recovery into a spiritual center like the church?"

As African American people we are spiritual by nature. The church has always been the focal point for African American people. It has always been that meeting place where African Americans come and talk about their cares, their problems, their hopes, and their dreams. The civil rights movement that we know today started within the church! For many African Americans, entering the Glide program is like coming home.

I call Glide a universal gateway of spirits. When I first came to Glide, I saw people of different ethnic groups and economic levels. I said, "Wow! This is what Jesus was talking about."

People in recovery, like us, desperately need an available extended family. Together as a Generation, we will become one another's immediate family, and all the others who come to Glide during the week and on Sunday will be our extended family.

And like a committed and healthy extended family, we stick together for the long haul. If someone slips and relapses, I won't kick you out the first time, nor the second. Neither will I enable you by accepting that kind of behavior—that would be codependent.

But as long as I see people dying from drugs, I and the rest of the staff at Glide will dare to be innovative. We will dare to try to come up with some kind of treatment that will contribute to the longevity of your recovery. My ego is not so big that I know everything or that Glide has everything you might need. You must be an active part of your recovery. We are here to help you in your recovery.

The way I see it, we African Americans are great sprinters. You give us the 75- or 100-yard dash to run, and we will bring home the gold every time. You give us the marathon, and that is too long a race for us to run with ease.

Many of us can stay clean for a few days or weeks, but it's the long haul that is difficult. This Generation Addiction Education Class will teach you endurance and train you in recovery skills that will help you to keep running the marathon of lifelong recovery.

There is no blue-ribbon cure waiting to be pinned on anybody a few months down the road. Yes, there are weekly Celebrations, picnics, and parties along the way, and finally a graduation ceremony. But remember, the ultimate finish line is nowhere in sight. We win in recovery by staying on the track, one day at a time.

Now, I know that some of you don't read well. I know some of you didn't exactly love school. But you are here to learn. We will use lots of audio and visual techniques. I'll take my time in bringing home the important concepts of self-definition, cultural identity, and recovery skills. I don't want to miss anyone.

Every few weeks we will have tests on what we have covered. Several people in the class have told me they have problems writing. I will test anyone orally who feels his or her writing skills are weak. I will grade all of your tests. The tests help me to see how much of the addiction information and recovery values you are putting into your toolboxes to help you along in recovery.

There is one other kind of test you'll be expected to take. Every week there will be random urine tests to check for drug use. These tests help us all stay honest.

We test the staff, too. Anytime I or one of the other Facts on Crack counselors asks you to take a test, go immediately to our office. If any of you has a urine test that comes back positive for drugs, you won't be dismissed from the program, but you can bet you and I will sit down to do some serious talking. We know that people slip up; we also want to help you make it all the way through to drug-free living.

The first skills or "tools" we will teach in the Generation classes are self-definition, self-esteem, and self-discovery.

You probably feel bankrupt—spiritually, physically, mentally, emotionally. Most of you have lost everything. I've been there. You've been told all your lives that you are no good and you aren't going to make it.

Let me tell you the truth. Being an addict doesn't make you a bad person. Each of you has a crippling disease that can be overcome with time, compassion, and the truth.

We all have problems with self-esteem, self-definition, and self-love. A lack of self-love is one of the reasons we turn to drugs. Why would we have spent so many years of our lives on a suicide mission if we loved ourselves?

Each of us is looking for something or someone outside ourselves to validate us. When I was a kid, nobody could get me out on a dance floor without the false courage I found in a wine bottle. Think back to your first drink and your first hit. Did you throw up? Did you cough or get light-headed? Your body was trying to tell you something even way back then. We haven't been listening. In the first four weeks together we are going to learn how to listen to ourselves.

Once you start to define yourselves and gain some self-esteem, then we will study the mental and physical effects of drugs and poly–drug abuse. Most of you think *you know a lot about Crack. You are experts on buying it, smoking it, and dealing it. But I'm going to make you experts on what the chemical process of addiction does to your body, your brain, and your children.*

Once you know the truth, you will have the tool of knowledge. Knowing the facts will help you stay away from self-destructive behavior.

Let me give you a quick taste of what we will learn in depth.

Cocaine isn't a new drug. In fact, coca leaves were chewed hundreds of years ago by native Peruvians to mask hunger and thirst, cold and fatigue as they worked, often as slave laborers for the Spaniards who owned the silver mines.

In the 1800s cocaine was inhaled or chewed by many prominent people in the Western world. Sigmund Freud, Queen Victoria, and Pres. Ulysses S. Grant are but a few of those who praised its beneficial effects. And Coca-Cola was first made popular when cocaine was an ingredient.

Then violence and destructive behavior changes were linked with cocaine use. In 1914 Congress passed the first legislation regarding drug use and cocaine was banned. Other drugs took center stage for several decades.

Crack is a concoction of cocaine hydrochloride powder mixed with bicarbonate of soda (or rat poison, or baby powder) and water that is heated until it forms a crystallized, rocklike substance. When this "rock" is lighted and smoked in a pipe, it makes a cracking sound. That's where the name Crack comes from.

Crack was first seen in Brooklyn, New York, in 1984; it showed up in Los Angeles later that same year. You and I all know that Crack is easily manufactured and cheap. I'll bet y'all have cooked some, and some of you have spent a year's salary on the stuff.

With a few dollars anybody can buy Crack. Before Crack came on the scene, cocaine was a drug available only to those with money to buy enough to inject or snort.

<u>Crack produces a quick, almost instant high.</u> Since Crack is smoked, the lungs absorb the cocaine more quickly than when cocaine is snorted or injected. The high that results is immediate, intense, and lasts from a few minutes up to an hour.

After the first Crack high, we have been trying to recapture that first hit, or "blast" as the street terminology goes, by smoking and smoking. No matter how much money somebody has to spend for drugs, it is never enough. Crack addiction hits the broad spectrum of people, not just minority people like us who are on the lower end economically. The law of diminishing returns applies to Crack users of all kinds.

<u>Just because Crack is smoked rather than injected, it is not safe.</u> Few people associate serious drug use with substances that are smoked. How many of you previously dabbled in marijuana? How many of you smoke cigarettes?

Most of us.

Most folks know the danger of injecting drugs but smoking nicotine, marijuana, or cocaine is thought to be fairly harmless. It's anything but harmless.

<u>Crack is highly addictive.</u> Have you ever wondered why you could try other drugs, then take them or leave them alone? But Crack, you crave it. Right?

Crack affects and disrupts many more of the neurotransmitters in the reward/ pleasure center of the brain than heroin or LSD. Things like the smell of cigarette smoke, the sight of a match being lit, the sound of running water, simple things like that can set off the neurotransmitters and tell them to start sending "Gimme more" messages to your brain until you have nearly unbearable cravings for a hit. Many people who have been able to handle using other drugs discover that they have an uncontrollable desire for Crack after only a few hits.

Crack has serious physical effects. Smoking crack increases your heart rate, blood pressure, breathing rate, and body temperature. Crack constricts the blood vessels and leaves you wide open to seizures and heart attacks. A user's appetite disappears, and most users become mere skeletons. It becomes hard to sleep. Some people experience blurred vision, hair loss, skin darkening, memory loss, and even paralysis from smoking Crack.

Traci, you and the rest of the women listen carefully. Are you with me?

The menstrual cycle of women users is often completely disrupted. Premenstrual symptoms such as headaches, dizziness, sleeplessness, body aches, and irritability are intensified.

Crack and pregnancy don't mix. Pregnant women who smoke Crack have a higher risk of miscarriage, stillbirth, or premature birth. When a fetus is exposed to Crack, it can have a heart attack or stroke in utero. If carried to term, a Crack-exposed baby can have deformed kidneys or sex organs. A Crack-exposed infant has a higher risk of brain seizures. Crack (and the Crack habit) can be passed on to a baby through breast milk. As they grow, children exposed to Crack may experience learning and motor skill difficulties and delays as a result of their mother's Crack use.

Prolonged Crack use can result in cocaine psychosis. Some of the most frightening aspects of Crack use are the behavioral symptoms that often follow extended use. Many users suffer from cocaine psychosis and experience a break with reality. They begin to have hallucinations and become paranoid, fearing that everyone is out to get them.

Now, this psychosis can appear to be just like schizophrenia. Even the medical people don't understand Crack. They'll send you to the psych ward quicker than you might believe.

A few months ago I got a call from a technician in the psych ward of a local hospital. He told me a woman who was in one of the previous Generations had been admitted. Before the woman had even seen a doctor, the staff had pumped her full of medication that could have had harmful side effects. They hadn't even asked about her drug history.

I went over to the hospital and brought this woman back to Glide. We worked with her through her withdrawal after her relapse. She's doing fine. She has her job back; she completed the program. I keep the bottles of medication the hospital gave her in my desk drawer as a reminder of what ignorance can do to someone.

Crack often leads to violence. Users who become fearful do crazy things to protect themselves. Dealers will do anything to keep from getting caught selling Crack or from giving up their profit to anybody else on the make.

Anyone here want to testify?

Before Crack, the cocaine trade was controlled by big money from organized crime and South American drug cartels. The ease of "cooking" Crack made it cheap, readily available, and a perfect product for teenaged gangs and under-capitalized, small-time dealers to sell for a quick profit. And as these new deal-ers entered the drug trade, helping to created the Crack explosion, they armed themselves. The danger of Crack is manifold.

Is there anybody here who hasn't carried a gun or had one pointed at you be-cause of Crack?

One or two of you have been lucky, I see.

So Crack is dangerous. It is addictive. It is cheap. But why do you use it?

<u>Crack is a potent painkiller, an anesthetic.</u> When you smoke Crack, you can forget about pain, forget about any need or desire for food, sleep, or sex. You can forget about your mother, father, sister, brother, daughters, sons, or lovers. By simply lighting the rock and puffing on a pipe, you can feel euphoric and ab-solutely powerful for a brief few minutes. That is the lie of Crack. Crack makes us believe a chemical lie for a short, short time. Once the high is over, Crack makes you into a slave. No longer are you in control of your life. The need for Crack becomes a false God and makes your reality a hellish pit of deep despair.

<u>Crack recovery means total recovery.</u> When we say clean and sober living around Glide, that means abstinence from all mind-altering chemicals. You can't substitute one drug for another drug—one dependency for another dependency. Just because you've stopped smoking Crack doesn't mean you can drink all the al-cohol that you want. Alcohol is a drug—a sedative hypnotic. Some of the mem-bers of earlier Generations thought if they stayed away from Crack, it was okay to close down the bars. Now, I am removing the excuse factor.

When we talk about clean and sober living, that is what we mean: clean and sober.

We'll study the facts about Crack for the second month of the program. Then we'll learn the "tools" of faith and resistance that we have because of our African American heritage.

I know that most of you are trying to recover while living in the Tenderloin. We want to teach you that the drug culture is not black culture. We know you don't have the money to relocate and move away from the inner-city areas while you recover.

Through this Generation program we offer you an intensive outpatient pro-gram right here in the center of the Tenderloin. Alcoholics Anonymous teaches a person to get oneself together and go on out there in society and fit right in. The "society" that surrounds Glide is a drug culture; most of us know how to fit in there all too well.

We'll learn together that the drug culture is a pseudoculture. The truth is that it is not black to smoke Crack. We'll look at the African American experience by studying the lives and contributions of African Americans who changed history, like Harriet Tubman, Rosa Parks, Martin Luther King, Jr., Malcolm X. We'll listen to tapes of our culture bearers, like Maya Angelou. When she reads the poetry our ancestors wrote while they were slaves, you'll feel pride way down deep in your soul. We'll watch movies made by black filmmakers, movies like Roots, Do the Right Thing, *and* Eyes on the Prize.

We'll talk about the black experience. We're all black here. We know what being black is like. We'll spend time talking together. Most of us never learned about ourselves and our ancestors in school. History was always told from a European perspective. Many of us grew up watching our big brothers and community role models making it "big" through selling drugs.

Our African American ancestors fought for liberation. As we learn the truth, we can begin to claim our rightful places as heirs to the role of liberators of ourselves and our people.

The goal of the Generation program is to help you recover, get healthy, and go back home to your communities and make them conducive to recovery by being a positive, drug-free role model.

I know that most of you live in neighborhoods where many of your longtime friends or family members are involved in drugs. You can't move them out of those places, but you can lean into the recovering community of Glide. Here you can find drug-free people to laugh with and hang out with, people who will encourage your new way of living.

We must combat drug use in our families and in our neighborhoods. It's well known on the streets of the Tenderloin that Glide won't tolerate dealing outside our building or while standing in line for meals. We will get involved. This is our neighborhood, and we want it drug-free. Individuals, families, and the whole community are the focus of the Facts on Crack program.

We also know that when each Generation completes the Facts on Crack program, all of you must enter the mainstream of society. Some of you might find that world foreign and frightening.

I mean anyone who has been homeless, is currently unemployed, and hasn't worked in ten years should be afraid. Each Generation has to relearn life skills. During the final weeks of our seventeen weeks together I will ask you to build on what you have learned about yourselves and develop a two-year "career" plan.

Some of you will be ready to enter the job market immediately. Others of you might start your career plans by focusing on getting some vocational training. Each member must determine his or her exit plan, for it takes dedication to remain in recovery while taking on the additional responsibilities of managing money; providing housing, food, and clothing; and coping with life. The more you can think through now, the easier it will be then.

We'll help you to identify skills and interest areas. *During a recent Generation class, one member declared she wanted to pursue licensing as a foster-care provider as her next step. Another wanted to go back to school to learn to read. One man was getting his general equivalency diploma and was planning to attend City College in the fall. He said, "It may take me ten years, but I am going to be an engineer. I know where I am going."*

Some of you may want to enroll in Glide's Computers and You program after completing the Generation class. There you can learn computer, data processing, and literacy skills. Others may enter the job training program, which specializes in job readiness, placement, and follow-up.

We'll practice decision-making skills. *Many of you may need help learning that choices have consequences. Some of you think you have all the answers, and through role playing we'll learn new ways of evaluating situations. For example, one of the members of an earlier Generation said, "On my last job two people got in a fight. I saw the whole thing, but when the supervisor came to ask me about what happened, I said that I didn't see anything. The key to survival is to take care of yourself. Look out for number one—that's the key to survival."*

So I turned the situation around by saying, "Now, what if you were the supervisor in that same situation, what would you do?"

Now, he liked the idea of being the supervisor, but when forced to make a decision on who was responsible for the fighting, he said, "I'd fire them both."

The class jumped in. "No, man, that isn't fair. Those people probably have families and need the money. You gotta find out who was at fault," one woman declared. "Why couldn't you ask the two who were fighting to recreate the fight to see if you can tell who is lying?" suggested another member.

They came up with solutions and discussed how each method would have certain consequences. Through practicing problem solving, the Generation members realized they had skills and responsibilities they hadn't considered before.

We'll prepare resumés, practice filling out applications, and talk about personal grooming and presentation during an interview. *Many of you have been on the streets for a while and haven't been sending out too many resumés, have you? Some of you may have a hard time filling out job applications. Near the end of the Generation classes we'll practice filling out some sample applications.*

During one of the earlier Generation classes, one member got frustrated and said, "Man, everybody already knows this stuff, Eddie. Why do we have to fill out these applications?"

Just then someone else said, "One of these blanks asks for my military status. I've never been in the army. What do I write?"

Someone yelled across the room, "Write N/A, for nonapplicable. That is a shortcut way to say you don't have a military status. You can put N/A in any blank that doesn't fit. Then the employer will know that you aren't just leaving that space blank."

The guy who had complained about practicing with applications looked at me a little embarrassed. "I didn't know that," he said.

"Yeah, we all have some things to learn," I reminded him.

Later that same class session I said, "I'm going to go on a job interview. Watch me."

I grabbed a chair, noisily slid it across the floor, plopped down in it, and proceeded to toss my head. "Yo, homeboy," I said. "I'm the man for the job you got. How's 'bout it?"

The Generation broke into laughter, just like you guys did.

I asked them, "Now is that how you talk during a job interview? What did I do right and what did I do wrong?"

"You ain't done nothing right, Eddie," one of the members yelled. "You can't call someone you want to work for 'homeboy.' That's street talk, not job talk."

So we'll talk about "job talk," proper behavior, appropriate body language, and appearance.

Day in and day out for seventeen weeks, this Generation will meet together all afternoon, every weekday. We will become close to one another. This group is a safe place. You can be real here. You can let your emotions out. You can trust your brothers and sisters in this Generation to handle your anger or your tears. As a Generation you'll find that when given some basic tools, you can solve your own problems. Now that's empowerment.

What makes the Facts on Crack program unique is that it is as close as someone can get to an inpatient program without being in one. When you come to Glide, you can stay here from early in the morning until the evening. You can eat your meals here and volunteer between meetings if you choose to. Talk to me if you need someplace to stay. We are a part of the city shelter system; we'll work on finding a decent place for you to stay.

We don't have a magic wand at Glide. What we do have is a circle where you come to talk about whatever is out there that is bothering you. The Generation meetings are an extension of the circle meeting; they don't replace them. The only limit to what you say is that you must honestly talk of and about yourself, since you are the only one you can control.

As Eddie went over the schedule for the next day's meeting, I slipped out of the room. As I did, I patted Eric warmly on the shoulder. He'd come a long way.

If there was ever a toxic hustler on the loose, it was Eric when he first arrived at Glide. The way Eric handled himself showed his middle-class upbringing, but his drug use had taken him right into the heavy heart of poverty and homelessness. His polite ways and easy smile made him a charming hustler.

I knew I was taking a risk when I took Eric and Traci with me to Texas to speak to a group of people interested in our recovery programs. I knew Eric had slipped up in his recovery. But I gambled that telling their stories to a group of strangers would really make them face themselves. It did.

After they spoke, Eric and Traci seemed amazed that there were people in another state who were interested and genuinely concerned about their lives. They also learned that day that they had the ability to impart their power and their pain to others in a way that furthered the recovery process for all who would listen.

Rebirth: Eric's Story

I WAS TWENTY-NINE YEARS OLD when I got out of jail on a Saturday in October of 1990. I got on a bus that dropped me off at the San Francisco bus terminal. I didn't know anything about the shelters or San Francisco so I spent the night in the terminal near the BART station. The next day was Sunday and I was just walking around and I saw all of these people coming in to Glide, so I came in the church. I don't know why I came to church; I was really dirty, but I did.

It was a graduation ceremony for one of the Generations. That's how I first heard about the Facts on Crack program. I remember it was the Sunday after one of the women counselors in the program named Janean lost her baby. Everyone was talking about it that Sunday.

Someone told me about the food program at Glide, so I went downstairs and ate. On Monday I went and got on general assistance and used my prison money to rent a room and get some drugs. I was back at it again.

I needed recovery when I got out of prison because of the mentality in jail. I mean everybody says stuff like, "When you get out man, look me up. I'll fix you up with whatever drugs you like." There is no recovery program in prison; everybody is just waiting to get out and go back to doing just what they were doing before.

I tried to get into a drug treatment program, and they told me they were too full. They referred me someplace else, but I didn't have enough drugs in my system to get in. Then I found out more about the Glide program.

I volunteered at Glide, and they accepted me right away. Nobody told me to come back later. One of the door monitors told me that the meeting had already started and I could go on in.

Before I went to prison, I finished three years in college. When I was on the basketball team, I got hooked up with some of the other players who were into big-time drug dealing. These guys were driving around in Cadillacs and Mercedes. I wanted one. I started selling drugs, mostly marijuana at first, before I started using drugs. Crack wasn't the big thing back then. Most of the action was around weed. Crack hit the scene in 1984. You could go corner to corner and buy Crack cocaine.

I got introduced to it in 1985. I started using it because I wondered why all these people wanted to buy this rock. Why did people pay me $20, $100, $300, and then come back in fifteen minutes wanting more? I started using it to find out what was so fabulous about Crack.

Then I met some other people who were into Crack, and I started selling and transporting it. I came out here and got busted and put in jail. That was my first time going to jail, and I did three years of my life in the penitentiary.

When I got out of prison, I couldn't go to my family. When I had started using Crack, I really messed up things at home. When you use drugs, you get these crazy visions and you steal for more drugs. You do wild things. I got caught up in the limelight of fast money and expensive cars.

I was so bad when I was using drugs that when I went to my brother's and my sister's house, they made me sit outside because they knew if I came in, I would steal something and go and get more drugs. Still my family always loved me, and they never put me down. They always tried to get help for me, but I was in denial. I thought, "I'm all right. There's nothing wrong with me. You're the ones who are tripping!" I tried to put my problem back on them, but my problem was me.

After I came to Glide and got into the Facts on Crack program and was in it for a few weeks, some people gave me a job. I worked for three months; then I started back using drugs. I started to think that I was hot stuff. I thought I knew enough about recovery to get high the "right way" so that nobody would know. I kept telling myself, "You're a big man; a tiny little rock can't mess you up."

Cecil and my parole officer had encouraged me to get in the program, and I wanted them to still think I was clean. I thought I could smoke a little and still be in recovery; nobody would know.

I came to the circle meetings, and I thought nobody could tell that I had used. When somebody is getting clean from Crack and it is in his or her system, others can smell it. They can tell.

Everybody knew I'd been using so I quit the Tenth Generation and went back to the streets for a month and a half.

After a few weeks of smoking Crack, I came back to Glide. My drug "friends" whom I had been smoking with saw me on the streets and kept telling me, "You're crazy. Don't go doing no program; programs are shit, man." But I came back to Glide on May 22, 1991. I had to get out of my denial and go through the program as a man this time. The first time I started the program, Cecil wanted me to get in the program, and so did my parole officer and the people at general assistance. That first time I was doing the program for everybody else. This time when I came back to the program, I did it for myself. After a month I did go out and use, but then I came back the next day and started all over again.

My girlfriend Traci and I have gone hand in hand through recovery. I met her downstairs in the dining room after a circle meeting. She was volunteering. We were getting ready for a black literature class. Something just told me to talk to her. My friends were trying to rap at her like some big macho men. I started talking with her and being real with her. She told me about how she used to sell drugs. I told her, "You are a beautiful black woman. Why don't you go upstairs and get some recovery?" I asked her to come on up to our class, and she did. Afterward she walked home with me to the shelter where I was staying. She told me where she was living. I didn't want her walking back to that hotel that late; I knew what kind of place it was. I asked the workers in the women's side of the shelter if there was any place for Traci to stay. They had room upstairs in the woman's program. I woke her up in the morning, and we've helped each other to grow physically and mentally.

When I relapsed and went out and smoked Crack, I left Traci here at Glide. I knew what I was doing, and later I had to apologize to her. What I did was wrong.

I still have urges to use Crack. But I have a tool to use; I have the extended family. When you're being clean and sober at Glide, a lot of people acknowledge you and help you. I've had some recent job offers. I've had people who wanted to help Traci and me. The people in the children's program want us to talk to the kids. How can you use drugs and then come to church and talk to an audience about being clean and sober? My recovery is getting so strong that I don't want to use drugs. Every day is a happy and emotional day.

If Traci has a problem, she comes to me, and I go to her. We don't put too many problems on each other because we are both dealing with our recovery. We have to take it one day at a time. We are still early in our recovery; we have our circle meetings to help us get our emotions out so that we won't mess up our relationship. When we are dealing with the outside world, we keep reminding each other to use our tools; that helps us keep each other strong. My relationship with Traci is beautiful to me. I love her to death because this isn't a drug relationship. She gives me all the love I need.

When I met her, I couldn't go to my family to get the love I needed because I didn't want them to know that I had been using drugs again after I got out of prison. My family knows everything now. I called and told them everything. My father flew out from Georgia one Sunday in July just to see his son in recovery, doing good, getting himself together.

The last time my family had seen me I weighed 150 pounds, and I'm six feet three inches tall. I was torn up. Now I weigh 215. That Sunday my sister called me and asked Traci and me over for dinner, something she hadn't done in about four years. When we got there, we were sitting there watching TV and in walked my father. They didn't even tell me he was coming. They got me; I wanted to cry. It was so emotional and touching for me because the last time I had seen my whole family, I was all messed up. I missed out on years of birthday and Christmas celebrations. I hadn't spent a Christmas with them for four years. My family life during those years was a blank. The only family

I had during that time was drugs and the dudes who were dealing and the girls I got high with.

Now things are different, better. I can stop over to see my sister or spend the night at my brother's house when I want to. Before they wouldn't trust me. They knew if they had money laying around or a VCR, I would steal it.

My recovery is so beautiful. My mother called me last week and wanted to take Traci and me out to eat with her. My whole family now asks us to go places with them.

These days I volunteer at Glide and when I'm out on the streets, I tell other people about my program and my recovery. Lots of people know me from when I was using and now they see that I'm getting myself together. The light is shining on me. They come to me now and ask, "Eric, how did you do this?" I tell them, "I'm going to Glide." People could be in an inpatient program for fifteen years and still come out and use drugs. But if you come into an outpatient program like this, it is up to you 'cause you have to go home at night and still stay away from drugs. You can only lie to yourself; no one at Glide will let you lie.

The other day I took Traci over to see my house in Oakland. I'm not ready to move back there because of my recovery. I showed Traci how the front of the house got all shot up. There are fifteen bullet holes in the door. When you are into drugs, you got people who are jealous, people who are envious of you because you are making more money than them. Then you have people who want drugs but ain't got no money. They're on a mission. They'll kill at will. I got robbed before for two rocks. Four guys pulled out shotguns and threw me on the ground. My life could have been over for forty dollars worth of rock.

By the grace of God, I'm alive. One night I was in my house playing the keyboard and something told me to look out the window. I saw a guy get out of a car with an Uzi and start shooting. That guy thought that some dude who had hit him with a shovel lived in my house. I found out two days later when I had to go to court that someone who I thought was my friend had hit this guy in my yard. If he had really been my friend, he would have told me about this incident. That's how messed up people get over drugs. People will kill; they'll do anything.

My mother and God are the ones I have to thank for my recovery. Without the prayer of my mother I wouldn't be here today. I stole things from my mother. Still my mother never denied I was her child. She would have whopped me if she could have, but I was twenty-three years old when I came back to Oakland and was selling drugs. What could she do to me then? I took advantage of her. I never hit her, swore at her, or smoked dope in front of her. I was never that low. I would use drugs and then come home to her house, but she knew what I was doing.

She had people praying for me. She told me, "That isn't you. You weren't raised like that." My mother and father went to church all the time. I was raised in a Christian family. I just got caught up in the lime-light of using drugs.

My brother and my sister were mad at me while I was using because I had always been a role model in our community. I played basketball in junior high and high school. All the youngsters in the neighborhood idolized me because I was a ball player. I'd come home with trophies and stuff. I was only the third guy from the neighborhood in Oakland who went to college. When I turned to drugs, all the respect was gone.

It was like hell. I smoked away all the love and emotion I felt from my family and community. Losing the love of people I care about is one of the reasons why I refuse to get high now. I get mad when people try to get me to use. I can't go back to living like that.

My mother took nine months to birth me and years to raise me; she didn't go through all that for me to be a drug addict. My mother loved and cared for me. She never turned her back on me, even when I was using drugs.

As I recover, I'm not going to put myself on a high pedestal and fall. God only lets you go so high. Long as I have that faith and Spirit in me, I'm gonna do what is right. I don't think bad. I walk the beach, lay back, breathe the air, sit in the park.

Life is beautiful after death. This is after death. I'm proof of it. I did drugs, and I got shot at, shot, and beat up. Traci got stabbed, beat up, and robbed, too. By the grace of God, we are still here. Still living.

Community: Graduation of a New Generation

When I left my office and walked through Freedom Hall to the sanctuary on a recent Sunday morning, I saw the newest Generation as they were getting ready to graduate. They had congregated early, all dressed in black and red, their chosen class colors.

As I continued through the lobby, I saw small huddles of people loitering outside on the sidewalk. Some were dressed in Sunday finery, while one poor soul was searching the trash cans for a thrown-away cup of coffee. As I made my way slowly upstairs, I understood why so many were outside. They were the overflow from the eleven o'clock Celebration, unable to find even a place to stand inside the sanctuary that teemed with hundreds of clapping and shouting people.

As I dodged and twisted my way to the platform, I could hear the Glide Ensemble belting out the words to an anthem Janice and I rewrote for the First Generation.

Jesus loves you.
Get on off of that cocaine,
Get on off of that Crack.
Get yourself together,
Get your mind back.
Can't you see what drugs are doin'?

The congregation was alive.

"Grab on to somebody's hand," I said, when I got to the front. "It's Sunday morning, Lord," I began to pray. When I finished, as is traditional at Glide, we all stopped to embrace everyone around us, stranger or friend alike.

Then I announced, "Now we are going to have a graduation ceremony for our Facts on Crack program, but here we call graduations a rebirth. These folks are starting new lives.

"I want all the newest Generation of people in recovery to come on up here to the platform. Drug counselors, you come on up here, too. Don't worry where you gonna stand. We don't worry about that; we'll work it out somehow."

Just as they formed some semblance of rows, the words *It's Recovery Time* were projected onto an overhead screen. The congregation, as if joined into one body, leapt to its feet in a rowdy ovation.

One of the members of the Generation stepped forward and hushed the crowd. "Today I am giving my husband and children the best present they could want, a mother and wife who is clean and sober."

The place went wild. People started stomping and crying and hugging.

Another man stepped forward. "My spirituality is what helped me recover. I'm so happy today that Glide has a spiritual recovery program. I'm a new man today."

"Eddie, c'mon over here," I called out.

Eddie Franks then read each Generation member's name. Each one stepped forward and was handed a Bible and a certificate for completing the seventeen-week course in recovery skills. Then I draped each one's shoulders with a scarf woven of red, green, and black while saying, "These are the proud colors of the country of your ancestors. Let them remind you who you are. You are a new person, a liberated person."

When they each held a certificate and wore their colors, I called their families forward. Husbands, brothers, sisters, mothers, fathers, and more than a dozen children pushed their way up to the crowded platform. Side by side, the New Generation stood with their extended families. Together as individuals, families, and a community in recovery, we clapped for them, for us, and for the future of a race.

That Sunday we had a graduation of a Generation moving from death to life. Generation by Generation we keep moving, doing, and living. Person by person we are seeing the rebirth of a race.

▲   ▲   ▲

CHAPTER SIX

Women on the Move

Recognition: The Importance of Self-Definition for Women

One day while I sat in a circle meeting and listened to the First Generation of women tell their stories, an awful truth dawned on me. One hundred percent of the women in the First Generation had been seriously abused. One after another, each woman told a horror story of incest, battering, rape, or severe emotional abuse. Not one of the women had entered Glide unscathed. The women's stories, their tears, their courage to fight for their very lives left no doubt as to the truth of what they were saying.

The sheer magnitude of the abuse they suffered staggered me. Were these women unusual? Or was there a silent avalanche of abuse crashing down on woman after woman in our society?

When I went back to my office that day, I closed the door and looked closely at the lives of the women I knew the best—the women in my family. Did all women experience abuse?

I started with my mother. When I was a boy, my mother instilled respect for women in her sons; indeed she commanded it. But when I thought back on her life, I began to see that my mother had experienced racist abuse all through her life.

Once when I was nine years old, we had a little extra grocery money. I went with my mother and baby brother Reedy to the store in the white section of San Angelo; it had better food and a wider selection. We had to wait a long time in line that day, as usual. The white customers got served first, even if they came in after we did. When we finally paid, two street cops awaited us outside.

"Hold it, Auntie," one of them barked at my mother. "Lemme see your stuff," he said, leering at my mother, who was a very attractive, light-skinned woman. "We wanna see what you got in them bags."

"What for?" Mother replied as politely as she could under the circumstances.

"Ain't you got no sense at all? We wanna see if they all yours. Some y'all steal."

The crowd that gathered tittered. For them, the humiliation of a black woman and her children was as good as any circus sideshow.

"We'll do what you say, officer, but can't we go 'round to the side? I don't want my children—" my mother persisted.

"Dammit, nigger woman! You gon' do it right here, right now."

In front of the laughing crowd we reached into our bags while the cops checked every item against our receipt. When they could no longer prolong their little game, the cop said, "One thing—we gon' watch y'all next time you come around. You niggers can't get away with nothin' here."

That was the final humiliation. Mother glared at the cop. "You're not ever gonna get me to take my groceries out of the bag for you again! None of us steals. If my groceries come out again, you gonna have to take them out yourself."

The cop looked at Mother with surprise and contempt, his eyes bitter. "Why, you nigger bitch!" he spat. "Don't you tell me anything! You'll take them out if I tell you to!"

When that cop called my mother a bitch, I wanted more than anything in the world to reach out for his .45 caliber gun and shoot him for humiliating my mother. It was the only time in my life that I wanted to shoot a white person. Even as I remembered the incident from the safety of half a century, I clenched my fists until my knuckles were white.

How much my mother must have endured; how much I will never know.

Then I thought of Janice, my wife. Her struggle to face childhood molestation had brought the issues of self-esteem and personal empowerment into our home. But sexual abuse wasn't the only gender-related abuse she had experienced.

A incident from the early 1980s rushed back in from the recesses of my mind. Janice and I had traveled to Mexico to participate in a conference on liberation theology. I was scheduled to speak and Janice was slated to lead a panel discussion. When we arrived, I gave my speech and Janice reviewed her notes. Then one of the conference conveners came and told Janice that they didn't want a woman to lead the panel.

These macho theologians were threatened by Janice's very presence. The irony of the situation and the blindness of the conference conveners amazed me. We had all gathered to discuss liberation for the oppressed and empowerment for all races and classes. How could these men hope to keep Janice from talking solely because she was a women?

Janice fought back. I fought with her, as did some of the others in attendance. Janice lead that panel.

I flew home from Mexico asking myself how could ministers, men of the cloth like me, presume to live out the principles of liberation theology and still sweep women aside?

I knew, as a man and as a minister, that women's liberation issues had a lot to do with me. The struggle for women to claim power over their own bodies, minds, and souls affected me. I knew then that I had a long journey to take inside me. How was I living like one of the oppressors?

In the ensuing years, as Janice claimed her power and responsibilities as president of the Glide Foundation, I had to give up my male insensitivities to her leadership. I had to let go of having things my own way. If she made decisions that I would have made differently, I learned to leave them in her hands. She would handle the consequences—good or bad. When choices were hers to make, I had to step out of the way and follow as she lead. Her ways of leading are different than mine—not better, not worse, just different.

I had to adjust at home, too. Janice tells people that she makes her side of the bed in the morning and I make mine. That is literally the truth. Without effort from both of us, the bed would go unmade. I iron my own shirts and sew on my own buttons. I fry my own fish because I like mine battered and crispy. Janice likes her raw sashimi with rice. I no longer expect Janice to do things I grew up thinking were "women's work." In earlier days I would have expected her to take care of my domestic needs.

After Janice became the director of programs at Glide, I had to readjust my style of making decisions. Previously I just made single-handed decisions and demanded that they be enacted. When Janice had pivotal decisions to make, she often came and discussed them with me or with whoever was involved. I could see that her mutual style of making choices really empowered people and helped them to take an active part in the work at Glide.

I wanted to learn how to work in a more mutual way. But one of the hardest journeys for me to take when I faced a crucial decision was the walk out of my office and across the hall to Janice's. At first I used the excuse that she was always on the phone; I couldn't get to her in time. Then my excuses showed themselves to be simply excuses. Now many times I have made that journey from my office to hers, and she has crossed from hers to mine; Glide is stronger for it. Together, we've learned some important lessons. Janice can lead powerfully, and I can take care of myself.

That day, as I considered the women in my family, I thought also of my daughter Kim. My first wife and I had adopted Kim as a tiny newborn. One of Kim's biological parents was black, the other white. Over the years her kinky hair grew long and honey-colored and her skin glowed golden, the color of coffee with extra cream. Her bright hazel eyes are wide and complemented by full lips that link her surely to her African bloodline.

Tall, lovely, and bright, Kim faced her own internal war. Was she black or was she white?

Kim did not have to face the horrors of segregation or the trauma of incest. Yet her own venture toward self-definition was painful and uncharted. I had tried to shield Kim and my son Albert from the painful racial rejection that I had experienced as a child. But I could not shield my daughter from the luring influences of drugs that so beckoned her generation.

On a Saturday in 1989, soon after the First Generation began, I was in a rush to get to Oakland to speak to a drug task force that had emerged out of Glide's Death of a Race Conference. While I was on my way, I sat on the passenger side of the car and perused the morning newspaper. A small article on a recent drug bust caught my attention; as I read further, my heart nearly stopped. Kim Williams, whom the article correctly identified as my daughter, was one of those arrested.

Here I was a minister fully and publicly engaged in the war against drugs, and my daughter was one of those playing with the fire of the drug trade. What was I going to say to those who were coming to hear me speak that very morning?

When I arrived and looked into several hundred expectant faces, I knew there was only one story I could tell, and that was my own. I told them about my daughter's arrest and my struggle as a father and as a minister.

When I finished, many in the audience came out of their seats and gathered around me. In turn, they told me their stories. Their daughters, nephews, nieces, and grandchildren were also playing with the deadly fire of Crack and other drugs. As parents and extended family, we moaned and wept and wailed together. The drug problem wasn't just a social issue that we wanted to conquer; it was a ravaging scourge that was destroying our own families.

Before my daughter's arrest I knew that she had experimented with drugs before Crack came on the scene. She had tried freebasing cocaine for a short

while. One of the consequences of drug addiction—especially to Crack cocaine—is that it causes compulsive lying on the part of the addict. Kim created outrageous lies to obtain more money from me for drugs. One of the
lies was that Crack dealers were going to kill her if she didn't pay them the
money she owed them for drugs.

In 1987 she came and told me the truth about her lies. I told her that I
would not support her financially or help her out of her mess. Kim began
to feel like she was out there by herself. So she had quit using drugs, but
now, through the newspaper account, I learned she was still hanging around
the mix and mire of the drug world. She had been arrested for being with a
man as he sold marijuana.

After she was arrested, our family planned a family intervention. All the
nearby relatives and some of her lifelong friends converged at my brother's
house. One by one we told Kim that she would no longer hustle us. We
would not excuse her for being an accomplice to drug trafficking just because
she wasn't dealing or using herself. She still needed recovery; participating
in the drug culture, using or not, would lead her nowhere. We all declared
that we would not enable her behavior any longer by helping her out of her
trouble. She would have to take full responsibility for herself.

After that family meeting, Kim went into recovery. She sought the professional help that she needed. She enrolled in business school, and she put
renewed energy into being a good mother to her small daughter.

Kim's experience taught me perhaps the most essential lesson about
women's recovery that I have learned. Anyone's daughter can get caught up
in drugs; only she can decide to come clean. The extended family could encourage her in the direction of recovery, but her life was hers, and hers
alone. As I reflected back, I realized that each woman in my family, no matter the devastation and trauma meted out by others, had to claim responsibility for her own life.

Like all women, my mother, my wife, and my daughter are responsible for
their own lives. As women, they have helped themselves and one another.
Neither I nor any man could have done for them what they have done for
themselves—they have defined themselves in the midst of a culture that
screams out messages that encourage them to passively accept the degrading
names and identities handed to them, like "nigger woman," "incest victim," or "the dealer's woman."

The women in my family have suffered greatly, and yet somehow they
have found the courage to reclaim their lives. My mother stood up to those
cops and so many others like him by standing her ground and refusing to

accept their racist, dehumanizing labels. Janice fought against feeling invisible and declared in her poetry and in her life, "Who is singing this song? I am." Kim pulled away from the deceitful promise of false power found in messing with drugs and reclaimed her life.

That day as I reflected on the lives of each of these three wonderful women, I felt different. I saw that as each one had defined herself, she became more than mother, wife, or daughter to me. No longer was I only my mother's son, my wife's husband, or my daughter's father; I was also their brother, their friend—a partner who continues to marvel at the power each has claimed and has shared with the extended family.

Self-Definition: The Women on the Move Program

The lessons I learned by taking a look at my immediate family were reaffirmed as more and more women joined the recovery programs. The connection between sexual, physical, and emotional abuse and Crack addiction became undeniable. As the women began to see and hear their plights echoed in the words of other women, they began to congregate after the circle meetings.

Sometimes they gathered on the stairs on the sixth floor. When the men in the recovery program noticed that the women were gravitating toward one another, some got nervous. Inevitably one of the men would find some reason to stick his nose into the women's meetings trying to figure out what invisible force propelled the women together.

Arguments between the men and the women erupted in the circle meetings when the women claimed that recovery for women was different than it was for men. "Recovery is recovery, no matter who or what you are," some of the male members protested.

Edna tried to help the men understand. "Even if it is just the way Crack affects our bodies, women's recovery is different."

Still the women kept gathering. They talked about their emotions, their addictions to men, their struggles to take responsibility for their lives, and the changes taking place in their bodies as they withdrew from Crack. The meetings were informal, spontaneous, and initiated by the women.

One of the women told me how important the women's meetings were to her recovery. "Hearing another woman's pain and courage helps me to say to myself, 'I don't have to stay down. I can move up. I can get my leg up to hoist myself over this mountain of addiction and abuse. I have the power to say no to that man who beats me up because she did it before me.'"

As each woman shared her story, she tied one more knot in the lifeline to which the other women held fast.

All during this time the five o'clock open microphone meeting continued to draw hundreds of people daily to Freedom Hall, where any who wished could take the platform. The women who had been gathering together started announcing that there was a new support group for women. Soon flyers were printed and distributed at check-cashing facilities in the Tenderloin—sure places to find unemployed women with dependent children on the first and fifteenth of the month. The number of women joining the recovery program swelled.

As the number of women in the program grew, so did the number of preschool children. One day in the circle meeting the group members decided to spend their time listening to what the children had to say about drugs, but the children wouldn't talk. Someone wisely went and found paper and crayons. The children graphically drew the fearful monster of drugs, some in the shapes of pipes, needles, marijuana joints, liquor bottles. The children knew everything.

If any of the women weren't serious about their recovery before, many saw the stark truth that day. They needed to stop using not only for their own sake but also for the sake of their children.

One day as the women met in their support group in room 618, they decided to choose a name for their group. Lots of names were thrown up for consideration, but none matched the core reality of who the women felt they were becoming inside. As they talked, they kept coming back to the reality that they were women who were moving on beyond addiction and abuse. They were women moving forward to start something that made a difference in their attitudes, in their relationships, in the recovery program at Glide, and in the community outside the walls of Glide.

Then someone simply said, "We are women on the move."

The women immediately knew that their name had been spoken.

ADVOCACY AND COUNSELING

Over the course of several years the Women on the Move office has become the living room for many of the women in the Facts on Crack program. The well-worn sofa offers a safe resting place, and all the posters and mottoes taped to the walls serve to infuse the women who enter with hope and renewed determination. Taped on the walls are posters of African queens as well as pictures and news clippings that feature successful African American women.

The Women on the Move logo is the lotus flower. Rosa, one of the Women on the Move counselors, suggested it because the lotus flower is one of the most beautiful and fragrant of flowers, but it only grows in mud. That's a symbol for the women who enter the doors looking for help. Even lives early nourished on muck and misery can grow strong and beautiful.

The Women on the Move program offers one-on-one counseling, small group meetings for recovering women, and advocacy to help them maintain or reunite their families. The Women on the Move counselors are peer counselors, women who have broken free from the very chains that each new client drags in behind her. The counselors specialize in prevention and counseling to help women face the hard issues of abuse, self-hatred, and poverty that prompt the women to turn to drugs.

From Monday to Friday, Rosa, Janean, and the other staff counselors provide support and encouragement to women who are seeking to make positive life changes. Rosa and Janean dispense hope as they offer information regarding Facts on Crack, local shelters, family intervention, health care, life skills, money management, self-esteem workshops, and support groups that deal with codependency, incest, and physical abuse issues.

Recently as I walked by the Women on the Move office, a man and woman were arguing in the hallway. Janean came to the door and said, "Angie, Joe,* come in here. Now what is going on with you two?"

Angie stepped inside the office. Janean straightened to her considerable height and leaned toward Joe. "Let me remind you that no one tried to interfere with you when you came here looking for recovery. Now that Angie is the one coming for help, why are you trying to talk her out of it? I want you to get out of here for a while."

Joe was angry with Janean. "That's my woman. I married her six months ago; I got rights."

Janean, as usual, took nothing from this guy. She had been working with the two of them for several weeks, trying to get Angie to stay and talk to her for a while. Janean knew by now that drugs served as a powerful glue in their relationship. More than once, one had led the other back out to the streets and straight into another round of drugs and another cycle of battering.

---

*These people are composites; their names are randomly chosen.

"Yeah, I know. When Angie gets her head together, she'll know where to find you when she wants to."

Angie, who had slumped down into a well-worn easy chair just inside the door, looked out at her husband and hissed, "Maybe I'll be here, maybe I won't."

Angie looked like a limp rag doll without a smile. Her hair was uncombed, and she wore a tattered raincoat over an ill-fitting pair of jeans. The soles of her shoes were coming loose, and she wore no socks.

While Janean dealt with Joe, Rosa took over with Angie. "Let's see what we've got in this bag that might fit you," she said, digging through a bag of new clothes searching for a decent pair of shoes and clean clothes to fit Angie.

Rosa handed a pair of sneakers and a pair of socks to Angie. By that time Janean was freed up and Rosa had to go facilitate the eleven o'clock circle meeting in Freedom Hall.

"What's going on, Angie?" Janean asked. Angie seemed distant and despondent.

Janean's tone of voice had softened. "What is it that you want from me? Why have you come here today?"

Angie only mumbled. She fidgeted and had a hard time concentrating. Her body language sent a clear signal that she was high on Crack.

Janean got down to the nitty-gritty. "Do you need a place to stay tonight?" Angie nodded, and Janean made a call to the Crisis Care office where one of the staff started to work on temporary shelter.

While Janean was on the phone, Angie slumped down and began to cry. Janean moved from behind her desk and sat with Angie as she began to moan and piecemeal describe the drugs, the squalor, the abuse with which she lived.

"Honey, you don't have to live like that," Janean assured her. "If you are willing to work at your recovery and come here every day as a part of the program, you can make it."

One to one, Janean walked Angie through the day. "Have you eaten today?"

Angie said no.

Janean offered her some coffee and encouraged her to go to the dining room downstairs. "I'm not that hungry," Angie protested, seeming uneasy about venturing into the crowded dining room.

"Hey, I'll go with you. Today I won't let you out of my sight. You need to eat; a good meal will help you as you come down from that high. Detoxing from Crack is different than coming off heroin or alcohol. You have to drink lots of water and eat."

After lunch Janean led Angie back to the office and gave her a list of support meetings and recovery groups that would be available after hours if she needed help after Glide closed for the day.

Janean then asked, "Do you have any children who are not in your custody at this time? If you do, sometime in the near future, after you've been clean for a while, you can talk to one of our advocates who will work with you to get your children back."

Angie has one child, a son who is living with her grandmother.

By the time Janean finished asking questions about Angie's situation, it was three o'clock, time for the circle meeting. Janean took Angie to Freedom Hall and sat down next to her. Angie squirmed during the first few minutes. Then abruptly she stood up and ran from the room. Janean followed her and caught her at the door.

"Angie, whenever anyone is coming down from Crack, she panics and wants to get out. What you are feeling right now is normal. It will get better. Just sit in and listen to the people in the circle. Some of the others in there only have two or three days clean. You're not the only one feeling afraid."

Angie seemed startled that Janean so clearly pinpointed her feelings. "Yeah? Some of the others in the circle have used this week? I'm not the only one?"

"Hardly, sister." Janean took Angie's elbow and guided her back to Freedom Hall.

AFRICAN QUEENS REVISITED

Once women like Angie begin the struggle to leave drugs and the life of powerlessness behind, the largest battle to win is often an internal one. The women believe after years of abuse that they are worthless victims, unsuitable for a better life.

The Women on the Move program was designed to introduce the recovering women to a new, empowered way of being, believing, and living. Specifically, since the Women on the Move program served mostly black women, one of the questions to be answered by the staff early on was, What will help to empower and educate African American women? How can they come to know and benefit from the legacy of faith and resistance forged by their foremothers—the powerful black women who paved the way in earlier days?

The answer walked in the doors of Glide in December of 1990 when Rosa entered Glide for the first time.

For fifteen years she had traveled with Stevie Wonder as his hairstylist. She had lived in opulence and mingled with the jet set. But there came a time, when her kids were grown, when she just decided that she wanted to be of service to her people somehow. Rosa called her aunt, Maya Angelou, and told her what she was thinking.

Maya introduced Rosa to me and to Glide. When she first came in to talk to me, she told me that she wanted to teach the women how to sculpt hair so they'd have a skill they could use to make money. But I could tell by listening that Rosa had a natural inclination toward counseling. Her clear eyes were like deep wells. She carried herself as royalty might, and she spoke softly with compassion and conviction. She was a truly spiritual woman who was rooted in her hard-won self-identity and steeped, rich and brown, in African history. She could help the women raise their sights and believe in themselves.

When Rosa arrived at Glide, she started the African Queens Revisited component of Women on the Move. It is a self-esteem-building course based on the belief that as women get to know their cultural roots and are introduced to the great women of Africa who succeeded, who came up out of the mire and became queens and leaders of their people, the women will begin to see who they really are and where they really come from. So many of the women who come to Glide seem to think African American culture originated with slavery. Rosa, as a student of African history for twenty-five years, has collected stories, books, and pictures of strong African women, and she brings them in and shares them with the women.

One day I asked Rosa to educate a group of visiting interns as to what the African Queens Revisited program was all about. I was curious, too. I'd never been to any of the women's meetings either.

Rosa lifted her chin and, sitting poised and powerful, told us about Queen Makeda, the Queen of Sheba, who is written about in the Bible and in the Koran. Queen Makeda ruled what is present-day Ethiopia for fifty years during the tenth century B.C. The Queen of Sheba is renowned for her visit to King Solomon; she traveled far to test his wisdom with her hard questions, and Solomon hid nothing from her. Before she left, she gave Solomon some of her riches—gold, spices, and jewels. In return, he gave her everything she desired. Other history books and legends mention a love affair that ensued between Solomon and the Queen of Sheba, resulting in an heir who later ruled Ethiopia.

Rosa also told us about Queen Ann Nzinga, female leader of the army in Ngodo, present-day Angola. Queen Nzinga lead the Jaga tribe as it fought against Portuguese occupation in the early seventeenth century.

Rosa said, "These women from history inspire the women in their recovery. It isn't unusual for a woman to come to a meeting after learning about the queens and proudly introduce herself with her chin held high: 'I'm Denise, and I am an African queen.'"

The African Queens Revisited course is one way the Women on the Move program builds some self-esteem in the women. In addition to learning about the queens and other modern African American women, Rosa tries to find ways to tap into the women's sense of self and spirituality. She starts most of the meetings with a meditation, followed by a prayer. Then she tells them stories about our ancestors and stories from her own life.

I know from my own life that these women can make it. When they first come in here, they look at me and think I must have it made. As time goes on and I tell them stories from my own life, they come to know that I've been where they are. I am an incest survivor, and I've taken every drug that is out there at one time or another. But I haven't touched anything in seven years. If I can recover, so can they.

As a group we do exercises that help the women look for the good in themselves. In an early meeting I wrote the words I Am Somebody Because . . . on a large sheet of paper and asked the women to find five good things about themselves.

Someone said, "I am somebody because I want recovery." Another said, "I am somebody because I take good care of my kids." We went around the room, and everybody came up with something. It was amazing to see the women start to realize they were worth something.

Another time I had each woman turn to the woman sitting next to her and tell her what she liked about the other woman. One said, "I like the shape of your face; it's a perfect oval."

The woman who heard this grabbed her face and moaned in disbelief, "You like the way I look? I hate my forehead; it's so high."

The other responded, "Yeah, I think you are beautiful, especially when you laugh."

The other almost cried. She, like all the women who have come through the program, has heard and believed for years that she is unattractive and worthless. I try to provide opportunities for the women to see themselves through another person's eyes.

Some of the women in the self-esteem groups have made affirmation angels, which are wooden angels with mirrors for faces. Each woman paints her own affirmations about herself on the angel's wings. Every morning when a woman gets up, I encourage her to look at herself in that mirror and repeat the affirmation. The truth starts to seep into the women's souls when they say daily: "I am recovering," "I am a wonderful woman," "I am black and I am beautiful."

When the women start believing they are worthy people, they usually start caring about their outer appearance again. Repeatedly, I've seen the women go from not bathing or brushing their teeth when they first start coming to Glide to looking and feeling really good. Once a woman who owns a cosmetics firm donated a box of skin-cleansing products. I had a great time showing the women how to care for their skin.

Recently a group with a research grant came in asking us to choose a couple of women graduates from the Facts on Crack Generation program who were looking for work. They wanted to study what would happen to a new worker's job performance if all the material and logistical obstacles faced when trying to get a good job are removed. They individually took the women shopping for a new wardrobe. Then they helped the women tailor their resumés for a job fair they had organized.

I'll never forget when one of the women came into the Women on the Move office with her bags full of new clothes. Piece by piece, she pulled out a beautifully cut plum suit with brass buttons, a black flowing jacket and print skirt, and a couple of casual outfits, with shoes and accessories to match.

"Look at this necklace. I want to wear it in my hair," she declared, putting it over her braids like a headdress and pirouetting around the room like an African queen. With outstretched hands, she said to Janean, "I thought of you when I saw these earrings. Do you want them?"

Janean shook her head and looked the woman straight in the eyes, "You are worthy of every single thing you have. You keep it all for yourself."

"Yeah, I am worthy," she reminded herself. "I'll look in my closet tonight and remind myself of that at ten o'clock when I start feeling like I'm nothing, like I usually do."

Janean smiled, "Enjoy this moment."

"Can I put on this jogging suit, right now?"

Janean threw her the keys to the rest room, and a few minutes later the woman came back strutting like a peacock in a turquoise and violet outfit. "I never thought I could wear stuff like this; I thought I was too fat."

By this time several people had come into the office to see what was going on. One of the men piped up. "You look pleasing, baby," he said with admiration.

She threw back her head and laughed with sheer delight and said, "This is recovery."

Times like that are what keep me working as a counselor here. People who knew me when I was working for Stevie Wonder and making really good money sometimes ask me where is the reward or payback for working here? When I see a woman stand up and declare that she is not going to take it—drugs, abuse, degradation—anymore, when a woman takes charge of her life, claims it for herself, that is where the reward is found.

But I've got to be honest, the rewards are few. So many of the women come in here when they are so low. One young woman who came in here last week told me she had been on the streets since she was ten years old. Now she's twenty-seven. She spent the day here at Glide, and when she left, her pimp was waiting outside. Someone told me later he said to her, 'What made you think you can go in there and get recovery?'

He beat her up in the park across the street. I wish I had been here. I would have done something to stop him. But that woman came back the next day all bruised up. It happened again that night, and she came back the third day. She said that she kept coming back to Glide because people had offered her a helping hand for the first time in her life.

It is amazing to see these folks come in here, not even expecting to be loved. Most of them have never experienced a parent or a friend who really believed they were worth loving. They have a hard time accepting love.

Most of the women don't deal well with other women at first because their lives have been spent manipulating men. It takes work for the women to trust one another. Many of the women don't trust other women. Out on the streets they vie for men's attention and sometimes compete for the money or drugs that can be had for sex. A lot of women don't like being with other women. They've been taught all their lives that power and protection come from being with a man. Even when men have abused them or offered them much misery, most of the women just start looking for another man instead of looking to themselves and their sisters. As they get clean, the women learn that it is other women who'll support them as they get on with their lives.

Sometimes I just open up the African Queens Revisited meetings for the women to talk about whatever they are dealing with. Inevitably the topic turns to three familiar subjects: shame, relationships with men, and fear of responsibility. The women are afraid of taking responsibility for themselves; they are afraid of parenting by themselves; they are often afraid of success because they have had so little in their lives. Success and health are new to the women.

Nobody talks about health without prompting. The women as a whole ignore physical pain, chronic aches, unnatural discharges. They don't want to think about what drugs have done to their bodies and their spirits.

Recently some of the women came to me asking if we could set up a prayer chain. They wanted to be able to contact somebody if they had a need. It has become important for them to know that the others in the group are linked with them in prayer and support. The women are starting to be there for one another. They understand that they have something valuable to offer.

When Rosa finished talking to the group of interns, I asked Janean to address the group, not as a counselor but as a member of the First Generation of the Facts on Crack program.

Janean obliged, for she knows like few could that when women walk into the Women on the Move office, they are spiritually and emotionally broken. Standing strong, with a dignity born through overcoming suffering, Janean told the truth about her life.

Rebirth: Janean's Story

WHEN I FIRST STARTED ON this journey of knowing myself, I was terrified. I was a stranger to myself. I had never been with me. I had always been the caretaker and rescuer of my family, which meant that what I was feeling and what was going on with me didn't matter. Everyone relied on me.

I always felt inadequate, but I never would have admitted to others that I couldn't take care of their needs. I lacked honest love in my life, so when someone needed me, it really tapped in on my need for approval and acceptance. Any request from somebody else seemed like a great opportunity to show people that I cared.

I have a paradoxical background. I'm Cape Verdian. My grandparents are from the Cape Verde Islands. That means I am African and Portuguese, but I was brought up as if I were only Portuguese. As a matter of fact, blacks were talked about really badly in our family.

When I was born, my parents were famous musicians. My mother was a singer, and my parents did a lot of traveling. My grandmother would take care of my brothers, my sister, and me.

We lived in Boston. I was brought up as a "museum child." We had to be perfect, proper, extremely well dressed. We couldn't get dirty or go out and play with the other kids. There were always managers and jazz groups coming through our house.

The real secret in our family was that my mother had a son before she met my father. This son is darker than the rest of my family because his father is black. My father is extremely prejudiced against blacks. My mother's family were darker Cape Verdians so my brother's coloring didn't matter to them.

When my brother was eight months old, my mom met my father. They married and soon after, my father started beating my brother when my mom would leave the house. At first, my mom thought that there was something wrong with my brother because he was always getting hurt. My mom told me recently that she should have known what was going on because any time she would leave, my brother would beg her not to go. My father was really abusive.

When my brother was three years old and I was less than a year old, my father threw him all over the place. My brother ended up with broken ribs, a broken wrist, and internal injuries. He had fist-shaped bruises on his stomach. After my father beat him, my mother took my brother to the hospital; he was hospitalized for a long time.

My mother was in a lot of denial, and the doctor told her that either he'd been hit by a car or truck or someone in the house had beaten him. My mother said it couldn't have been the baby-sitter; she wouldn't do it. At the time she never considered it could have been my father.

My brother is thirty-nine today and has a scar from the top of his ribs down to his groin from the operation they had to do to save him. He still has intestinal problems from that beating.

My mother told me this whole story last year. I had only heard bits and pieces as I grew up. When she told me, I felt terror and anguish; I realized I was reexperiencing feelings that I had all through my childhood. I had recurring nightmares for many years, and as my mother told me the truth about my brother, one of the dreams began to make sense.

After more than thirty years, I realized that I was in the room that night my father beat my brother. I asked my mother about one of the bureaus that always showed up in one of my dreams, and she told me it was in that room where my brother was beaten.

All my life I had this great terror of my father that I didn't understand. My father was physically abusive to me, but he was more emotionally and mentally abusive to me. What I experienced didn't account for the kind of fear that I had for that man. Today I know why.

I've always been afraid of the dark. I know that being in the room when my father beat my brother late at night has a lot to do with it. I'm not afraid of walking around on the streets late at night. I'm afraid of being in the house, in my own home, in the dark—it has something to do with someone being in the room and it's dark. The fear is just as real as any gut terror I've ever experienced. When I'm in the house alone, I always feel like someone is there looking at me.

The social workers took my brother away from my mom after that incident and placed him in a foster home. I was so young when all this happened that I didn't even know I had a brother until I was five years old. My mother didn't know where my brother was, but one day when he was outside playing, she saw him. He had became mute and seemed to have forgotten everything he had learned. He was like a mummy.

After that, my brother's foster mom would let my mother sneak over and visit him. One day my mother told the foster mom that she and my dad would be performing on television that night. My brother hadn't seen my father since the day of the beating, and when he saw my father's face on TV, he went bananas. He started crying, "The hands, the hands." When the foster mother told my mother what had happened, my mother knew what my father had done. She confronted my father, but he denied everything.

My mother was young and soon lost her singing career because of my father. She would get ready to go on tour, and he wouldn't let her go. He would beat her at night when we kids were sleeping.

My parents are both very handsome people. My father looks like Ricardo Montalban, with that Latino look. He is tall and muscular.

The paradox of my family is that we had a great image in the community. We were one of the few families of color that owned a house back then. Mom and Dad were making a lot of money. At Christmastime the living room would be so packed with toys that no one could walk a straight path though the room.

We were brought up with rigid, strict rules. If my father tried to teach me something and I didn't get it the first time, he would say, "Janean, if you had a brain, you'd be dangerous." My father always complained about me because I didn't do well in school. Schoolwork was foreign to me. All I remember about school is staring out the window and hoping my mother would be alive when I came home every day.

I just lived in fear. If I had known a way to commit suicide back then, I would have. I had three brothers by the time I was in elementary school, and they picked up some of my father's oppressive behavior. They cruelly teased me and pulled the heads off my dolls and talked to me like I was a nobody—just the way they heard my father talk to me.

I was the only girl in the family for a long time. There were some okay times when my brothers weren't at home and my dad was at work. When it was just my mom and I, she would call me her princess and be really good to me. But when my father was home, she was an entirely different person. If the house was not inextricably clean, she knew that she was going to get it.

There was no alcohol abuse in my family. Sex was the drug of choice in my family. My uncles, aunts, and cousins had sex with one another. I believe my great-grandmother was a madam.

Our family was always getting together. When we would have family reunions, the adults would put on some music and tell us to dance and shake our money-maker, and they would put money in our pants.

My grandmother was a nasty woman. Sometimes she would pull her breast out and try to get one of us to suck on it. When my grandmother would greet us, she would put her hands in our private areas and say, "Is it clean down there?" Then she would sniff at her fingers and laugh.

My father had lots of affairs. He even had sex with some of my aunts. I know one of my aunts was a prostitute, a call girl who made $500 to $1,000 a night and drove fancy cars.

When I was six or seven, my father took me into the bathroom, real suspicious-like. He pulled a bra out of his pocket and put it on me. He said, "It's too big for you," and then he stuffed it with tissue.

There just were no boundaries.

We never had outsiders come into our home. In many ways I was brought up to be abused. One of the predictable realities of an abused woman's life is isolation. She has no friends. The man cuts off all relationships around her. My mother never went shopping by herself. She was not allowed to be friends with anyone but her in-laws.

Since my mother got beaten regularly, it felt normal to me when I started getting beaten myself. I didn't like it, but I figured that was how it was supposed to be. My older brother remembers seeing my father beat my younger brother. My mother always told my older brother that there was a good angel and a bad angel. The bad angel would stay on the left shoulder and the good angel would stay on the right shoulder. Mom told him to always listen to the good angel when it whispered in his ear.

One day my brother went to my mother and asked if daddies have good and bad angels, too. She said yes. My brother responded, "Daddy must be listening to the bad angel when he punches my baby brother."

I remember my father once beating my mother in front of all of us. He said, "This is what you do to bad mommies. This will happen to you if you are bad."

When I was about ten, my mother tried to break up with my father. She couldn't sell the house without his permission, so she went on welfare and we moved into the projects.

This new neighborhood was predominantly black, and I would get beat up most every day. I definitely didn't look black—I guess I must have looked East Indian or Spanish. My younger brother used to get beat up at school, and they called him Poncho because he had straight hair.

My brothers and I had never seen a cockroach before; we thought they were cool and began collecting them. The other kids thought we were weird. Even our food was weird—we ate Cape Verdian dishes.

After we moved away from my father, my mother met this white guy named Michael and fell in love with him. My mother didn't want to be with my father anymore, and he couldn't accept that. He was always watching the house and driving by or calling.

Michael was much younger than my mother. He wasn't at all like my dad. He frolicked with us, and we had fun. He would bring his stereo system over and teach us dances that he made up. The period when Michael was around was one of the times in my life when I was conscious. I lived my life as if I were invisible. I was like a walking shell—a child who would come out every once in a while, and if I saw everything was still painful, I would just crawl back inside and numb out. I still have those moments of becoming invisible now.

I was so glad to see my mother happy again, but my father hated it. One day he called and asked to speak to me. He was so nice to me. This was the first time my father had ever acknowledged me, and it tapped into a lot of my need for his approval. He wanted to see me. I was in awe. He said he wanted to come by and take me out on the town—just me.

My father told me to get ready and to leave the front door unlocked, because he didn't want to disturb anyone else. He asked me, "Your mommy is home, right?" He then asked, "Is Michael there, too?"

I answered, "Yes, they're in the bed sleeping."

He said, "I'll be over in a few minutes to pick you up." I sat there eager, ready to go.

My father arrived soon enough, but he walked in the unlocked door with the police and social service workers. The police took Michael and my mom off to jail. At that time it was illegal for a woman on welfare to have a man in her house. She was still legally married to my dad. The police told Michael that he could either go to jail for being with a married woman or leave the state, and that's what happened. After Michael was long gone, my mother realized she was pregnant.

For a short while, my mother had to go into a mental institution—the whole thing made her crazy. I never knew where my mother was at the time. I just knew she came to visit once in a while, and she wasn't the mommy I knew.

My dad tried to get us away from my mom, but he didn't really want us. When the social workers realized he didn't really want custody, they left us alone. My auntie took care of me.

I was blamed by the whole family for letting my dad barge in and mess up our lives. As an adult I've had to come to grips with the fact that I'm not responsible for what happened, but throughout my childhood I felt responsible for everything bad that ever happened to my family.

After my mom came home again, I had to be taken to a psychiatrist. I had these very, very bad dreams; I got cramps in my legs and I'd sweat. The psychiatrists told my mom that I was acting out because I wasn't getting any love from my dad.

Soon after my mother came home, she had the baby. The doctors left part of the placenta in her and she had to be hospitalized with an infection. When the ambulance came to get her and we were going to be separated again, I went crazy. My mom was my only refuge—the only person I could cling to. My baby sister was put in a foster home.

At thirteen I met this guy, and after having sex with him, I got pregnant. My father disowned me. When I had the baby, my mother helped me give the baby a name and taught me how to take care of her. Then when the baby was three or four months old, my mother asked me if I thought I could take care of the household while she went to

Maine on a singing tour. Her request tapped into my need for approval, and I readily agreed. She talked to my boyfriend, and he moved into the house. She was going to mail money to us, and he was supposed to help take care of me and the baby. But he was really abusive, and he would beat me. He was having sex with lots of women, and we got the crab lice.

Then my boyfriend started having parties and became an alcoholic. When my mom came home, the baby was eight months old. She was making a lot of money off of her music royalties again and was living high.

I married my boyfriend, and we had another child. Then he moved us off to North Carolina to an isolated place. He was selling drugs, was gone most of the time, and never gave me money to feed us.

That relationship didn't work, so I came back home and met another guy. He had the fool's gold. He was making big money and drove a Cadillac. He liked me and my kids. He did the same things as my first husband. He moved us to Texas and became as abusive. We were in Texas for about five years.

I was ashamed to tell anyone back home. I'd already messed up one marriage, and you know it always goes down on the woman if it doesn't work out. I could just hear them: "Can't you do anything right? I swear!"

I convinced myself that life wasn't so bad because we were living in a great house and my husband was making $60,000 a year. I compromised because this man was taking care of my kids, but he would beat my ass late at night, just like my dad had beat my mom's. When the beatings became regular, I started smoking marijuana. Then I turned to hard drugs.

I started being able to tell when I was going to get my ass beat. I could tell by his tone of voice. Sometimes I would pretend to be asleep when he would come home real late at night all messed up. He would do things like put matches out on my back or tip the bed over so that I would fall out. No matter what he did, I never got angry; I wasn't brought up to be angry. I never saw my mom get angry or bad-mouth my dad. She never complained, so I never did either. If my man beat my ass, I just behaved a little bit better the next day. It was awful. I had to wear long sleeves to hide the bruises.

My husband used to stay out all night and be with other women, and I would be in such terror that he wouldn't come back. I'd be all bruised up, and he'd go out and come home the next morning smelling like a whore with lipstick all over his clothes, and all I felt was relief when he got home.

I didn't know anyone, didn't know where to go. Once I did call a shelter for battered women late at night after he left. They put me on their waiting list. Weeks and weeks after I had called, they had an opening and could have taken me and the girls into the safe house, but by that time my man and I had made up.

When he was home, I couldn't make phone calls. He was so overbearing. If I wanted to go to the store, I would have to walk because I hadn't learned how to drive. He would always want to know why I took so long.

The paradox of my choice in men is that both my husbands were very handsome, bold-looking men. The second one could have been a model, just like my father.

When he left me, I really lost my mind. I had never been on my own in my entire life.

He moved me into an apartment I could barely afford. My girls and I had bills based on the previous amount of money he was making. By this time I had a job. He had forced me to get a job. He took me downtown and was there when I filled out the applications. He'd call me on my lunch breaks to check up on me. About this time he taught me how to drive.

I would have done anything to be with this man again. I'd go over to the house where we had lived and bang at the door and cry. Sometimes I'd go over late at night and peek through the windows and watch him be with another woman. I was really out to lunch.

One time I wrote "I love you" in lipstick all over his front doors, his windows, his car. I mean, I was obsessed.

My husband talked me into dealing drugs. Then I snorted some cocaine, and that was the beginning of the end. In 1986 I snorted two lines, then I went up to half a quarter, then up to a half. Then I heard about this freebasing stuff.

When we first broke up, I was working eighty-five hours a week. I'd come home, spend ten minutes with my girls, and then leave again. They were adaptable. They were so glad I had broken up with that man. They didn't care what Mommy had to do as long as I didn't bring him back. He had finally hit my older daughter once when she tried to rescue me. I had tried to fight back, but it only made it worse. I'd roll up into a fetal position and hide under a table or crawl into a corner.

Then he'd get mad because he couldn't get me the way he wanted to, and he'd kick me in the ribs. I was pregnant with this man twice, and I miscarried both times.

As my addiction became bigger and bigger, I wasn't able to pay my rent, but I didn't know I had a drug problem. I thought I just didn't know how to handle money. It was at this time that I began calling my family. My sister suggested that I move to be with my mom, who now lived in San Francisco. My family sent $2,000 to move us, and my cousin flew in to drive us to California.

When I arrived in San Francisco and the Jones* started kicking in, I began to admit to myself that I had a drug problem. What I used to smoke wasn't doing anything for me anymore.

At that time my uncle introduced my children to Glide. Every time I came home my girls would say, "Mommy, you've got to come to Glide. You'd love it there." They were spending their afternoons at Glide, going to the various children's programs. So one Sunday I decided to come. But people were too happy and too joyous for the state I was in. I was just the opposite. I left and got high.

Eventually I stole $1,200 and jewelry from my mom, and she kicked me out of the house. I had never been homeless before. I was like a babe in the woods. I'd been a housewife addict, and I had to start learning the ways of the street. I even learned to prostitute for a brief moment, and that was sickening. Then when I got hungry enough, I came to eat at Glide.

I went back to my mom's house and begged her to still love me. I started lying, telling her that I was clean when I wasn't. One day I wanted some drugs, and I didn't have any money. I had a good lie, but I was afraid that she was going to say no to me. The addiction in me was asking, "What are you going to do if she says no?" Inside I answered, "If I have to, I'm going to hurt my mom to get the money." I felt like a volcano was erupting in me.

She gave me the money, and I sighed with relief, then started crying uncontrollably. She walked me to the door and asked what was wrong. I said I wasn't feeling good; I told her I loved her. When she closed the door, I hurt so bad; I felt I was going to blow up in pain. I had just lied to my mother and knew that I would have actually hurt her to get cocaine. That was the bottom for me.

---

*Jones is a term for the need for more and more drugs to get the same high.

I went to the streets and got the drug, sure that this high would be different; I planned to get high like I'd never experienced before. I thought if I could just get high once more, then everything would be okay. That Friday and Saturday I kept smoking, but I couldn't get high. The lighter broke on me; the pipe broke. Nothing was working. I was miserable.

My sister came and found me on Sunday morning. She had a rock of Crack that was so small that it looked ridiculous. By now my addiction was the size of the room. Her rock was beyond trivial. I started to pray, "God, I don't want to live like this anymore."

I remembered it was Sunday morning and my kids would be going to Glide in a few hours. I was just compelled. I went to my uncle's and thought I could be cool, but as soon as I walked in the door, I fell apart. I cried and I cried. I was just ruined. I kept screaming, "I don't want to do this anymore. I don't want to hurt anybody anymore. I don't want to lie anymore." He didn't know what was wrong.

Then I told my uncle that I had a drug problem. He got on the phone and immediately got me in a twenty-eight-day treatment program. Glide didn't have a drug program in 1987.

I moved into a recovery house, and I started coming to Glide on Sundays. Cecil was always talking about issues that connected with my life. My uncle would hold me during the services because I would cry because of guilt. One time Cecil was talking about incest and abuse, and it just really messed me up. I looked forward to climbing down those back stairs after the Celebration to get a hug from Cecil.

When I graduated from the inpatient program, I had about nine months clean, and I started coming to the Facts on Crack program that was just beginning. I started volunteering; I wanted to show other people that there was a way out.

After a few months I moved out and got a new job as a cook, working on Sundays so I couldn't come to Glide anymore. Soon I got fed up with my job. I started coming to the circle meeting groups to air my problems. Eddie Franks told Cecil about me.

One time I came and shared at the circle meeting, and Cecil was there. Right during the meeting, he pointed at me and said to Eddie Franks, "I want this woman at the Crack conference we are planning. You see this woman? She's a miracle!"

When I was fourteen months clean, I got into this relationship. I fell in love with this guy who asked me to have his baby. It took us nine months to get pregnant. I learned through this relationship that even though I wasn't being physically abused anymore, I was allowing him to emotionally abuse me. I didn't know any better. I felt that as long as he wasn't kicking my ass and throwing me across the room, putting holes in my body, everything was fine. I had to learn the hard way.

I was seven-and-a-half months pregnant when I went into the hospital. My son was born prematurely. He died of a simple stomach infection, two days before my birthday. My life hasn't been the same since my son died.

This last year has helped me to grow up a whole lot. It was hard. I wanted to commit suicide when my baby died and my boyfriend and I broke up. I didn't want to live. Eighteen months of grief followed. I was a zombie with a shield of pain over my eyes. I prayed, "God, when are you going to take me off this earth? God, when are you going to let a car hit me? God, when are you going to let someone blow me off this earth?"

It has only been in the last three months that I've been happy again. I've accepted my son's death. I've really gone through a lot in seeing how my former boyfriend was abusive to me. I can recognize abuse today in all its forms. I see everything, down to the little point of the guys around Glide calling me "Hey, baby." I don't let any of the men in this building call me that anymore. Men in this building respect me because I demand it. In years past, if a man stepped on my toe, it was me who said "Excuse me." However anyone wanted to treat me was fine. I figured I deserved it.

It's not like that today. I've moved into a cute little apartment, on my own. At first I was terrified, and most of the time I stayed at girlfriends' houses. Then I really started working on self-loathing, self-alienation, self-isolation, self-doubt, and fear. I started coming closer to my pain, and I grieved for my childhood. I grieved at how my father wasn't there for me. I grieved at how my father beat my brother. I grieved at how my mom wouldn't leave that violent man. I grieved at how I was groomed for everything that has happened to me. It's been a long process, but well worth it. Today I want to live.

Sometimes I'm in awe of why I was chosen to walk this path. To be on the other side of self-oppression, society's oppression, men's oppression—the whole works is amazing.

Today I'm independent and am embracing my power. I know that what I say and what I feel matters. I'm trying to learn how to be single.

I have friends in my life now, but I'm selective. My friends are wonderful to me, and I am wonderful to them.

I haven't done drugs for four years—not even when my son died. I stay clear-minded and concerned with what I have to do for myself to be healthier and more mature so that I don't ever have to be locked in to being abused.

Today I really listen to me. If my perception says that something ain't right, I respect that. I respect me like I respect a hot iron. If you unplug an iron, you still touch it with caution for a while.

I may have been unplugged from drugs for a while, but I know that abuse of any kind could cause me to go right back out on the streets and use drugs. I've got to be serious about my recovery. The self-esteem I have today is brand new, and if I don't keep on strengthening, disciplining, and working on it daily, I can go right back to the old stuff, just like that.

It's been an incredible journey.

Community: Recovery and the Gender Gap

Over the years women have flooded into the Facts on Crack program, and as they feel safe enough, more stories of incest and battering have poured forth like a never-ending stream. But as the women told their stories and moved on in recovery, they found they couldn't flourish and grow as long as they held fast to the identity that had been given to them through their victimization.

Those women who became empowered, able to change, and able to live new lives were those that came to no longer understand themselves as victims. As long as woman thought of herself as a victim, she couldn't accept the responsibility for her freedom. The women began to experience the reality of moving beyond past experiences of victimization. One of the keys to unlocking that pathway that led to becoming a survivor rather than a victim happened when the women began to struggle with the issue of forgiveness.

As I heard the painful stories, I thought it would help if I preached on forgiveness. For several Sundays that's what I did. Usually most folks at Glide tell me after the Celebration services that I've touched the truth of their experience by being honest about my own. But after those services many of the women told me differently.

Janice minced no words. "For me, forgiveness is denial."

The forgiveness that I preached about sounded in the ears of many as something that magically erased the past—and for the women who have been abused, this was not helpful. To forget the past would be to send the abuse they experienced back into the hidden realm of silence, where many had already lived for years.

The women helped me to learn more about forgiveness. In the context of incest the child is made to feel at fault. It takes an act of self-definition to break through the shame, to realize that the abuse is not "my fault." The power of self-definition begins to shatter the shame. Forgiving is not about excusing the perpetrator's actions. Forgiving is about gaining personal freedom by breaking free from the power of the past. One can then begin to let go of the traumatic pain that has taken control of one's life. I've come to understand that letting go and living on is truly forgiveness.

The women's willingness to define forgiveness, to forge their own ways toward empowerment and change made me believe that victims of abuse, regardless of age or life circumstances, don't have to be fatalities. When each of us who has suffered grave injustices begins to realize that we have choices, we can begin to let go of past victimizations. We each have the choice and responsibility to let people know when they are hurting us. We also have the responsibility to ourselves to stay away from people and circumstances that would continue to beat us down. Too often, victims learn to say, "I'm sorry, you are standing on my foot; go stand on the other one, too." Victims all to often allow everyone to abuse them, even after they have the skills to stop it. Anyone who sees herself as a victim needs a perpetrator or abuser to maintain her identity as a victim.

Victims know all too well how to cope with pain. Survivors are those who learn that it is possible to live some days without all that pain.

Edna articulated the task of forgiveness and reclaiming life when she declared, "Giving up our pain is the hardest thing we do in life. Die, pain. Let go, pain. Let's get on to living."

As the women became empowered, the climate at Glide began to shift. The women and men had to relearn how to interact. The whole issue of gender relationships escalated quickly in the fall of 1991 during the Senate confirmation hearings of Clarence Thomas, soon-to-be Supreme Court justice.

By gender, the women and men were divided when Anita Hill took the stand and raised the issue of sexual harassment, as the nation watched. The men and women at Glide argued about who was telling the truth. When Judge Thomas was confirmed, the argument continued, but the disagreement was now less about Clarence Thomas and Anita Hill; it was more about the men and women struggling with their own pain.

Janice and I decided we needed to face the issues of gender divisions and sexual harassment with the staff. Janice gathered the women together in the Green Room. Women who worked in the basement with the food programs, women who worked in the recovery programs and in the Celebration office on the first floor, women from the business office and the children's program on the second floor, and women from the sixth-floor computer training center all converged.

Janice began by stating aloud that every woman at Glide, if a client or a member of the administrative staff, would have recourse at Glide if she were ever sexually harassed. No one would be allowed to harass anyone at Glide without action being taken.

That set the tone for the meeting. Women would be listened to. One by one, the women spoke. Unanimously they claimed that they felt powerless during the hearings and that they were fighting despair now that it seemed clear that Anita Hill had not been believed.

Around the room women told of being harassed in former work settings. For some, harassment had been meted out in raunchy, dirty, and sexually charged words. For others, the harassment had meant being pinned against the wall or being raped by co-workers. Without it being explicitly said, the truth came out: Anita Hill's complaint was hardly extreme.

The women shared that in the midst of the abuse, many had been single moms with children. They had that feared speaking out would mean losing a much-needed job.

An intimacy born of shared struggle created strong bonds among the staff women that day. Before the meeting concluded, the women shared strategies on how to handle future instances of harassment.

Janean got concrete: "Here's what I did yesterday. I was walking up the stairs and this guy acted like he'd never seen a woman climb stairs before. He described my every move.

"When I got to the top of the stairs, I turned around and said, 'I understand your sexual affirmation of me, but today I would also like to be affirmed for my keen thinking and mental attributes.'

"That stopped him cold. It made me feel good, too. There would have been a time when I would have ignored him and gone on my way feeling naked and vulnerable. Then there would have been a time when I would have screamed every put-down I knew back at him. Today, I'm proud to say, I turned around and told him how I expected to be treated."

Other women shared other ideas on how to act when harassed. By coming together they broke through the isolation that is always the greatest tool of powerlessness.

A few weeks later after the staff women first met, a few gathered again and reflected on the ensuing weeks. A difference had come over Glide. The staff women felt more intimate with one another. One recalled a day when she had dressed in clothing that some of the men had responded to as provocative. Another woman on the staff had asked her, "How are you doing today looking so good? Are you ready to handle what might be said? Get ready. Be strong."

Together the women also acknowledged that while the men had been behaving better, they women themselves had changed, too. They were standing up for themselves, believing in themselves. Knowing that their sisters would stand by them no matter what made all the difference.

At Glide the women are on the move.

CHAPTER SEVEN

▲　▲　▲

Men in Motion

Recognition: Living the Dream

When civil rights prophet Martin Luther King, Jr., stood before the Lincoln Memorial and cried out "I have a dream!" before the hundreds of thousands gathered on August 28, 1963, I was there.

I stood, riveted, as this black brother, a minister like me, voiced the truth that had stirred for years in me and in the soul of the black community. I stood near the front of the march with a group of black clergy. We had left a conference in Chicago early and had caught the train to Washington.

I had followed the movement of Martin King and the NAACP ever since the Montgomery bus boycott had quickened my spirit in 1955 when I was in seminary. It was then that I started actively demonstrating for civil rights in Dallas, then in Kansas City, Missouri, as a cochair of the Congress for Racial Equality. I then met Martin when he came and spoke at a church when I was studying again on the West Coast. The way he carried himself, moved, and spoke was nearly enough to change my life, but ultimately it was the way he enacted his life that made all the difference.

Then I heard the plans for the march on Washington, D.C. I had to be there. The clergy group I came with had arrived at the nation's capital early and had a good vantage point near the Lincoln Memorial. I shall never forget that day. I didn't want to move one inch lest I miss something. I drank in everything I saw, heard, and felt as if I were an empty well waiting to be filled. I had a visceral feeling deep inside that this day would affect the rest of my life. And it has.

Martin's words baptized the masses with the fire of truth and set the course for a long struggle for justice.

Nineteen sixty-three is not an end, but a beginning. And those who hope that the Negro needed to blow off steam and will now be content, will have a rude awakening if the nation returns to business as usual. . . . The whirlwinds of revolt will continue to shake the foundations of our nation until the bright day of justice emerges.*

The dream of justice and equality burned in my soul, and that day I realized that it burned inside many, many others of all colors. I had never before seen so many folks marching in support of civil rights. From where I stood near the Lincoln Memorial, I could turn around and see wide ranks of folks that extended past the fountain to the end of the mall and farther, beyond where I could see. People of every race and creed marched side by side. Humanity moved together that day.

Martin reminded us all of the importance of working together for change. He challenged us to remember that freedom for African Americans was "inextricably bound" up in the freedom of our white brothers and sisters. Martin shook me to the depths when he declared:

The marvelous new militancy which has engulfed the Negro community must not lead us to a distrust of all white people, for many of our white brothers, as evidenced by their presence here today, have come to realize that their destiny is tied up with our destiny and they have come to realize that their freedom is inextricably bound to our freedom. This offense we share mounted to storm the battlements of injustice must be carried forth by a biracial army. We cannot walk alone.

Nearly thirty years have passed since that momentous day, and I have marched hundreds of time since then, yet I have never felt fear when standing firm for justice. Once I had seen the community of humanity flood the streets of our nation's capital crying out for justice, there was no room for fear in me. I knew that the community was always walking and standing, singing and praying, shouting and crying together, whenever and wherever we marched.

What I felt that day in Washington convinced me that as long as the extended family of humankind marched together, we would be propelled by the Spirit of freedom. When people march and hope together, something

---

*"I Have a Dream" speech delivered by Martin Luther King, Jr., on August 28, 1963. Transcript taken from *A Testament of Hope: The Essential Writings of Martin Luther King, Jr.*, ed. James M. Washington (San Francisco: Harper & Row, 1986), pp. 217–20.

that comes from us and goes beyond us—what we call the Spirit—moves us forward. Change takes place.

The anticipation I felt was as tangible as the hot, humid air that late summer's day. Sweat and tears of joy rolled down my face and my heart affirmed "yes, yes, yes" when Martin cried out:

> *We are not satisfied, and we will not be satisfied until justice rolls down like waters and righteousness like a mighty stream. . . . So I say to you, my friends, that even though we must face the difficulties of today and tomorrow, I still have a dream. It is a dream deeply rooted in the American dream that one day this nation will rise up and live out the true meaning of its creed—we hold these truths to be self-evident, that all men are created equal. . . . I have a dream my four little children will one day live in a nation where they will not be judged by the color of their skin but by content of their character. I have a dream today!*

That day I knew for the first time in my life that I was where I needed to be—in the center of the struggle for justice. And I also knew that I was what I needed to be—a minister in the church. My self-understanding irreversibly shifted that day; if I were to be effective as a minister, I acknowledged that I could not be a traditional minister. I would be a minister whose eyes would remain fixed on bringing liberation and empowerment to the poor, the outsiders in our land.

That day was a breakthrough day for me. In the weeks that immediately followed, I accepted the position as director of community involvement at Glide.

Twenty-five years later, the First Generation of people needing recovery came to Glide. More men that women were in the early Generations, yet it was the women who quickly embraced recovery and began fighting for their lives and power.

Most of the men held back, hesitating to talk deeply about their lives. Their body language and attitudes screamed out silent rage. When one or two took the risk to talk, hot, raging words of anger and humiliation that had smoldered in their guts all their lives erupted from their lips. Always being last in line for jobs, always being the first suspected when a crime was committed, and always knowing that they had a greater chance of going to prison than going to college had filled these young black men with fury.

As I watched and listened, I realized with great anguish that many young black men who have come of age in the last twenty years have been hard-pressed to find role models who have lived out a commitment to the dream of a better society. In inner-city neighborhoods often the most visible role models of success have been the drug dealers whose power comes from quick money and high-powered guns.

Many of the young men had lost a sense of identity. In so many ways they were searching out what it meant to be an African American man. These men were too young to have heard about slavery firsthand; most hadn't sat at the feet of a man like my grandfather, Papa Jack.

One of my formative boyhood memories is sitting on the porch with Papa Jack as he told a group of university students about his experience as a slave. Papa Jack's final words that day were spoken not to the students, but to me and my brothers and sisters. Papa spoke with anger and resolve when he said, *"Papa's an ex-slave. Now you all be ex-slaves, too."* Papa's declaration was seared on my soul. His resolute command helped me, in later years, to let the power and force of my anger loose for the cause of freedom. I understood the anger the New Generation felt. I had it, too, but Papa Jack had showed me how to channel and transform anger into the courage to resist racism at all costs.

Most of the New Generation were born after the mighty civil rights marches. Martin Luther King, Jr., was just another hero their parents talked about. They hadn't seen with their own eyes how Martin Luther King or any of the other great black men who had embodied steadfast faith in the dream had lived lives of nonviolent resistance.

Those raised in the inner city in recent decades have lost a sense of being a people of struggle. They do not share a self-understanding of themselves as inheritors of the great gifts of community, faith, and resistance that kept our ancestors alive. The New Generation had grown up admiring role models from the streets whose lives, all too often, were rooted in violence, or they idolized African American athletes and musicians whose exceptional talents had paid off in riches and fame. There certainly was cause for concern.

When Glide convened the first national conference on Crack cocaine, African American leaders came from everywhere. As we talked together, one of the most worrisome issues that raised its head again and again was the role of the black male today.

As black leaders we felt afraid that we were losing some of the ground that we gained through civil rights. Just when we have begun to discover our African roots and our strength born out of the faith and resistance forged for us by our slave ancestors, drugs and violence have nearly destroyed the black extended family, which has always been our stronghold in times of trouble.

For an African American male, if he doesn't have the extended family to fall back on, he really has absolutely nothing at all in life. For many blacks there is no longer any family. Even the recent family model composed of a single mother with children is ceasing to exist. Grandmothers and foster care are taking over the task of raising thousands and thousands of our children.

After that first conference we knew that developing a new kind of extended family of support, like we have at Glide, would remain critical to the survival of the African American people. When black men and women have the support of an extended family, they can and will put their own families back together.

The male's role today often demands that as a recovering person he no longer can define himself as a dominant person in the family. No longer can a man bring home a paycheck and assume that obligates his family to submit to his every wish or whim. The male's role is not to be the breadwinner but to become a breadmaker—one who offers nurture, sustenance, and compassion to the others in his family. A breadmaker in the family is like leaven is to bread—it brings together all the ingredients and helps them rise and expand. The new black family must be a community where there is justice, mutuality, equity, and unconditional love among the family members.

That is the dream, and it was far from reality for the men who were walking through Glide's doors for the first time. These young men were peers of my own son Albert. When I stopped to consider my own family, I saw that the dream had not been a constant reality for us either.

REBIRTH OF A RACE

As an African American man and father, I've always held an attitude about the generations that would follow me. I believe that each succeeding generation of African Americans ought to have better living conditions, more educational opportunities, and more power to vie fully for good jobs, adequate pay, and free mobility. Without really knowing it, inside me I held fast to the belief that my own kids and the others in their generation should not have to suffer the racism and injustice that I have experienced.

This attitude led me to try to shelter my children from suffering. I gave them every opportunity, but I can honestly say now that I didn't give them enough of my time. I was too busy to listen to them with my full attention. I gave the best of my time and attention to Glide. In the meantime, I achieved a level of fame, and my kids hated the extra attention and expectation that my notoriety thrust upon them. They wanted to be normal kids with a father who came home at the same time every night.

When their mother and I began to be honest with each other about the state of our marriage, Kim and Al were young teens. Their mother and I talked and talked for months until we reached a point when we both knew our marriage wasn't going to work. I felt harsh guilt inside. How could I, who was thought of as a successful man, a great minister by my congregation, admit that my marriage wasn't working? Up until then I had lived in a world of spiritual illusion believing that everything would work out how it was "supposed to be."

When my first wife and I divorced, she moved away, and Kim and Al stayed and lived with me. I became a single parent, and I had an awful time of it. The three of us struggled to establish some way of communicating, but we didn't have much to build upon. It was almost too late, for my kids were going their own ways.

I was a single parent for five years until I married Janice Mirikitani in 1982. Those five years of trying to care for and communicate with my teenaged kids brought me face-to-face with myself.

I had to deal with me and to honestly face up to the truth of what kind of father I had been. Up until then I thought I had been a great father. What I had really been was a great codependent. Whatever Kim or Al wanted, I gave. In my desire to shield them from suffering, I protected them from the realities of life, and like all kids, my children wouldn't learn from my mistakes; they had to learn on their own.

The struggle with my children was a vital part of bringing the need for recovery into my home and my life. My son Albert also had to experience suffering firsthand. Al comes across as very nice, serious, and kind. He was raised around people of all races and classes. His friends crossed all racial barriers. One of his closest friends today is a white Jewish friend he made in high school. After he finished school, he went to work for a major corporation in Southern California. Externally everything about Al's life looked good, but he was still a member of his generation.

Once when Janice and I visited him, I admitted to her that I had seen the signs of drug use in Albert. A month later Janice and I went to Southern California for another visit, and this time Albert wanted to talk. Albert told me his story.

"I started smoking pot years ago and then experimented with powdered cocaine in the early 1980s. I would snort a line of cocaine as a socially accepted thing to do with my peers. My friends and I used cocaine and didn't think of it as a problem. To us, doing cocaine was cool.

"I tried Crack because I wanted to experience it for myself. Some of my friends had already done it. I remember I first tried Crack in the summer of 1988. I knew what neighborhood to go to for drugs and I went and bought ten dollars' worth. I went home, mixed it with my marijuana, and tried it by myself. I had a pretty good rush. I was playing in a band after work, and one of the other members and I started smoking Crack before we went on stage. I told myself that I'd only smoke Crack on the weekends, but before long I was smoking every day. I built up a craving, as if Crack was a food that I had to have before and after work.

"After I had been using for a while, I came to San Francisco on a vacation. I'll never forget driving down Market Street and seeing your face on a billboard. You were pointing your finger and the ad said something about 'Don't do drugs.' I knew that I was involved in the very thing you were fighting against. I knew I was defeating your purposes. At that time, I was damn sure I didn't want to tell you what I was doing. I wasn't yet ready to quit.

"But this time I'm ready.

"There have been a lot of times living in LA that I missed having family around. When I've had problems, I either took a long drive on the freeway or went and got some more drugs because I didn't have anyone to talk to.

"I've been living a pretty unhealthy life-style. I've tossed up quite a few women while smoking Crack; I still go home sometimes and hope and pray that I haven't contracted AIDS along the way.

"But now I'm tired of drugs. It's no fun anymore. I know that I look shrunken in; my face is breaking out. Smoking Crack has become like hearing an old joke—it's not funny anymore."

At that time Al decided to move back to San Francisco. I knew when he moved home that he was ready to recover. I didn't know how or when he would start, but I was glad that he came back home to the family.

One of the hardest things I had to do when Albert moved home was to let him find his own way to recovery. In earlier days, before I started taking my own recovery as a minister and a good codependent seriously, I would have come down on him about using drugs. Then I would have made some phone calls to drug programs and told Albert, "Here's what I want you to do. I'll take care of this for you."

But I'd been around recovering people long enough to know that only Albert could redirect his life; I couldn't. I knew enough to stay out of his way and to listen when he wanted to talk.

On his own Albert came to Glide and attended some of the circle meetings. Today he works here at Glide running the food programs. He sought the job and was hired. Many people at Glide weren't even aware that Albert was my son. By working together, we've had to learn that we will always be father and son, but that we also have the roles of working together as co-workers. We don't give each other special treatment; there is no letting each other get by because we are family.

Recently we were together in my office when someone asked him what it was like to be my son and work at Glide. Albert answered, "There's only one Cecil. I try to learn from him. He's my role model. I admire what he does. His actions talk. Since I've come back to Glide, I am trying to learn about giving and helping people. Glide gives me a lot of strength as a support system."

I was amazed by my son's praise and overwhelmed by his understanding of Glide as an extended family. Albert had never told me anything like that before. Our whole family is in recovery and getting closer all the time. Recovery has brought us closer to living the dream.

Self-Definition: The Men in Motion Groups

When the Thirteenth Generation of the Facts on Crack program began forming, I invited a dozen men into my office. Twelve African American men crowded around the conference table, not knowing exactly why they had been asked to come in. After they were all seated, I said to them, "I'm especially concerned about African American men like you and me. A lot of us have been cut down by racism, slavery, and now addiction, the newest form of slavery that we must defeat together.

"I'm going to tell you straight—the African American male is an endangered species. More of us are in prison than in college. You and I are more likely to be murdered than to die of natural causes. It's time to start fighting for our lives—the black community needs us to survive.

"Every time I've visited Africa I've stopped in at the compounds, the villages where everyone shares with one another. In Africa individuality is important only in the context of the extended family. In the compound there are no outsiders. Children who are born become the children of the extended family.

"The African American community in earlier days has functioned as a compound. When my sister had a child out of wedlock, our whole community claimed that child as its own. There was no need for foster care. Just yesterday a woman came into Glide who had fourteen children. How did she make it? There had to be something there for her in the extended family or she wouldn't have been able to raise all those children.

"Today there are elements in society who would love to keep us African American males weak and anesthetized by drugs. When we are drugged out, we aren't full players in society—when we check out, the broader culture can pretend we don't exist. But let me ask you, who suffers most when we aren't strong? Let me ask you."

Then I lifted my hands silently asking with my open gesture for someone to answer my question.

Quietly one muttered, "We do."

"That's right, brother, you and I suffer most." I continued, "Our women and children suffer most. The black community suffers most. That's why I've called you together today. I want you to know that Glide is here for you as an extended family. You can bring your suffering here and we will deal with our pain together. Now I want Ed Jackson to tell you about the Men in Motion group that is available as a part of Facts on Crack."

I pointed to Ed Jackson, on of the Facts on Crack counselors who came through the program himself in the early days. Ed, a wiry, articulate man, leaned forward, his eyes clear and his voice intent as he spoke.

"Men in Motion started about three years ago. At the time I was recovering from more that just drugs; I was recovering from bad behavior, bad attitudes, and violence. I had a quick temper and was ready to go off at any time. I had learned on the streets that if something got to me, as a man I should take care of business, right then. If I didn't like what someone called me, I'd go after them, male or female.

"When I came to Glide, I didn't know what it meant to be a man. I thought a man had to be in charge and if a woman didn't listen, then it was the man's job to hit her upside of the head. Even after I became clean and sober, I still popped my woman when I got angry. As some of us men got into our recovery, we started feeling like this wasn't right.

"Before I got into the program I was married to the best wife in the world. I was working, making good money. I had a house and a stepdaughter. But then I decided to be a dealer. I stayed out all night with other women. I started feeling really bad about me and I took it out on my wife. I thought she'd never leave. I gave her money and a roof over her head. One night when we had a fight, I yelled at her, 'What more do you want?' She answered, 'You.' At the time her answer made me mad. I told her, 'Then get your shit and get out.' That night I came home and found a big sign hanging on the door that read, 'I didn't like what you was doing so I got my shit and got out.'

"About this time Women on the Move had started, and some of us started feeling that the women had so many outlets, but the men had nowhere to go to say the things they couldn't say in front of women.

"One day some three of us in the program were standing in the hallway talking and a woman walked in to the Women on the Move office with her two little boys. The boys were running around and roughhousing, and when we asked her what those boys were doing in the women's program office, the mother laughed and said, 'These are my men in motion.'

"Once we heard the phrase *men in motion*, we decided that described those of us men who were wanting to redefine what it meant for us to be men. So we started meeting together and inviting other men to join us.

"We talked about everything—drugs, sex, violence, rage. We talked about how it feels to go apply for a job as a black man and see a black woman hired before you every time. We talked about how it hurts to have the women in our families bring in the money when we want to support them but can't find work. We talked about turning to drugs to forget about being last in line time after time. But we did more than talk about it; we decided we didn't want to forget the pain by smoking Crack anymore. We decided to risk everything and tell the truth to one another.

"The women around Glide kept talking about being molested and raped, and when we got together, we could talk about how we've been treated, too."

At this point one of the men, a big, tough-looking man named Gene,* interrupted Ed. "Yeah, if I was to say I was molested, nobody would believe me—they'd laugh."

The emotional temperature in the room had risen. The men were beginning to identify with the issues Ed had raised.

Another man chimed in, "These days if a man is accused of rape, even if he didn't do it, he always will wear that jacket on his back."

Gene had more to say, "Rape is real for those of us who have been in prison. It happens. And I went to prison because I wouldn't tell the police

---

*Names, except that of Ed Jackson, have been changed.

what I knew about some stuff that went down. I thought keeping my mouth shut was a way of upholding my manhood."

Ed Jackson was nodding and smiling by this time. He was energized by the men's honesty. "Men in Motion is about redefining manhood. Our meetings are a place where men can get together without slinging fists or drinking. We get together to share our intellect. Addicts are some of the most intelligent people around. Street survival requires figuring out how to make it."

Jesse, the man seated next to Ed, had something to say about survival. "I came up under racism in the projects outside Chicago. If someone in the projects did something wrong, the city cut off our bus service. That's when the gang-banging started.

"Man, on the streets you learn that if you don't hustle everybody else first, they'll hustle you. You've got to scheme on how to keep your woman from smoking Crack and how to keep her away from some other Joe who wants her.

"I came to San Francisco about a year ago, and it is like the land of milk and honey. In Chicago you can't just plop down and sell some dope on any corner. Some gang already owns that corner. Here it's real toxic. Everyone has free reign.

"When I first looked for help, I went to another center down here, but it was a bunch of white folks telling me about black problems. I came to Facts on Crack to express myself as a black person to other black people."

When Jesse finished, Paul began, "I'm an addict and an alcoholic. The first day I walked into Glide, everybody was getting ready to go march on the Valencia Gardens housing projects.

"At that time I was just out of prison, living in a halfway house. I was going to Twelve-Step meetings, but everyone was white. When I walked into Glide and saw black folks talking about recovery, it was like something was lifted off me.

"When we marched into Valencia Gardens. I couldn't believe that we marched in there without guns. We carried food and music. It was raining when we got there, and then the sun broke through. Standing there in the sunshine, I knew that Glide was where I needed to be. I've left a few times, but every time I leave, my old shit starts shaking.

"When I got out of prison, I was carrying some deep resentments. I did two and a half years of a five-year stint in prison. I was sent up for dealing, but I wasn't a dealer. I was just hustling to feed my habit. When I got out, the judge sent me to a program, and I'll never forget what he said to me: 'I don't think you'll make it, but I'll give you a chance.'

"Man, that's all I needed was a chance. But it's been rough going. With the help of a therapist, I figured out that I'm scared of success. When things get going too good, I don't know what to expect. When things go bad, I know all about that. That's where I've been all of my life."

At this point in the meeting I decided to see if I could get a couple of the men who hadn't yet spoken to open up. I said, "Somewhere in our lives all of us have to have a trustful relationship with someone."

I pointed at Sean, one of the men seated near me. I knew him since he'd been around Glide for a while. I said to the other men in the room, "See this one—when he first came to Glide he was scared. He used to go off at anything. I want to ask you what made you so full of rage."

Before he could respond, someone else jumped in. "Feeling powerless makes us angry. When we aren't hooked up with our higher power, every time someone slams a door in your face, we go off."

I pointed back to Sean, "It's your turn."

Sean took a deep breath and said, "I remember seeing a play called *Wicked Ways*. Part of the play was drug-related. There was this girl trying to get her man out of the mix. Before he decides to get out, his sister gets killed for being in the wrong place at the wrong time.

"I felt like the woman in that play was talking to me. After the play, my girlfriend and I got to talking about my behavior. She helped me to start to hear how my voice gets wild when I'm angry. My girl told me, 'You got to stop that; someday somebody is going to blow your brains out.'

"The things my woman said got to me. I started to see that arguing isn't just about throwing words around; I never before thought about what would happen later.

"I've got a lot to learn. Right now my woman is gone. She left me, said she was tired of hearing me say 'I'm sorry.'

"I've got pain. I'm on parole. I'm trying to get out of that system. When I came out of the penitentiary, I was bitter. I had an attitude. I don't feel like I got a fair handshake, but that's the system. Anger has built up in me so that I go off on innocent people. I never mean to cause confusion for other people; I'm trying find new ways to deal with the pressure that has built up inside of me for so long."

Sean stopped and eased back farther into his chair. I probed further: "Last week when we had the big party here and you were one of the waiters, you were so good. What kept you from going off that night?"

Sean's answer cut me to the quick. "Because I was working again. Pulling my weight. I love to work."

I told him honestly, "Be patient, friend. In time there will be a job for you."

At Glide we hire from our constituency. Most every job at Glide is held by someone who has come up from the bottom.

Earl, a newcomer to the program, spoke next. "A friend of my mother's told me about Facts on Crack. I've seen death. I may have even been a part of causing death, but that's between me and the man upstairs.

"I served eight years and seven months on a fourteen-year sentence. I'm twenty-seven years old. I got sent up to the penitentiary from Youth Authority. The Youth Authority workers said I had an adult attitude.

"Any drug I wanted was available behind the wall. I did everything but heroin inside. That's what my cellmate was into. I didn't want to end up like him—throwing up his guts or lying there like he was dead. When I got out of the pen, I smoked Crack for three days straight. That's when my friend sent me over here. I'm still having trouble with my withdrawal.

"When I was behind the wall, if anyone did me wrong, I had the power to do him in. I had moved up in the ranks of power inside the pen. I've seen men raped behind the wall. I've seen dealers pulled apart.

"Now that I'm out, I got to accept my responsibility to care about the people I'm with. Last night my girlfriend's mamma really roasted me with her tongue. I felt like breaking out all her windows. I'm trying to control the evil gorilla inside me."

We all laughed; we all knew firsthand about that evil gorilla.

I then asked the group, "How can y'all turn around all the skills you've used to hustle and manipulate the system and use them to save yourselves?"

Jesse spoke up first. "We need to be brothers in the struggle. One of the reasons I started using drugs is that the black folks wouldn't stand together. In the seventies I learned so much from the Black Muslims about Allah and about being brothers in Islam, but when I asked why we weren't feeding the hungry people, I got no answer. It was like everyone was supposed to fend for himself.

"That's when I decided to get some of the good life for myself. I figured that if I could buy an ounce of cocaine, cut it, and double my money, then I had found my Puff the Magic Dragon. But it was a deadly dragon. Now I'm trying to figure out how to use those skills to work for us and not against us."

Paul offered an answer. "Addiction makes us lose all sense of value. If we all started a business, we could show our young brothers something better they could do with their lives than to sell hubba."*

Hubba is another name for Crack.

Ed Jackson added a dose of realism when he countered, "We are the reason our young brothers are lost. How soon we forgot *I'm black and I'm proud.* Now our young brothers say *I'm black and I sell Crack.* Kids think that without a beeper or a BMW you can't be anything. Money doesn't mean that much to them; it's the limelight, the status.

"Just yesterday around the corner from Glide, Eddie Franks and I went up to some little brothers who were selling drugs. They had bad attitudes. One of the them said to me, 'You don't know who you dealin' with. I'm a major player.' He didn't even know he was going nowhere. Wouldn't listen at all.

"Kids out there are like a lost tribe. We've got to get to them. They didn't grow up with fathers or big brothers to teach them about being men. They learned from the streets how to be men.

"We got to start teaching them what we are learning: If you don't respect yourself, you can't expect respect from others. We've got to get in touch with ourselves."

Ed had preached the truth. Now all that was left for me to do was close out the meeting.

I tried to summarize what we all had been touching on for the last hour. "Our survival as African American males depends on our being able to trust, to love, and to admit that we are beginning to feel something good about ourselves and others again. To survive we need to be able to say to one another, 'I'm black, you're black and we need one another.'

"Just like the brother said at the beginning of the meeting, all he needed was a chance. You are all a helluva chance to take, but we at Glide are going to take it. Thanks for coming in today. Come back to next week's meeting. You can all pick up where you left off today."

The men who left my office that day were just beginning the journey of becoming whole, truly male, and truly human. They have a long road to travel, but it is not an unknown road. Many men at Glide have stopped tripping and started moving forward. Jamal is one of those who has traveled a stretch on this road.

When I first met Jamal, I met a man full of rage. He would sit rigidly, quietly in the circle meetings. When he finally broke loose, anger poured out of him. He was surprised that the group was able to accept his anger. I think he thought his rage would scare us away. But Jamal found out, like anyone does who stays at Glide, that many of us feel angry and enraged at what life has dealt us. Hopefully we are learning to channel that rage into making the world a more just place. Today, as a substance abuse counselor and facilitator of Glide's job training program, Jamal is transforming his rage into the courage and power to change.

Rebirth: Jamal's Story

I CAME TO GLIDE IN June of 1988. Facts on Crack was about three or four months old when I got here.

I came to San Francisco from Manhattan, where I was raised. I moved because some heavy things were going on in my life. I was into drugs—selling drugs and smoking drugs. My life was in a lot of turmoil and confusion; I was literally losing myself.

So one day I called up a college friend and I said, "I'm coming to San Francisco." I'd never been to California before. I was born in Brooklyn and raised in Manhattan. I had been there all my life except for when I went to college. I finished college in 1983, but I never really found a career. I had managed two men's clothing stores. I had been out of college for about three years and really hadn't found anything in the business field that was turning me on.

Then I took the test for a job at the post office in 1986. I got hired and did that for over a year.

About Christmastime that year, my older brother got out of prison. He had committed a robbery and had served about eleven months on a three-year sentence. When he got out, he came and visited me and said, "I got a present for you." He gave me an eight ball of cocaine. Broken into pieces, it would have been worth several hundred dollars.

At that time I was a lightweight drug user. I smoked pot and drank beer, but I never did anything heavy-duty. I had snorted cocaine a couple of times during college, but I never really could afford it. I wasn't a hard-core drug user.

In 1986 most black people were still moving into heroin or the mainstream drugs like marijuana. I had never used cocaine seriously before my brother gave that eight ball of cocaine to me. I snorted some of it—it was really raw stuff; it burnt my nose. Then I stashed some of it for later, and I gave a little bit of it away to some friends.

To make a long story short, while I was still working at the post office, my brother asked me to get an apartment with him. By that time I was starting to make pretty good money. We got a furnished apartment, me and him. He started to sell drugs. At first I didn't trip or nothing; I thought, "That's his business."

I didn't know anything about selling drugs. While we were growing up, I'd been into the books. He'd always been the one into the tough stuff—the criminal element. Doing something real dangerous and not getting caught, that was my brother's biggest high. He thought getting caught and doing a little time in the penitentiary was almost like a rite of passage for a black man.

At first the only thing my brother asked me to do for him was to stash drugs. He'd give me four or five ounces and say, "Put this somewhere for me."

He kept bringing home huge quantities of cocaine and bigger amounts of money. I realized that dealing cocaine was a major-league thing. I actually became fascinated with it.

I got creative in where to stash the dope. I went to the Port Authority Bus Terminal and got a locker. I even stashed some under the plants in my mother's living room. I put dope in my aunt's house, my sister's car, behind the washing machine in my building—all kinds of different places. I discovered that the best place to hide stuff is right in front of people's faces. If you wanna hide something, the best place is in a place that is too obvious for someone else to ever think to look there. Nobody ever found my stashes.

I became my brother's stash man. No matter how much he brought me, I always found a place to hide it. I became obsessed with looking for places to hide things.

After a while I told my brother that I was ready to sell some drugs. I told him that there were a lot of people at the post office who make good money. I convinced him that I could sell cocaine to the people I worked with. I already knew a bunch of them were users.

At first my brother started me off with a sixteenth of an ounce; I guess that was worth about $175. I got rid of that, and he gave me some more.

I always made sure that I left the post office to deal. I'd sell it to my buddies while we were on break. They started buying in quantities for their friends; I told them never to use my name when they resold the stuff. That's how I graduated from being a stash man to dealing.

By dealing I started becoming popular, almost a little too popular. People at the post office started acting like they knew me—people that I didn't know, had never talked to before.

I started worrying. I knew that any one of them could be a postal inspector. The post office had narcs on the premises sometimes.

Then I sold somebody some cocaine at the post office; he turned around and sold it to somebody else and got busted. So I slowed down on selling for a while.

The postal inspectors were really watching everybody. Not just because of drugs. A lot of credit cards had also been stolen before they reached the individual mailboxes.

Working at the post office was a trip. I was selling dope, and other people were taking credit cards.

One day while the heat was on at the post office, my brother said to me, "Man, quit the post office, and I'll pay you three, four times what you are making."

I told him, "Four times my salary is about five thousand a week. You're gonna have to pay me that much." He said that wouldn't be a problem.

So the next day I walked up to my superintendent at the post office, told him I quit, gave him my badge, walked off the floor, got in my car, and left.

That night I told my brother that I had quit. At first he was in shock because it was almost like he had been bluffing. But then he and I just got down to business.

He and I drove all over the tri-state area: New York, New Jersey, and Pennsylvania. At first it was exciting, but then it got to be real work. I didn't get much sleep. It was scary having a lot a dope on me. I remember that at that time there was a brand of acid-washed jeans on the market, almost like overalls with big pockets. Four ounces of cocaine could fit in each pocket. I bought four or five pair of those jeans because of the pockets.

I was always nervous when we were driving in the car because I had figured out how I could undo one side of the pants and sling four ounces out of the car if the police tried to stop us, but how was I gonna reach across and empty out all the other pockets? I knew that if I was caught with eight ounces of dope on me, that I'd be doing a lot of time in prison.

My brother and I would make daily runs and drop an ounce off here, an ounce off there, until it was gone. Then my brother hooked up with some people he had been with in the penitentiary. We started selling kilos of cocaine. A kilo is equal to about 2.2 pounds and is usually packed like a regular parcel.

I began to get fascinated with the numbers, the weight, the scales, and all the mathematical side of drugs. I could translate grams to ounces in my head. I became a legitimate dope dealer; I was no runner.

I never stood on the corner for nobody. But it didn't take long in the big time until I knew that I wouldn't last long at that level of dealing. There was something inside me that told me that this was too big, too much. I always felt there were limits to what I could do. To sell large amounts of drugs you have to be ruthless. Your integrity and morals got to go straight out the door.

It's worse when women are involved in dealing. Women who deal aren't seen as women; they're objects. A man can't afford to look at a woman as a woman. If you do, she'll steal your dope.

To be a long-term dealer you have to have your mind just on the dope. You gotta be obsessed with getting the dope and getting rid of the dope. That's how the big-time dealers get their reputations.

Only a few people are responsible for the cocaine that gets to the street. Smaller dealers get their dope from them. Then the folks that stand on the street corners, and the kids who act as runners taking small amounts of dope everywhere, they are just the big guys' pawns.

When a dealer really gets big, he starts selling cocaine to other suppliers, not to the dealers, not to the users. The big dealers take turns pulling back and creating a scarcity on the streets. Each of them takes a turn because none of them wants to draw a lot of heat on himself for too long. That's when people start getting shot and killed. When someone in the big time pulls back, some local dealer who has made promises gets shot up.

I became engulfed in dealing. It was power, like power I had never known before. For once in my life I wasn't concentrating on trying to prove that I was equal to the white man or just as good as the white man.

When you get the type of power that comes with drugs and big money, you don't care about the white man anymore. You don't care because you can buy him. Or you can get his sons and daughters on the stuff.

My brother became so obsessed with the power that he started undercutting other dealers. He sold his cocaine for less than they did, and soon he had a lot of cocaine out on the street. Everybody knew his name. I was always known as my brother's kid brother. I even lost my name. I didn't even have an identity.

For a while I resented having no identify of my own. I wanted to get into the big dealer's club, but that feeling didn't last long. When you really sell dope, it's work.

The people who live out the real glamour and notoriety of drug dealing are the people at the top who never touch drugs. They arrange for the shipments to come into the country and how to get it to the dealers. They're the people who can afford the glamour.

But for the dealers, dealing is work. People are always sweating you to know if you got the drugs. Sometimes you're in a constant state of paranoia, but you can't show it. You learn when to give some cocaine away if you think someone's gonna open his mouth and gonna draw the heat on you. Dealers learn to give a lot away to women because women are the most vulnerable people out there. Most of them have no identity. They're looking for an identity in a man. And a dope dealer's their ideal person to look to for their identity because all they have to do is keep validating the dope dealer by saying the right things or by tossing up for sex.

A dealer ain't never gonna say "Hey, baby, I love you," but he may give a woman some dope or buy her a Gucci bag or a dress. He can't afford to let a woman tell him "I love you." Because when she starts talking like that, well, it's time to get rid of her.

When you are dealing, you can't trust anybody that much. You trust just enough to negotiate; you're really buying people. If you trust people, you'll get taken. Selling cocaine is a business. And one of the biggest liabilities is a woman because she can get to you easier than any man or any other dealer or any other user or any person.

Whoever you lay down with easily, she knows more about you than anybody. Sometimes you have to have someone to talk to; you have to have someone to confide things in; and you have to have the confidence of someone. Because it's a very scary life.

During those days I lost myself; I did not know who I was. My brother lost himself. Things that could never have come between us started to come between us—money disputes, cocaine.

As my brother and I started dealing in larger quantities, we started getting high. We'd sell dope and whatever we had left after paying off our suppliers, we'd sell and make our money. Then even after that, we started having dope left over. We learned how to cut the cocaine ourselves; we'd dilute it with some other tasteless powder, like vitamin

B-12. All it takes is a stop at the local drug or health food store, and you double your profit.

When you start cutting cocaine, that's when you start making money. You buy a kilo, cut it with a kilo of some other tasteless substance; then you sell two kilos worth of cocaine after buying only one.

At first we cut the cocaine one time. Then we started getting greedy. One thing about power and money, nobody ever wants less.

When cocaine comes into the United States, mostly from Colombia, the big guys cut it many times over before it gets to the dealers. Then the dealers can still cut it three more times before it gets to the street.

By this time my brother had started smoking Crack, but we never dealt with Crack. Crack is only 10 percent cocaine; it's usually home-cooked. I hadn't started smoking yet. My brother was smoking Crack, but he could take one hit and go out and do what he had to do. He didn't tweak, didn't trip; that was him. But me, I couldn't do that. Once I smoked Crack, I would lose every bit of thought. Until I came down from that hit, I was gone. I couldn't concentrate, couldn't focus.

I didn't like Crack the first few times. It gets you high too quick— instantly. I couldn't even put the pipe down; it was too fast. I wanted to get a gradual high like with pot or alcohol. But wheeew! Man, Crack was fast! But the more I smoked it, the more I got used to it.

Because my brother and I were selling cocaine, we never had to do the things the addicts on the street do for a hit. They smoke up their hard-earned money from their job; some take money from their kids; some rob, steal, or toss up to get a hit. We never did any of that so we thought that we were better than the street addicts.

But then my brother and I started having trouble between us. He pulled a couple of pump shotguns on me, pulled a pistol on me two or three times. One time he lost $16,000 in the house. He had tucked it under a sofa.

Another time he had ordered a special part for his Porsche 911 and when UPS delivered it C.O.D., he had to pay for it. It cost $700. He pulled $500 out of his pocket and turned to me asking, "Where's the rest of my money?"

I said, "I don't know."

He went nuts. He started yelling, "You have my money!'

I had maybe twelve, thirteen hundred dollars on me, so I gave him a couple hundred dollars to pay the delivery man. But my brother went after my money again. I tried to tell him that all the money I had on me was mine. I said, "I don't know what you're tripping on," and I went into my room.

So I was in my room with my back to the door. I felt his presence in my room. He said, "I got a pistol here. Where's my goddamn money?"

I turned around and said, "Man, what are you talkin' about?" I moved the pistol out of my face. Then he cocked it and put it to my head.

He said, "Man, you better find my money."

Since he had his finger on the trigger, I started tearing up my room and saying to myself, "What the hell am I looking for?" I finally talked him into letting me out of the house by pretending I had hidden his money somewhere else.

I went to my cousin's house and looked in his car. I knew there was nothing in his car, but I told my cousin what was going on. I wanted my cousin to be able to tell my brother that I had been looking if he ran into him.

Finally I knew there was nothing I could do; I didn't have his money. So I went back home. My brother was standing there with the money in his hand. We started laughing; he said, "I'm not gonna say I'm sorry."

I really was mad. I didn't speak to my brother for maybe two, three days.

The second time my brother pulled a gun on me was over a girl. He had his girlfriend and her sister there. He told his girlfriend right in front of us all, "I wanna go to bed with your sister."

His girlfriend responded, "My sister wouldn't go to bed with you if I told her to."

I could see this was going to get messy. I said to her, "Don't say that. Don't dare him. Don't put him in a position like that; you'll lose."

And the girl said, "I ain't worried."

About three days after that my brother invited the girl and her sister over to our place again for dinner. When we were done eating, he pulled the sister into his room and his girlfriend followed them. My brother said, "I'm glad I got both of you in here. I got a question to ask y'all. I wanna go to bed with you," he said to the sister.

The woman looked at the her sister and said, "No, I can't go to bed with you."

My brother wouldn't let it go. He pushed his girlfriend out of the room, and he locked the door. The sister was yelling, "Stop! Don't do this." She finally told my brother she just couldn't sleep with him because her sister was around. She told him she would some other time. That got him to stop.

Finally he unlocked the door, but he was all riled up. So he pulled that money thing again. This time he accused me of taking $800 out of his leather jacket when I had worn it the day before. He yelled at me, "You took my money again." And like the last time, he pulled a gun.

I told him, "Oh, man, we gotta go through this shit again?" So I went in the kitchen and got some E&J Brandy; I took a drink and said, "Man, I'm tired of this. This is getting old." I slammed the glass on the kitchen counter.

And he said, "You gotta problem?"

I said, "No. You gotta goddamn gun." And then I left.

A few days later I called my cousin. It was on my mother's birthday. I said, "I want you to take me downtown to get something for my mother." So he took me to this mall. I went in the front door, walked around, and went out one of the other exits while he was still waiting for me.

I caught a cab and went to Kennedy Airport. I was scared. I walked around the airport, slept in a couple of chairs until the ticket counters opened. I didn't have any reservations; my ticket cost about a thousand dollars. I took some money from my pocket, counted it, and gave it to the agent. He gave me a ticket, and I got on a plane.

It was 7:30 in the morning, and the plane was leaving at 8:15. I had to fly through Atlanta and lay over a few hours. I got off the plane in Atlanta, found a clothes store, and bought a suit; all I had with me were the clothes on my back and several thousand dollars in my pocket.

My college friend picked me up at the San Francisco airport and took me to a hotel. I stayed there for a couple of nights. Then I moved to the Hilton, right across the street from Glide, but I never noticed Glide was here. From the Hilton, I moved to a cheaper hotel. I finally came back to the Tenderloin and stayed at a nearby hotel.

Every day I went out, spending money with my friend—drinking, giving waitresses twenty-dollar tips. It didn't take me long to blow nearly six thousand dollars. I acted like I was on vacation, but I was on the run.

When you live with a lie, you're engulfed in a lie. After a few weeks I couldn't pay my hotel bill. I was kicked out; I had never been homeless in my life.

I stayed at my friend's house for a few days until his mother told me, "The city has this general assistance thing; they'll find you a place to stay." She took me to GA, dropped me off near the office.

I had never before seen so many people so bad, so confused, so out of control. There was madness everywhere. I just stood there; I was in awe.

I signed up and found another hotel to live in. About this time a friend took me to a Jesse Jackson rally; he was gearing up to run for president around then. At the rally I picked up a Glide Facts on Crack pamphlet.

I read the pamphlet and figured Glide must be near my hotel. I read the pamphlet but didn't think too much about it until I stood in the food line later that month. Then I realized that this was the same place that the pamphlet was talking about.

So one day soon after, I came in the building and asked one of the door monitors, "You have a drug meeting in here, right?" And they said yeah. And I said, "Well, I'm goin' to the drug meeting," and he pointed to the room where I should go.

I came back again and went to another meeting. I started volunteering. I'd get here at six o'clock in the morning; I'd get a meal, volunteer until the eleven o'clock meeting, volunteer some more, then go to the three o'clock meeting.

Volunteering gave me something useful to do. One day I was hanging around outside, and I saw the kitchen manager making trip after trip downstairs to bring up food. He was loading up a van with all sorts of things for an off-site dinner. I told the man I would help him carrying and transporting all of that stuff. I could tell he needed help, and he sure was going to need help unloading everything at the other end.

I wasn't doing anything else. I also just wanted to ride in the van and drive around to see some of San Francisco. Since I had arrived and landed in the Tenderloin, I hadn't been out of the area much. I just wanted to see some houses, not just hotels, stores, and homeless people.

The kitchen manager hemmed and hawed, saying, "Man, I don't know you very well." He needed the help, but he wasn't sure if he could trust me.

Meanwhile Dave Richmond, the deputy director of programs at Glide, was loading the van with some other things from the office. He overheard me offer help and he told the guy from the kitchen, "Jamal's all right. You can trust him. I've been watching the way he works around here. He's a good man."

What Dave said really did something to me. Next to Cecil and Janice, he has the most responsible position on the staff at Glide. Dave

was the first white man who ever opened up to me. He treated me like
an equal. Whenever I had dealings with white men before, they made
it clear that they were at a different level than I was. But Dave isn't
like that. He tells people just how he feels. He isn't hiding his hand,
waiting to play the trump card when you're down. He is real.

Dave and the others around Glide made me see that breaking
down stereotypes is important. People are people, no matter what
color they are.

Soon after I first came to Glide, the First Generation started meeting with Cecil, and I joined. Cecil kept using words like "Be authentic," "Tell your story," "Have some integrity."

Cecil would ask questions. "Is this happening with you? What is
causing this Crack problem?" I don't even think Cecil consciously
knew what he was doing, but he trusted his instincts. It was almost
magical. Here was this minister asking this group of people to tell him
their story; everybody was coming out with what was happening with
them. I ain't experienced nothing like that in my life.

I really started to like Cecil. At one point, I was almost in love with
his spirit. I mean what we shared in the group was very, very intimate.

I decided that what we had in the groups was what I had been looking for. Cecil didn't give any of us answers. He would make us bring
the answers out ourselves. When we discovered what we really needed
to know, he'd say, "I knew you had it in you." Talking with the group
and with Cecil helped me peel so much stuff off myself.

When I came to Glide, I was mad at the world. I was mad at my
brother for what he had done to me. I hated women with a passion
because I only saw women playing the victim role. And then I had seen
women on drugs who had put themselves in certain situations; then
when bad stuff happened to them, they blamed everybody else. I didn't
like hearing that victim stuff.

Actually when I first started coming to the circle meetings, there
were hardly any women who came. Women would only come to the
five o'clock meeting when there was an open mike. Freedom Hall
would be packed. Everybody was free to take a turn. Standing in front
of the mike was magic; it said to everyone who stood behind it, "It's
your turn. Say whatever it is that you've been going through."

When it came time to graduate the First Generation, some of the
first folks to come in were gone, smoked out, smoked up, and still

smoking, in denial and lying. The group of us that stayed endured and went through all the stuff because we wanted recovery. This is the recovery program that worked for me.

The program worked because Cecil set up a trust factor right away. The man didn't know anything about Crack, but he knew the only person who could tell him about Crack addiction was a Crack addict. He listened; then he learned. He learned the language.

Cecil believed in us, and he made us believe in ourselves. He let us talk, get it out; we told our story everywhere.

Cecil took the boldest step when he asked the congregation to form the Placenta group. We started having meetings together on a regular basis.

I would never say anything. But then we were in room 618 one night, and all the anger started to come out of me. "Is this a hobby for you? Are you a bored housewife with nothing better to do?"

This was my way of testing them, shaking them up. I was trying to see if I could break a couple of them down. A couple of them answered back with spunk and said, "No, we're here because we want to be here." They came back at me.

I said, "Damn! These some bold white people." I didn't intimidate them.

I knew the average black male could intimidate a white person. It helped me break down a thing about stereotypes. When the white people fired back at me, I was shocked. They were not your average white folks. They were intense about wanting to help.

That was different for me. The Placenta was getting together folks from different backgrounds, different cultures. This was the first time I had to deal with white America. In college I was one of the few blacks who had gotten into Maryland. When you go through what you go through on the flip side, being vulnerable and listening to these people made me want to give it a try.

Interacting with people who cared made a difference for the First Generation. Even though we were homeless and had no self-esteem, the women would say how much they saw in us. I really developed some quality relationships with people in that group that I'm still friends with today. No one could have planned what happened.

On graduation day there was a lot of crying on the part of the Placenta members. They never knew how coming outside themselves would help them. Some of them were alcoholics, incest survivors—all sorts of problems. But by coming out of themselves and helping someone who was a little bit more disadvantaged than themselves, it was a good experience for them, too.

I kept going to the circle meetings, even after I graduated. One day Cecil announced that Glide had been given some money to help some people with the rent deposits for first and last months' rent. Lots of people in the group got really excited: "I need some of that." "Look over here, Cecil; count me in."

I got bothered by some of those folks always getting excited about a handout. I knew many of them weren't working. What good would help with the first and last months' rent do if you didn't have any money to pay the in-between months? What good does it do to get into a place and then be evicted in a few weeks when the next rent is due?

So I decided to tell Cecil what I thought. I went into his office later and asked his assistant if I could make an appointment to see Cecil. I was really impressed when he came out and told me he would be glad to see me the next day. But then I got scared and didn't show up the next day.

Before the circle meeting the following day, Cecil saw me on my way in. "Weren't you supposed to come and see me yesterday?"

I said, "I had an appointment."

Cecil's face told me he knew that I must have been afraid but he just said, "How about today then?"

"How about right now?" I answered before I lost my courage.

Cecil and I went into his office. I told him that the offer of first and last months' rent didn't do someone like me any good without a job.

Cecil caught on fast. "You want to work, don't you?"

I nodded. We talked for a while and then he offered me a job on the spot.

That was three years ago. Since then I have completed my training as a substance abuse counselor. I left Glide once and got fired once. Getting fired was the best thing that happened to me. I had started to think that Glide needed me too much, that they'd never mess with me. I had an attitude.

When I got fired, I stayed away for a while and checked out some other groups and places. But I came back. I never found anything else like Glide.

I remember the day that the Women on the Move program started. It was September 22, 1988. I remember it because it was

Cecil's birthday. There were still not a lot of women coming to Glide. There were some pretty heavy dudes around here—men with a penitentiary attitude. Some of the women were afraid; others who were still tossing up for drugs on the streets didn't want to come in and see a bunch of men they'd performed sexual favors for.

Lots of women came in that day, and Cecil announced that Glide was a safe place where women could come and not be threatened. He told them that if men called them bitches or harassed them at Glide, he wanted to know about it. He promised to deal with it.

There were a lot of men around Glide at that time who were really down-and-out and didn't want to admit it. When men are like that, they often want to take out their own shit on someone who they feel is weaker than they are. Nine times out of ten, that person is a woman.

Before I came to Glide, I didn't have any platonic women friends. I only wanted women to go to bed with. After I came to Glide, I started letting my guard down more than I ever have before in my life. I looked up the word *platonic* in the dictionary and it means "a close relationship with a person you aren't interested in having sex with." I have some of those friends today.

Today I'm working on trying not to put women, or anybody for that matter, into categories. I'm trying to learn to respect women as women.

But it's hard. A lot of women don't respect men at all. I've had women say to me, "I know your type; you want to go to bed with every woman who comes through the doors." That kind of comment hurts me. I've been called a wolf or a dog by women. That would be considered sexual harassment if I was a woman. Why do some women think it's okay to put down all men?

I especially hate it when women say "Men ain't shit." I've heard women say that casually, but comments like that cut me to the bone. I know that women have been oppressed, but sometimes I want to holler out, "I am not the one who did that to you. Don't treat me like I did those things to you."

But it's hard to know how to treat women. Some of the women at Glide have been through so much that I don't know how to act or how to come off. Some of the women need to work on their attitudes toward men, too. Women aren't the only ones who have been victimized. There's a double standard in society that allows women to talk about men as if we are all perpetrators of rape or incest. Now I'm not denying that there are some black men who treat their women and daughters wrong, just like there are some white and every other color of men who do, too. But every man isn't a molester or a batterer.

Black men know what it means to be oppressed, too. When women start talking about the "men in power," they aren't talking about black men. We've never been in power. The "powers that be" doesn't include me. Sure, a few black men have risen above the oppressed, but most of us are still pushed down, too.

I think that women want to be respected, treated equally, and validated. But that's how men want to be treated, too. For me, respect, equality, and validation are the general format I want to try to stick to in any kind of relationship. Glide helps me to do that.

I come here every day. I even come on Sundays, even though I've been a Muslim since I was thirteen. Sunday is the day I can let Cecil be my minister rather than my boss. Being a Muslim simply means to be one who follows the will of God. Even though Cecil would never claim to be a Muslim, he follows the will of God. He'd make a good Muslim for the way he acts with the poor and how he helps people. I sing in the Glide Ensemble, and when everyone sits down to listen to the sermon, I stay standing by the platform door. I listen to every word Cecil says. He's always out there on the edge; what he says is important to me. But I know that everyone out in the congregation doesn't like what Cecil says. Every kind of person comes to Glide. I stand like a sentry by the platform door. You never know what could happen. People have threatened Cecil before. Nobody has ever asked me to keep my eyes open, but I want to offer something back to Cecil. I mean if someone has reached out a hand and pulled you up from the bottom, you'll never forget it. That is what Glide has done for me.

Community: Recovery and Relationships

One day while sitting in the circle meeting, I asked, "Why are black men so angry?" The answers that followed were like a barrage of deadly bullets shot indiscriminately in the air.

The men were angry that they couldn't get jobs. They told me, "Black women can get jobs quicker than we can. Affirmative action has helped our women maneuver in the work force dominated by white male employers, but the bosses don't want us.

"We're angry because everyone treats black men like we're all crazy." Through story after story they proved that the old racist adage "Watch out for those crazy niggers" never has been fully put to rest in society.

One man said, "The black man knows that one of the ways he is effective at frightening the white community is to act 'crazy' by letting his anger and rage out. Some of the white male community have always warned their young, 'Be careful. Black men are violent; they are angry. They will kill you, destroy you. They are inhuman, oversexed, no good; they have no sense of responsibility. They are unpredictable and will be waiting for the right moment to take you by surprise.'"

As the men in the early Generations talked, they proved that in many ways the black males coming into manhood in recent years have lived up to the negative expectations of the white community. Some of the young males selling dope do so to get money quick and easy. They have learned that there is power in money.

As one young man put it, "We are just using the white man's ways of profit. They control downtown and do their business in the stock exchange on Wall Street. We are just playing the same game, only we do our exchanging on every street of this city."

I quickly saw that the young dealers see people as customers and use sophisticated skills that keep their customers regular, their profit steadily rising higher and higher. Drugs are their product and, heaven knows, there are enough people out there looking for a quick fix to poverty and pain.

No one, black or white, willingly gives up power. The Wall Street shysters use electronic tools like computers and cellular phones to protect their power. Young black men resort to using the most effective tools they have at their disposal—intimidation and violence. A lot of pushers and others in the community will protect what they have by using their guns and their anger. And it isn't only pushers who are angry or who resort to violence.

There is some truth to another myth that whites hold about black men as violent members of their own families. But black men don't batter because they are black; any man who batters does so because he is angry, insecure, afraid of losing what he has.

Where is a man who feels castrated by society because he can't find work and can't support his family going to take out his rage? Probably on his mate or children. Men who feel they are nobody in society—that they own nothing—are going to try to own something or somebody. Many men act like they own their wives or children. If your woman threatens to get away, you beat her. When men can't control anything else in their lives, then at least they will control their families with the most effective tools they have at their disposal—intimidation and violence. And the tools of intimidation and violence are most always fueled by drugs or alcohol. Additionally, the drugs and alcohol offer an excuse. After the battering, a man can blame his actions on the effects of taking a drug or downing too many drinks.

A man feels like a powerless, impotent nobody so he takes a hit of Crack to forget. Then he goes home and rages and flails in his anger, and he discovers that no drug ever lives up to its promise to take away the pain—it only deepens it.

Black males, being at the bottom end of society, have been taught by generation after generation to be toxic hustlers. *The system rewards those who learn how to manipulate the system for their own benefit.*

Married women with children get less money from Aid to Families with Dependent Children than do unmarried women. So why should black couples get married at all?

The way to get what you want is to outhustle, outmaneuver, outfight, and outcompete everyone else who wants what you want for yourself. Integrity doesn't pay the bills when you are unemployed and statistically the last in line to get hired, but hustling on the streets might just pay for a few groceries and next month's rent.

Recovery for the men meant more than getting free from drugs. They would have to find new ways of defining themselves. They would have to learn to measure their worth and power by new standards. Trying to measure up to the materialistic promises of the American dream had brought them nothing but addiction and false hope. They would have to find better answers for themselves.

Recovery starts with each of us individually and then extends to our relationships. Albert said it well when he told me, "Recovery has made me appreciate relationships more. I appreciate life, living, and having a good relationship with other people, male as well as female. Having somebody you really can trust is important. I remember friends that I hung out with before and after I started doing drugs. One of my friends stole my television after we started doing drugs. I knew that the thief wasn't my real friend; Crack had made him into something he hadn't been before. Drug friends aren't real friends. Drugs are the glue that hold you together. When the drugs are gone, so is the friendship."

The lessons in recovery that Albert learned were lessons many African American men at Glide learn over time.

AFTER THE HEARINGS

When the Clarence Thomas hearings captivated the nation's attention, the men at Glide were no exception. So I sent the word out that I wanted to meet with all the male staff members in Freedom Hall. Twenty-five men filled the room when I entered.

We reviewed the details of the trial, and then I opened the floor for the men to express what they were feeling. One or two spoke, and then I was called out of the room on an emergency. I left Albert in charge.

When I got back to Freedom Hall more than an hour later, the men were dispersing. I asked one of the men, "What happened while I was gone?"

He smiled and puffed his chest out wide. "Cecil, we decided not to call women bitches anymore, and we made that choice without you here. We did it by ourselves." He was certainly proud of himself.

Later that afternoon I caught up with Albert and asked him to tell me what had transpired in my absence.

Albert told me that most of the men felt that Clarence Thomas had been set up by the Senate; none of the men felt that if Thomas had been white, the sexual harassment charges would have been detailed before the American public. Only a black man running for high office would have been subjected to that. After they agreed on that point, little was agreed on for the rest of the meeting.

Opinions differed widely. Several men in the meeting took Anita Hill's side. When some coarse remarks were made about Anita Hill, one of the men said, "You are shallow in your thinking." Then the place erupted. Words were flung from far and wide. Instead of talking about Clarence Thomas and Anita Hill, the men began to talk about themselves. They began to redefine their feelings about sexual harassment.

"Man, the other day a female pinched my ass and said, 'You have some cakes, baby.' I said back to her, 'What would you think if I did that to you?' She said, 'You can't. Men just can't.' Now I ask you, how's that fair? How come that's okay? There's a double standard."

Another stood up and said, "Men get falsely accused of everything. Women don't understand what we go through."

He was followed by another. "Hey, wait a minute. Some of the volunteers around here are always hitting on the women in the food line. They act like Glide is a meat market. I think that's why some men come here. That isn't right."

Another responded jokingly, "Isn't that what the thirteenth Step is all about? After you stop using Crack, you got to redirect your vices? What's wrong with enjoying women?"

Some laughed. Others shook their heads in disbelief.

Somehow the meeting turned to calling women bitches. One man vehemently said that his woman called him a bitch and every other imaginable name, so he did it back. It was their way of communicating.

Someone else countered, "If you want people to treat you with respect, you've got to treat them that way."

Several others protested that aggressive, irreverent language was a part of their homes and always had been. They really had never considered that calling a woman a bitch was disrespectful.

Finally one man said, "What is this meeting going to do for us? At least we have brought out how we feel. What else can we do?"

That's when the men came to a consensus that they would no longer call women by derogatory terms; they would call the women at Glide by their given names.

After Albert recapped the meeting for me, I felt glad that the men had aired their feelings and decided to take a positive step together. It may have been a small step, but they chose to make it by themselves, and that in itself was clear progress.

That's the kind of movement possible when men are in motion together.

CHAPTER EIGHT

It's Compassion Time

Recognition: AIDS Is a Recovery Issue

On New Year's Eve, 1991, I telephoned Ron, a member of Glide, who was acutely suffering in the final stages of AIDS. We chatted for a moment and then Ron asked timidly, "Cecil, would you come and see me tonight?" I detected a quiet urgency in his voice. Janice and I agreed to stop by for a short visit on our way to Glide's first clean and sober New Year's Eve party for the people in recovery.

When Janice and I walked into Ron's one-bedroom apartment, his face brightened with pleasure. We talked for some time, and between the lines of hopeful banter, it became clear that Ron was scared. He knew that he didn't have long to live. He also felt ashamed and frustrated that his once virile and agile body lay listlessly, nearly useless to him now. He couldn't control his basic bodily functions, and in the middle of our visit the home nurse on duty had to rush in from the other room to care for his needs.

When the nurse beckoned us back into Ron's bedroom, I embraced him and held his fragile torso in my arms. He wrapped his bone-thin arms around me and squeezed with all his might. He wouldn't let me loose. Locked with him in an embrace, I began to rock back and forth, almost cradling him in my arms. Then I began to cry.

Ron whispered what his embrace had already communicated. "Thank you for loving me. Thank you for not forgetting about me."

To Ron, my coming to visit him meant that the community, the extended family of the church, had arrived to offer comfort. Ron held me so tight because he never dared hope that the church would really show up and be present with him in his darkest hour.

Glide had fully welcomed Ron and his partner Derek into the church with open arms many months earlier. Ron and Derek, both deeply spiritual and compassionate people, had been ostracized by other churches because they were gay. When they came to Glide, they waited to see if we really would embrace them fully. Glide did what the church is supposed to do: Glide rocked Ron and Derek in its bosom as our much-loved sons.

As Ron and Derek realized that they were loved, both had responded by showing up every time the doors were open. They lived their lives with courage and openness at Glide. It was as if they were messengers sent to us to teach us more about love and acceptance.

In September of 1991, the Glide family had surprised me on my birthday during a Celebration service by letting dozens of helium balloons go free after singing "Happy Birthday." After I finished preaching that morning, representatives from various groups in the church came to the front and offered birthday greetings and warm words.

Derek had hobbled up to the front. He looked like a man who had long been in a concentration camp—his body was shrunken, his face hollow, and his voice weak. He had willed himself to get well enough to leave the hospital so that he could be the bearer of birthday tidings to me. I was so touched.

Two weeks later I had to announce to the congregation that Derek had died. I wanted so much to find a way to offer comfort to Ron in his bereavement. Ron's own precarious health was weakened by his grief. Grief had struck the Glide family extra hard that week. First, Derek had died; then the mother of a family with seven children had died unexpectedly. I needed to find a way to offer comfort to all those in the Glide family who were wading through deep emotional waters.

I asked Ron and the woman's children to stand as I walked down the center aisle. Then I opened my arms, gesturing to Ron and the other family, and I started to sing some old, wise words of consolation:

There is a balm in Gilead
to make the wounded whole.
There is a balm in Gilead
to heal the sin-sick soul.

Sometimes I feel discouraged,
and think my work's in vain.
But then the Holy Spirit
revives my soul again.

Then I sang the final verse to the Glide family as an invitation to keep loving all of God's people, white or black, gay or straight, addicted or drug-free:

If you can't preach like Peter,
if you can't pray like Paul,
just tell the love of Jesus
and say he died for all.

Silence filled the sanctuary. The spirit of consolation swept through Glide that morning doing something to us. Glide is rarely quiet, but in the stillness of those moments wordless tears flowed, a balm to grief-filled hearts.

Three months later, on that New Year's Eve, Ron and I shared that same wordless closeness—a quiet understanding that flows between those who share unconditional love and acceptance with each other.

When Ron and I finally loosed our embrace and wiped away some of our tears, Janice opened her arms to Ron, and in her embrace he cried. Janice, as a partner in the ministry of Glide, offered Ron acceptance and love as a woman, a mother, and a sister.

When the hugging finally stopped, we all joined hands and I prayed, "Lord, thank you for letting Ron be a messenger to me. Thank you for sending Ron to help me and the Glide family feel more deeply and to hold on tighter to him, to Derek, and to all people who suffer with AIDS." Ron had helped me to move closer to suffering without fear.

When we said good-bye, Ron's smile said everything his heart felt. It was very difficult to part. Three days later Ron died peacefully.

Ron and Derek were not the first people with AIDS to find their way to Glide. The specter of AIDS has been haunting Glide since 1984 when a member of the Glide Ensemble suddenly hung himself without warning when he was diagnosed with HIV/AIDS. I learned of others struggling with the news of a positive HIV test in the ensuing years. I watched as some dealt with their diagnosis with destructive behavior, silence, or despair.

In 1986 a member at Glide asked me to visit a friend of his with AIDS who was in the hospital. When I arrived on the ward, the nurses made me don a robe and encouraged me to put on a sterile mask, gloves, and cap before entering the room. I choose not to wear the extra protection. It seemed so inhuman, so limiting to talk to someone about love and hope when covered with sterile garments.

When I walked into the room and greeted that man, I was shaken to my core. I have seen death many, many times during my life, but I had never before seen death literally creeping, moment by moment, into a person's body. The man was shrunken, emaciated, and had the hollowed-out look of one who had suffered long.

It wasn't long after that visit that the people in recovery at Glide started to tell their stories. Several of them told of struggling with a two-edged sword of suffering: addiction and a positive HIV test. HIV/AIDS all too often goes hand in glove with drug use. Intravenous drug users are at high risk for contracting HIV through shared needles. Crack use also lowers users' inhibitions, and many engage in sex in exchange for drugs. Fast living, be it in the homosexual or the heterosexual community, puts people at risk. Rarely when high on drugs does anybody practice safer sex.

Soon other people with HIV/AIDS in the extended Glide family stood up and told their stories, too. They found the Spirit, and we began to see people living with HIV/AIDS who were reclaiming their lives and living whatever time they had with renewed courage.

We then decided that AIDS is a recovery issue. Whenever people feel alienated, isolated, and rejected, they need recovery. Recovery at Glide is about offering hope to people who need healing in body and mind, soul and Spirit.

The same stench of death that led us to open our doors to Crack addicts permeated the lives of those suffering with HIV/AIDS. These folks needed recovery. People with HIV/AIDS have to deal with devastation. Their bodies are destroyed by this disease. Their minds and outlook on life can be dimmed by long suffering. Their Spirits are often crushed by rejection from friends and family who run in horror and dismay at the first mention of AIDS. People with AIDS usually have to find a new extended family, a community of support, to be present with them as they live as fully as possible while dealing with the medical realities of the disease.

Self-Definition: The Glide/Goodlett AIDS Project

After hearing the stories of some of the people in recovery who were also dealing with HIV/AIDS, I came back to my office and, convinced that AIDS could not be separated from recovery, gathered together the staff at Glide. I asked them to start thinking with me about what we could do for people with HIV/AIDS.

We came up with three specific ways we could act. First, we would visit those with HIV/AIDS in our community, offering acceptance and comfort. Second, we would gather information about the existing AIDS services in

San Francisco and pass it on to those who were infected. Third, we would ask the head of the city health department to come and speak on a Sunday to educate our people about HIV/AIDS in hopes of teaching the Glide community how to prevent further spread of the disease.

We began doing what we knew to do; as we did, we made a crucial discovery. The minority community was underserved, and few agencies were focusing on the specific needs of African American persons with AIDS. In fact, the black community as a whole was still pretending that AIDS was a gay white man's disease. The black community was believing lies by living in denial about AIDS.

In 1987 I started preaching about AIDS at Glide. No one was too surprised; I have always focused on people who live on the edge, precariously tipping toward death and in need of a loving, stabilizing embrace. In my preaching I advocated something very simple—reach out with comfort to those who suffer. I preached what I had learned as a boy in the church: People need to be rocked in the bosom of the church.

Soon some in the congregation caught the Spirit and decided to act on behalf of those suffering with AIDS. A woman at Glide who was a member of the health commission secured some funds from a local foundation, and Glide cosponsored a conference on AIDS for clergy and caregivers in Oakland. About seventy people—clergy, doctors, scientists, men and women with AIDS, and churchgoers—came together to share what we knew and to discuss what the church could do for people with AIDS.

Through that conference I met Louis Ashley, a minister raised in the Baptist tradition who sang, laughed, and prayed with fervor. Already he had fought mightily to break through the strongly held denial in the black community regarding HIV/AIDS and homosexuality.

Louis sat on the board of several local AIDS agencies, and he was familiar with the agencies who worked specifically with the black community. Soon Louis joined us at Glide and we began putting together an AIDS project that targeted the special needs of the African American community.

As the AIDS project was in the formative stages, Louis asked me what I thought we should name the project. We talked about wanting a name to convey compassion and an awareness of the special needs of African American people.

Immediately the face of my longtime friend Carlton Goodlett flashed across my mind. Dr. Carlton Goodlett, M.D., has been a powerful, compassionate voice for the black community in San Francisco for decades. On the West Coast Carlton Goodlett ranked with Martin Luther King, Jr., as an advocate for civil rights and world peace. Dr. Goodlett owned and operated several newspapers across the country through which he advocated for racial and social justice. In the early 1970s he had been the first African American to run for the governorship of California; I had been his campaign manager. Carlton Goodlett early championed the cause of AIDS and publicly and privately found many ways to express his concern for those who were HIV positive.

I suggested to Louis, "What about calling our program the Glide/Goodlett AIDS Project?"

Louis agreed enthusiastically, and we launched the program one Sunday in 1989 with Dr. Goodlett in attendance. Dr. Goodlett cried, embraced, and embodied the compassion that we hoped our program would extend to those suffering from HIV/AIDS in our community.

Even before the program was fully funded, Louis started reaching out. One of his first acts was to organize an outreach day for the people in the Tenderloin. Louis marshaled representatives from community AIDS organizations, set up tables in Boeddeker Park, and unabashedly approached the people in the park. Louis would talk to anybody. He was a master at community organizing and education.

As often happens at Glide, the Glide/Goodlett AIDS Project (GGAP) began operating before all the logistics were worked out. Before the fifth-floor office was cleared for Louis, he held court on the landing between the first and second flights of stairs when he wasn't out on the streets talking to anyone who would listen about HIV/AIDS.

Louis was a magician when it came to enlisting the help of others. County supervisors, medical doctors, and volunteers flocked around him. One of the professionals conscripted early on was Leon Baccheus, Ph.D., a slight, efficient man who had founded an AIDS agency and operated a private counseling practice on the East Coast for people with AIDS. Louis helped to convince Leon to move west from his Philadelphia home for a while. On a borrowed computer, Leon and many others helped Louis to formulate what has evolved into a thriving program of prevention and education through street outreach, individual counseling, support groups, and HIV testing for those who are AIDS-affected or at risk in our community.

Today the GGAP daily sends outreach workers to the streets to heighten awareness among the very transient and downtrodden population of the Tenderloin. The outreach workers herald the news that HIV/AIDS can be prevented, that support for those already infected is available, and that there is a place where they can come and find welcome.

STREET OUTREACH

Around noontime on a recent Wednesday Roscoe, a forty-eight-year-old outreach worker with a no-nonsense approach and a deep conviction about honesty, left the fifth-floor office of the Glide/Goodlett AIDS Project and headed outside with a new volunteer in tow. Roscoe was to initiate the new recruit into the realities of educating the transient, tough population of the Tenderloin about the dangers of HIV/AIDS. Roscoe carried a briefcase brimming with safer-sex kits, a pad and pencil, and cards printed with the address and phone number for the AIDS project.

First Roscoe headed up through the lunch line where several hundred people waited for the next seating in the dining room. "Today, free AIDS testing upstairs on the fifth floor," Roscoe announced to the crowd. "Have you been tested?" he stopped to ask one streetwise woman.

"Are you paying?" she asked pragmatically, as she knew that an earlier group had come to the Tenderloin and paid people twenty-five dollars to get tested. Unfortunately, after people were paid, few returned to learn the results of their tests.

"No, sister, getting tested is about your health. You need to do it for you," Roscoe answered without batting an eye.

Roscoe stepped a bit farther down the line and repeated the news. A black woman with a neatly turned-under pageboy covered her ears. "Ohhh, I don't want to hear about AIDS."

A man behind her asked, "What room?"

"Take the elevator to room 518."

The man continued, "How long does it take?"

"Only a few minutes. Go on up after you've eaten lunch."

Roscoe stepped clear of the lunch line and crossed over to Jones Street. Midway up the block he reached into his briefcase for a safer-sex kit and extended his hand to a black man dressed in a plaid jacket who leaned against the fence that surrounds Boeddeker Park. "Here's a safer-sex kit for you. Have you taken the AIDS test?"

"Yeah, a couple of weeks ago."

"Good for you, brother." Roscoe congratulated him and moved on to the next person leaning on the fence, a thin white man who appeared to be in his early thirties.

The man said low as Roscoe approached, "Wanna buy some pot?"

Roscoe answered with a question of his own.

"Have you been tested for HIV?"

The man answered while staring out into the street, "Yeah, in 1986."

Roscoe started to encourage the man to retake the test as the incubation period for HIV to appear can be six months or longer, but the man shook his head. "I mean I've had it since 1986, but I don't practice unsafe sex. That's how I got it; I ain't gonna give it to anybody else."

As the man turned to face Roscoe directly, a line of purplish skin lesions on his neck became apparent.

Roscoe moved in closer. "Are you in a support group? Are you getting medical care?"

The man shook his head. "It's too depressing to talk about it. I don't want to tell anybody anything and don't want to listen to others either."

Roscoe persisted in a caring, factual manner. "Talking about AIDS can make it less depressing. Besides, you don't have to talk unless you want to. Why don't you come to the support group this afternoon at three o'clock?"

The man shrugged noncommittally, "Where?"

"330 Ellis. Do you know where Glide is?" Roscoe asked.

"Yeah, Glide's around the corner."

Roscoe pulled out his pad of paper. "What's your name?"

"Brian," the man replied.

"Brian, I'm writing down your name because I want to remember you. C'mon up to Glide and stop in to talk sometime. I'll give you more information on where you can get some medical treatment."

"Thanks," Brian said, turning his head up the street. He was done talking.

Roscoe crossed Eddy Street and stopped to hand safer-sex kits to several Hispanic men reading Spanish newspapers in the doorway.

"Here's a safer-sex kit for you," Roscoe offered to the first man. He shoved Roscoe's hand away.

Roscoe persisted, "Do you speak English?"

The man sitting next to him answered, "Sure he does."

Roscoe focused on the second man. "Ask your friend here why he doesn't want a safer-sex kit. While you are at it, ask him if he has been tested for the AIDS virus."

The man obliged, but his friend remained sullen behind his newspaper. Roscoe redirected the question to the second man. "How about you? Have you been tested?"

He shook his head and pointed to the safer-sex kit. "I'll take one of those."

"Sure thing, man. Take one for your friend here, too. And both of you think about getting tested."

Just then a construction worker passed by on his way to the liquor store. Roscoe offered him a kit.

"Don't need one—I'm married. My wife don't cheat on me; I don't cheat on her," he claimed, but he accepted one of the kits and examined the contents curiously as he entered the store.

Roscoe moved on up the street to the next doorway where two white men leaned against a brick building. "Here are some safer-sex kits for you. Have you been tested for the AIDS virus?"

"No, haven't been here long enough to need it. Just got here last night," one retorted.

Roscoe wasn't daunted. "You could have come upon the virus wherever you were before, too. AIDS is everywhere."

"Man, we just got out of the penitentiary. They test you for everything when you go in there."

Roscoe persisted, "You can get AIDS in the pen."

"Not if you ain't doing it," the man laughed cynically.

"When was the last time you had sex?" Roscoe challenged, his brow furrowed.

"Ten years, eight months ago. That's how long I was in for."

"Okay, man," Roscoe conceded, "but whatever you do from now on, practice safer sex. It's dangerous out here." The man nodded, and Roscoe walked resolutely on.

Just two doors farther, two women, one black and the other white, loitered in a boarded-up entryway talking to a male passerby.

"Here are some safer-sex kits for you ladies. How are you doing today?" Roscoe's polite presence made it instantly clear that he wasn't here to hustle the women.

The black woman grabbed a kit from Roscoe's hand and tossed her head. "I'm great, man. Gotta run!" She and the man left together.

The white woman who remained was visibly pregnant. Her chestnut-colored hair lay limply, unkempt at her shoulders. She seemed willing enough to talk, but her fidgeting, scratching, and squirming belied her Crack addiction.

"Are you pregnant?" Roscoe asked, already knowing the answer.

"Yeah, seven and a half months," she assented distantly, offering a well-rehearsed answer.

"Are you getting medical treatment? Glide has a clinic if you aren't."

"Yeah, I went there once. I'm okay."

"Have you been tested for the AIDS virus?"

She shrugged. "They do all those tests automatically at General Hospital when you're pregnant, right?"

"Not unless you requested the test and gave your written consent," Roscoe clarified.

"Guess I haven't been tested. Man, I don't want to know anything about AIDS while I'm pregnant." She dropped her head, weakly supporting it on her hand.

"Take care of yourself," Roscoe admonished her kindly and walked past another doorway where a man peeled away several bills from a small wad of money held tightly in his hands. Whatever he was buying remained hidden in the dealer's pocket. Roscoe shook his head and muttered to the new volunteer who walked beside him, "They deal everywhere. The police station is only a block away."

Roscoe continued walking to the corner where a group of Asian teenagers congregated. "Here is a safer-sex kit," Roscoe explained. One of the boys accepted the plastic bag eagerly; the others hesitated but looked with interest at the kit their friend was examining. Moments later another of the boys tapped Roscoe on the arm and extended his hand for one, too.

Like a wise, pragmatic parent, Roscoe shot straight with the boys. "Abstinence is the safest way, guys, but if you do have sex, use a condom. AIDS is deadly."

The traffic light turned green, and Roscoe crossed over to where a group of a dozen or so men were gathered around a dented big white car. "Safer-sex kits, here." Hands went out all around. One Hispanic man refused. "Why don't you want one?" Roscoe inquired, pressing him by looking him straight in the eyes.

"The pope says no."

Roscoe had heard this response before. "Yeah, the pope says no birth control, but using condoms is also a helpful way to protect yourself from getting the AIDS virus if you are having sex. Using the things in this kit could save your life. You gotta care for yourself, man; do you think the pope wants you to die?" The man remained resolute.

By this time Roscoe had given out all the safer-sex kits he had loaded into his briefcase. He turned and headed back toward Glide, choosing to walk directly through Boeddeker Park where dozens of people loitered. Roscoe stopped at several park benches to announce the availability of HIV testing. Most responded with unenthusiastic nods or a shrug of the shoulders.

One man motioned for Roscoe to stop. He said, "I know you. I've seen you out here before. Why do you do this?"

Roscoe answered with sincere compassion, "Concern. I'm concerned for your life. I want you and everybody else around here to protect yourselves. I know people are going to have sex no matter what anyone tells them to do, so I'm practical. I want to help you know how to prolong your life."

The man replied, "Just asking. See you around."

Roscoe said good-bye and headed on across Ellis Street and back through the doors to Glide.

Counseling and Support Groups

Just before three o'clock in the afternoon later that week, a black man nonchalantly entered the GGAP office in room 518. Annually nearly six hundred people enter that same door for one-on-one counseling or to attend the HIV/AIDS support group held Monday through Thursday.

The man asked the receptionist if he could talk to someone. In a quiet voice, almost a whisper, he explained that he had just received a positive result to the HIV test.

The receptionist led him into the office of Jean Jackson, one of the outreach workers and counselors. Jean's knowing eyes compassionately bored through the man.

Almost immediately upon meeting Jean, people can tell that little, if anything, will shock her. As a native San Franciscan who grew up prior to the civil rights movement, she has experienced, seen, or heard it all before. Her hearty laugh and easy welcome offer the intangible assurance of trust to those with HIV/AIDS who come into her office feeling fearful or wounded by rejection.

Jean motioned the man toward a soft chair. "Hi. My name is Jean. How are you feeling?"

The man introduced himself and sat in silence for a moment. Jean waited; she was in no hurry.

After a few moments the man began to speak in an lifeless voice. "My woman is outside waiting for me. She thinks I came into Glide to talk to a job counselor. I don't know what to do. I can't tell her I'm HIV positive. She'll know I've been stepping out on her."

This man's story wasn't unusual. Gay, straight, or bisexual, the majority of the people who come upstairs to the GGAP office are African American men. The men often venture upstairs after eating a meal or checking into one of the other programs at Glide. Since Glide offers help for all kinds of problems and situations, there is no automatic stigma associated with entering our doors.

Coming to a church for help is acceptable behavior for most black people. Many people have admitted that they would never have walked through the door of any agency that dealt only with AIDS—their friends and family would automatically suspect that they were infected. When people are just beginning to face AIDS as a personal issue, they need time and a safe place to come and talk, knowing that their condition will be kept confidential.

"How much do you know about HIV and AIDS?" Jean asked the man.

"All I know is that I got it," he sighed.

Jean went on to describe the high-risk behaviors through which HIV is transmitted—unprotected vaginal or anal sex, oral sex when one of the participants has open genital sores or cuts in the mouth, fisting* or finger sex without a surgical glove or finger cot for protection, and sharing needles during intravenous drug use.

The man admitted the risky activities that he had practiced. Jean then explained the preventive measures he could take to lessen the chance of his passing on HIV.

Jean explained, "So many people act like they are on a suicide mission after they find out they are HIV positive. They think all that lies ahead is death, so why not hurry it along? There are some people who feel so bitter that they don't care how many others they may infect by their behavior. It is my goal to let you know that you are cared for, so that you can care about yourself. I won't turn my back on you, no matter what. It'll take some time for you to believe that."

Jean continued, "Do you have someone you can talk to about your feelings and your positive test result after you leave here tonight?"

The man shook his head sadly.

Jean handed the man a card with the GGAP phone number and her work number. "I work from 6:00 A.M. to 2:00 P.M. every weekday as a computer operator at a hotel at Fisherman's Wharf. Call me if you need to talk. Don't be alone in this."

It was now time for the support group to begin. She invited the man to attend, but he declined. Jean encouraged him to come back again whenever he needed to talk. Then the man left her office.

---

*The practice of inserting the fist into the anus or vagina.

Moments later Jean emerged from her office and marshaled the half-dozen people who were waiting in the reception area down the hall to the meeting room. People settled into folding chairs around the long table. Then Jean opened the meeting by telling the truth. "Hi. My name is Jean. Since 1982 I've attended more than a hundred funerals of friends who have died of AIDS. I work the early shift at my job; then I come to Glide as an outreach worker. I'm a survivor of child molestation and a recovering drug addict who has been clean for nearly a decade. I'm here because I want to be here. Why don't some of you tell us why you are here."

A vivacious black man who had been around the support group for a while and had just become an outreach worker jumped right in. "I'm here to encourage everyone to educate their families and friends about HIV."

He explained, "When I first went to get tested for HIV three years ago, my scalp was peeling. I became aware of changes in my body. I felt like my insides were curdling, like when hot butter is poured over milk.

"The nurse at the hospital was so uneducated that she got all upset when I asked to be tested. She went on like I was already dead saying, 'You're so young. This is so sad. . . .' She freaked me out so I went into denial for three years until I came to Glide. Now I'm trying to educate others."

A white man with a mustache spoke next. "Ever since I first heard about AIDS, I knew all the time that I was infected. I was married. I got kids—thank God, they are not infected. I got one kid who was born in 1985, one year before I learned I was infected.

"After my wife and I both tested positive, we begun to learn more about AIDS. She died from it. I lost my business. I've been really sick this year.

"AIDS has changed my life all around. Friends who have known me all my life disappeared after I told them I had AIDS. Right now I have no friends."

The man talked without self-pity. He was just telling the truth about his life.

Another man told of going to his church and telling his pastor that he had AIDS. The pastor told him that AIDS was God's judgment and ostracized him.

The man's story riled up Jean. She spoke again with fire flashing in her eyes. "I feel like the church has turned its back on a whole lot of us. I'm not saying this only since the AIDS issue came about. But we were all raised to believe that God was for everybody.

"When any of us goes to a church and the son or daughter of some big member dies of AIDS, chances are that everybody calls it cancer. Who knows how many others in that church he or she may have infected?

"The church at large is keeping everything hidden in the closet or swept under the rug. My early experience with the church made me very bitter. When I came to Glide, I was able to have the freedom to believe in God the way I felt I should believe in him—with my whole heart, not the way somebody else told me to believe or act. And I can love anybody I want to love, not just those the church says are acceptable."

Jean was preaching by this time. "I tell people every day, 'Just because you have AIDS doesn't mean you have to be spiritually bankrupt. AIDS is not God's curse on homosexual men or drug users. AIDS is a disease.'"

The man who had spoken first illustrated Jean's point with his own life story. "I'm adopted but I called my birth family in North Carolina a while ago. I opened my heart, and they now have opened their hearts to me. At first my original father threw the Bible at me when I told him that I had AIDS. I said to him, 'Pop, if you can show me where in the Bible that it specifically says that I am being punished with AIDS for being gay, then I'll have to believe you.'

"He stopped after that. I tease him still when I call: 'Did you ever find AIDS in the Bible?' I don't have a problem with his religion anymore.

"My family is getting educated for themselves. They stopped listening to what their preacher said, because he didn't know anything about AIDS. They are now on a new search for the truth, for life. They have started wanting to know about me, not just what was written in the Bible. You all should educate your families, too."

Another black man in the group shook his head and intently responded, "If I were to get sick tomorrow, I don't think I would have the energy to convince anybody why they should love me."

Jean responded, "You're right. You shouldn't have to convince anybody. You are lovable, with or without AIDS."

The support group ended with people giving hugs all around. One or two of those in attendance scurried out the minute the meeting was over. More lingered talking, laughing, and finding strength in knowing that they were not alone; there were others who understood their struggle and their fears.

Some of those who initially come to Glide for support stay around and offer support to others. Mark is one such person. These days Mark is the first person a new client encounters in the GGAP office. Mark volunteers full-time as a receptionist and office manager. I first met Mark when he came down to the Celebration office to deliver some reports he had written for Louis, when Louis was out sick.

Those reports proved Mark's gift for writing and clear thinking. A little while later Mark volunteered to help answer the phones in our office during a special event. Mark's phone manner with people showed such compassion and caring. He listened patiently to each caller. Soon after he came to Glide, Mark began to accompany the staff whenever we went on speaking engagements regarding AIDS. Mark's life provides an example of what the GGAP offers to people of all colors. Mark is white, and he is a living example of what each person living with AIDS can learn to do for others.

Rebirth: Mark's Story

I TESTED POSITIVE FOR HIV in 1984 when I was eighteen years old and living in San Francisco. I had been in a high-risk group for a very long time by then. At first I got tested out of curiosity, and the test came back positive. I called and told my mother. That was the last time I talked with her before she died.

A little while later my doctor called me and told me that my test results had been mixed up with someone else's. I retook the test in early 1985, and it came back negative. I was relieved, but deep inside I really thought that the first test had probably been right. When the doctors started using a newer, more accurate test in late 1985, I went back in for the third time. I was HIV positive.

When I learned the truth for sure, I went on a sexual rampage for two years. I was in deep denial. By that time, even though people didn't talk much about safer sex, it was widely practiced. I didn't engage in activities that would have put other people at risk of getting infected by me.

In 1986 I moved from San Francisco to Fort Lauderdale. I had used cocaine before, but in Florida cocaine was so plentiful that I used it seriously. I literally could walk to the corner store and buy it outside. I began snorting three or four grams a day.

I was working in a fast-food restaurant and had to take on an evening job as a waiter to pay for my habit. I was good at handling the drugs for a while. None of my co-workers ever knew I did drugs. But there came a time when I couldn't get out of bed in the morning without a line of coke. Before I went to sleep each night I'd set out a line so that it would be waiting for me when I woke up.

I knew I had to stop using cocaine so I moved to Washington state, where I knew no one. I didn't know where to get drugs. That's how I stopped using.

A few months later I went back to Brooklyn, where I was born and raised. I had left Brooklyn when I finished high school. At seventeen, I joined the army with my mother's permission, but I had a short stint. When I needed a security clearance for my job, the army did a background check on me. I didn't know at seventeen that I had a background, but somehow the army found out that I was gay. They gave me an honorable discharge and booted me out.

When I returned to Brooklyn in 1989, I visited my grandparents. I told them that I was HIV positive; they didn't understand and really didn't want to know what it meant. They told me not to tell anyone, not even my sister who was visiting, too. I think they were afraid that my sister would freak out and take my nephew and leave.

Eventually I did tell my sister about my diagnosis; she's eleven months older than I am. At first my sister was shocked, but now we talk on the phone all the time. She has my power of attorney if anything happens to me. She and I have talked about my desire to never be hooked up to a machine for life support. When I get angry and need to holler at someone, I call her up. She's always ready to holler back at me, too.

When we were children, my parents split up. I chose to go and live with my father for a while. My sister stayed with my mother. After that, there was a barrier between me and my sister for many years. It took AIDS to tear that barrier down.

I moved back to San Francisco on September 13, 1991, after a brief stay in Phoenix. I had a job in Phoenix, but I ran into discrimination, being a person with AIDS. My employer's medical insurance carrier wouldn't pay for my medical needs; they said I had a preexisting condition.

That's why I decided to come back to San Francisco. I knew there were more services for people like me. When I arrived, I went to several AIDS agencies looking for housing assistance and help in finding new doctors. Those groups helped put me up in a hotel just a few blocks from Glide.

Up in my room I read a copy of a local independent newspaper and I saw ads for services offered by Glide for women, children, and those needing food. So one day I came to Glide and found out about the Glide/Goodlett AIDS Project. I took the elevator up to the GGAP office looking for someone to talk with.

The outreach worker was just getting ready to go out into the field to do some street outreach, but he said if I really needed to talk, he would make the time. We talked for over an hour before he really had to get out to the streets. Then he asked me if I was interested in answering the phones for a while until the other staff members returned. I've been here volunteering ever since.

Right now I'm on general assistance, and I have applied for social security insurance, but that sure is taking a long time. I can work but any employer has to understand that there are times when I get severe headaches. There are times when I have lots of doctors' appointments to keep. And then there's the cost of my medical needs and medication. The medication is not cheap. My doctors recently took me off AZT and put me on DDI, which costs about a hundred dollars a month. Right now I can't afford that, so I'm not taking it.

I have a roommate, so we share the cost of rent for our apartment. If I need anything, all I have to do is ask around Glide. Someone is always ready to help me, but asking is hard for me to do.

Working here makes me feel useful. Doing something to help other people is one of the ways I keep myself emotionally healthy. I volunteer here because I want to be here; no boss is forcing me to be here every day. I answer phones, talk to people when they come in, direct them to one of the counselors when they need to talk in-depth with someone.

I do whatever needs to be done. A few weeks ago someone who attends the Sunday Celebrations came up to me and said that she had a friend who lived in small-town America whose son has AIDS. She asked me to gather some information together for her to send to her friend. I gathered the information together, but it seemed so impersonal. I decided to write a personal letter to that man's parents, even though I didn't know who they were or where they lived.

Maybe at the time I was wishing I could say to my family the things I was writing to this man's family. I took out a piece of paper and a pen and started writing. I didn't know what I was going to say, but the words flowed out easily:

Dear Concerned Parents,

My name is Mark. While I don't know how you feel or what you're going through, I do know what your son is going through. I am 26 years old. I was diagnosed with HIV in 1985. Three weeks ago, my doctor told me that he was changing my status to disabling ARC.

My health I have learned to deal with. The hardest part of this illness is being isolated, ignored, and unwelcomed by my family. I urge you, please do not do this to your son.

However he acquired the virus should not be of any concern. Your concerns should be centered around his health, your relationship with him, and, above all, your love and support.

I have enclosed some literature and brochures. I hope that they will be of some assistance. I have modified one of them; I believe it will be more appropriate.

If you need anyone to talk to, you can write to me or call me at work. Also, your local clergy and AIDS organizations are excellent sources of support. Don't be embarrassed or ashamed. You are not the only parents with a son who has this illness. Love, care for, and support him. Live his life with him today, for tomorrow may not come.

I do hope to hear from you. If not, may God be with your family and guide you through the shadows of doubt.

Best wishes,

Mark.

I gave the woman my letter, and after she read it, a copy of it was given to Cecil and Janice. They asked me to read it aloud during the Sunday Celebration on World AIDS Day, December 1, 1991. I did, and then people from Glide started calling me asking for copies of the letter to give to friends who have family members affected by AIDS.

I'm glad my letter has been helpful to someone. I only wish that I could find a way to offer a message to teenagers, too. I would like to say one thing to teenagers who are curious about AIDS—I would tell them not to have sex. Period. Practicing safer sex helps reduce the risk, but it isn't 100 percent effective.

Still I know that when I was a teenager, if some adult told me not to have sex, I probably would have gone right out and had sex just because they told me not to. Maybe telling teenagers to practice safer sex works better; it might get them to do some serious thinking about sex before they go out and do something that could mess up their lives forever.

There is one thing about AIDS—you don't know how long you have to live. You don't know when the virus is going to get you; so if someone you love has AIDS, just be with him or her. That is what I want people to do for me—just be there.

Community: The Church and HIV/AIDS

In the fall of 1991 I flew to Atlanta to address a convention organized by the women's group of the Southern Christian Leadership Convention about HIV/AIDS and the church. The conference leaders had invited representatives from black churches in the greater metropolitan area to attend. The first day of the conference was a Thursday and about forty people showed up. I was disappointed. The conference leader told me, "I don't know what is wrong with the African American community. Church folks just don't turn out for things like this."

Later that same day Earvin "Magic" Johnson made the stunning announcement on national television that he was HIV positive. On Friday the crowd at the SCLC more than doubled, as many ministers, both male and female, snuck in for the second day of the conference.

It took Earvin Johnson's announcement to wake up the black community. It took the most famous basketball player, a cultural hero, to wake up our society. He woke up everybody to the fact that HIV/AIDS isn't out there somewhere; it is upon us.

I told the ministers in Atlanta that day about a hospital visit that I had recently made. I had stopped in to visit a man with AIDS who had been raised in the Christian church yet had not entered the doors of any church for many years. The man's mother asked if I would visit him. Her son had not gotten up from his bed for days. When I walked through the door, I could tell that this man was wary of me. I decided to try something I hadn't done in years. I opened my Bible and read from the first chapter of Genesis, "Now God said, Let us make humankind in our image, after our likeness . . . So God created humankind in God's own image . . ."

I closed my Bible and simply said to this man, "If I am made in the likeness of God, so are you."

He shook his head, "But I'm gay."

I looked him straight in the eyes and said, "If I am created in the likeness of God and I'm a human being, that means you are made in the likeness of God, too. You are my brother in humanity. You are made in the likeness of God."

Now this man had been told all of his life that he had a quirk, that he was awful, that he must feel guilty, that he had a sickness that could only be healed by becoming heterosexual. He had come to believe that God didn't love him.

I repeated the words again. "You are made in the likeness of God."

This man's hardened look crumbled. He visibly relaxed as if a slab of concrete had been lifted from his shoulders.

We chatted for a while and then I left. Later that day that man's mother called me. Her voice sang with joy when she told me, "I don't know what you said to my son, but he's been up out of bed, rearranging his room, humming, and looking out the window."

I rejoiced with this man's mother. I hadn't done anything other than to tell this man the truth. The truth freed him to embrace his life. The truth always frees people.

So much of the church has spent so much time pointing a finger at groups of people, like homosexuals or Crack addicts, out of a belief that because they behave differently, somehow God stops loving them. Thinking that others aren't spiritual people created by God because they aren't exactly like us is an untruth. Believing that is believing a lie.

The Spirit isn't concerned with one's skin color or sexual orientation; the content of one's character is what counts. It's who we are and how we live our lives in relationship to other people that matters. God loves people who are embracing the Spirit and seeking recovery, but God also loves those who remain closed to change. God's love has no boundaries.

The church is the only place I've been that told me to never give up on myself and on the dream that the world could be a place where everyone made in the likeness of God could live deeply and honestly. But the church hasn't always lived up to the dream. That's why the church needs recovery.

Some of the ministers at the SCLC cornered me and tried to quote scriptures to prove that HIV/AIDS is God's punishment for gays, drug users, or promiscuous people. My blood boiled and my eyes flashed with anger when I said firmly, "The God I serve does not punish people. Our God is a God of compassion."

My blood still boiled the next Sunday when I returned home. I preached with an edge in my voice.

Every once in a while something happens in history that symbolizes the fact that our eyes, ears, and hearts have been closed to the suffering of humanity. We have not heeded those who have no fame or wealth, those who have died in isolation, or those whose cries have been unheard.

When Magic Johnson said before the world that he had HIV, he was flung into history to make a difference. He could have easily gone to some big public relations firm and said, "Protect me, cover me up. Make sure the public thinks I have something other than AIDS. I'll pay you whatever you need."

Instead of doing that, Earvin Johnson admitted that he is human. He took the "magic" out of his name for a moment and faced his finiteness. He's finite just like every other human being. Nobody is infinite.

Earvin did what we have been trying to do at Glide. He went public with his pain and his problems. He told the real story. He was honest about his life.

Earvin Johnson played in the National Basketball Association for twelve years. In those twelve years his greatest talent was in making assists. He made 9,921 assists. An assist takes place when one player helps another to score.

When Magic dribbled down the court, he always kept his eyes on his teammates. He knew where they were, and when he had the ball, he somehow could find the one in the clear who was able to score. He had this amazing way of looking one way and throwing the ball perfectly in the opposite direction. He had an uncanny ability to assist others so the team would win.

On last Thursday, Magic stood before the world and made an assist like we have never had before. He lifted us all. By telling the world, he made sure that something good comes out of his suffering. To use a church word, Magic was "ministering" last Thursday. He was helping others by telling the truth.

It's time for all of us to open our mouths and tell the truth. It is time for us to open our eyes so that we can see, open our ears so that we can hear, open our hearts so that we can love.

In this church there are people who have said nothing about this disease, but today I want each of you to leave here and tell everyone that you meet that there is a church on the corner of Taylor and Ellis streets whose people are going to reach out to everybody who has HIV/AIDS. We are going to embrace our brothers and sisters, whoever they are. The real church is made up of those who can be trusted. Real church folks are courageous. The church is found wherever folks are who are willing to sit with those who suffer and give love to those who have no love. The church is that group of people who are different because we act, feel, and live differently in relationship to our brothers and sisters. The church is made up of those people who offer unconditional love. The church is found when people decide they will not desert their friends or their children, no matter how sick they are.

A long time ago at Glide we decided we would not let anyone with HIV/AIDS go through our doors without support and help.

Next week we are going to extend our commitment to y'all. I want everybody here this morning to see something. See this bag that I'm holding here in my hand? This is a safer-sex kit. Starting next Sunday we are going to start handing out these kits to the congregation. Each week these will be available in Freedom Hall after the services. Also starting next week we will offer free, confidential HIV testing during the church services. If you haven't been tested, go on upstairs to the fifth floor. Everybody here needs to have proper information and proper protection. Your life matters to us. HIV/AIDS is a terrible disease. We must all do what we can to stop the spread of HIV.

The safer-sex kit I held in my hand that Sunday contained information about AIDS and the GGAP as well as condoms and other protective shields for various risky sexual practices.

Most of the congregation applauded. Many of those who didn't like what I said called me up, sent letters during the week, or asked to speak privately with me. The national media also started lining up to talk to me. The idea of offering HIV/AIDS tests and safer-sex kits on Sunday during church somehow was newsworthy.

But it wasn't congregational approval or news coverage that I was after. I simply had seen too much needless suffering. I'd seen so many vital men and women die young. We had too many babies with limited futures being born to mothers infected with HIV.

Just as I had known that Glide had to do everything we could to help the Crack addicts in our community, we also had to do whatever we could to inform, educate, and give our young the tools to protect themselves from HIV before it was too late.

As I preached that week, little did I know then that the next person at Glide whom we would need to embrace and rock in the bosom of the church would be Louis Ashley, director of the GGAP.

During Thanksgiving week Louis couldn't keep food down. His doctor prescribed some medication, but it made him high. The night before Thanksgiving Louis was hospitalized, and he deteriorated fast.

Early the next week, I was working at home, trying to recuperate from our Thanksgiving week frenzy of serving six thousand meals and offering special services when I got a call that Louis had suffered a stroke and was on life support.

I got in my car and drove to Berkeley where he was hospitalized. When I got there, one of the nurses recognized me and said, "Is Louis Ashley some important person? A prominent black minister from Oakland, two city supervisors, and now you have come to see him today. And this crowd of people, black and white, keep showing up to see him."

I nodded and said, "Yeah, Louis Ashley is a very important person. He is the director of the Glide/Goodlett AIDS Project. He's a member of the Glide family."

When I got inside Louis's room, an oxygen mask covered his nose and mouth, and his eyes were closed. I'd been told he wasn't able to respond.

I began reading stories from the Bible to Louis. I read of the blind man whom Jesus healed. I read the words: "A blind man was sitting by the roadside begging, and hearing a multitude going by, he inquired what this meant. They told him, 'Jesus of Nazareth is passing by.' And he cried, 'Jesus, Son of David, have mercy on me.'"

Right then I stopped reading, reached out, grabbed Louis's limp hand, and said, "Louis, did you hear that? Jesus is with you, Louis. Healing and mercy are available, Louis."

Louis clenched my hand and waved our hands vigorously side to side in affirmation. I knew Louis was testifying with his hand; if he had been able to talk, he would have been shouting and singing and dancing. I'd heard and seen him do it before.

That Bible story was Louis's story. In that moment, despite the doctor's words to me that Louis probably was unresponsive, Louis proved that his Spirit was very present and steadfast.

The next week Louis was still hooked up to life support; only the pumping of machines kept his body functioning. The doctors honored the wishes of his family and friends and unhooked the life support system. The doctors told those who gathered for his final hours that it would probably be only minutes until Louis breathed his last breath, but Louis held on.

Members of his immediate family and extended family from Glide kept vigil. Gospel music was played continuously. More than nine hours later Louis died.

A week later, after the Sunday celebration, the Glide family gathered to remember Louis. For years Louis had fought to break through the denial in the black community about AIDS and homosexuality. Now Louis's work was done. Others would now carry on, building upon his legacy of compassion and his commitment to full acceptance for all God's people in the church.

IT'S COMPASSION TIME

People have asked me why I consider AIDS to be a recovery issue. Why spend so much time and energy on a group of people who probably won't be around long?

Well, that's what others had said about Crack addicts: "Let them go. They are too far gone."

My answer has been and will always remain the same: "*We can't let them go. We won't let them suffer alone, for these are our folks. These are our brothers and sisters. These are our family.*"

Glide's family includes those who are isolated and alone, fragmented and hurting. A lot of people feel that no one cares about them. They believe from previous bad experiences that the church is not concerned about them. They think that the church is only concerned about them when they are good, successful, and have money to give. When they get sick, they long to be honest and to say, "I'm sick," "I've got AIDS," "I'm scared," "It hurts." But they think that nobody will listen.

The silence of churches, synagogues, and mosques across the nation—the refusal to listen with love—serves to push aside people with HIV/AIDS. The church, and that means all people, must stop pushing away our brothers and sisters with AIDS; we must stop trying to put them out of our lives and out of our families. The church is supposed to be about bringing people into the community. The church is supposed to bring people together, not to leave them out in the cold. The church is to be a place of healing.

And that's what people with HIV and AIDS need. That's what Crack addicts need. That's what we all need.

We need the church to respond with compassion. No other group can offer the Spirit—that's what the church has, and in Spirit and in truth the church can offer recovery and healing.

We can't get caught up in theology. It's time to get caught up with compassion.

With love.

Love bears all things.

Love believes all things.

Love hopes all things.

Love endures all things.

If any of you have any inclination or desire to turn your backs on your brothers and sisters, turn around. Face your brothers and sisters with compassion.

It's compassion time.

▲ ▲ ▲

An Attitude of Recovery

Now, there is only one Glide; it can't be duplicated. Yet the Glide attitude is one that can be chosen and adapted to any church, community, or city. Anyone, especially you, can take the risk of telling the truth and living in the Spirit.

Begin today. Take a chance on yourself. Risk extending a hand and being honest with your brothers and sisters. Put your whole life into the present moment. Let go of the past and take your eyes off of the future.

To cultivate the Glide attitude you must first come to see that all people are made in God's likeness. Then you must begin to wrestle with your previous conclusions and labels about people. Perhaps you once thought you could identify who was "in" with God and who was "out" by categorizing people.

Maybe you thought drug addicts or gay people were "out" no matter the content of their hearts or character. Perhaps you thought that white, middle-class, or married people probably were "in" regardless of the quality of their love or care for one another.

Our appearances or labels are not what count with God or with one another; it's who we are and how we live our lives that truly matter.

Over the years, people have labeled me as a crazy minister, a touched man, or a holy fool. None of what others call me matters much. What matters is that I live out the likeness of God that is found in my humanity. I must be who God created me to be. So must you.

The kind of attitude I'm talking about leads to true spirituality, which is discovered through self-revelation and self-definition. The power of the Spirit is set free when the truth is exposed. When someone stands up and tells the truth, others can feel it. The divine likeness that we all share enables us to recognize the truth and the Spirit when they are shared. When the truth is felt, the Spirit moves to action those who hear the truth. Living rightly, acting in love and then reflecting, is more important than believing any certain way.

Telling the truth does something to you. Have you tried it lately?

Telling the truth builds community; it creates a new extended family where people can find love and healing. It is critical for hurting people to know it is okay to stand up and be vulnerable. If we're honest we must admit that no one in the world, however downtrodden, has done anything so terrible that the rest of us wouldn't do it or at least think about it if put in his or her circumstances for a while.

Once a community catches the Glide attitude, it is natural to want to share it. The gift that the Glide attitude offers is the ability to survive. This gift allows me and you to carry on, endure, and live through suffering. This gift tells me never to give up.

Many years ago, when I was a boy, my mother and my father took me to the church, and the church was the only place that ever told me never to give up. Through the testimonies, the stories, the songs, and the hardship, I heard the community saying, *Look, we have to live across the tracks and deal with racism and segregation. We don't have good jobs. We don't always have enough to eat or decent clothes to wear, but you are goin' to go to school, boy. You are going to learn something. You are going to be somebody. Don't you ever give up. Don't ever give in. Keep on goin'. One of these days things will be different.*

The belief of that community propelled me on. Today the New Generation of young people needs a community like that, too.

I have a need to survive; so do you. Those of you who have been through addiction or incest, just think about the fact that you are still here. You somehow have held on to a thin thread of survival. Keep on living one day at a time. If you did it today, you can do it tomorrow.

To survive means to choose life every moment and every day. Hold on, don't give up. Choose life, then offer the gift you have to your community.

When we as a community of people in recovery offer what we have together, then everything begins to change.

I especially believe that the African American community has something important to offer to our troubled society. Because of the fact of slavery, because of the truth that our ancestors tilled the soil and in many instances died because of inclement weather and beatings and humiliation, we've learned the importance of faith and resistance.

In the end our ancestors held fast to something that allowed them to survive, to choose to live, love, and go on. They made sure that they never gave up.

My grandfather, who was an ex-slave, once told me, "I could have given up a long time ago, but I had to make sure that my sons and my daughters made it somehow. I wanted to do what I could to make sure my grandsons and granddaughters made it somehow. I had a strategy for survival."

The community at Glide is committed to seeing the New Generation survive. But we also want more than survival for them and for ourselves.

There is more to life than just making it. We want liberation and empowerment for all. Liberation means choosing freedom. Empowerment means claiming your power to change.

The power of decision allows movement; it lets us move beyond what we have always been and lets us change and do things we have never done before. We can overcome some things we have never overcome before. That's when recovery takes place.

We need to keep telling those all around us who are caught in addiction, "You can be stronger than before. You can turn in a new direction. If you've been beaten down all your life, those beaten-down days are over. Stand up for yourself."

Liberation is really redemption. You reclaim your life and live it. You release your brothers and sisters to be themselves.

Liberation is not the loss of tradition; it is the renewal of a lost tradition. I think some of the early Christians and Jews might have acted like some of us act at Glide. In the early Christian era people of different classes and races came together.

Glide also hearkens back to the Early American underground railroad, which told those who were caught in slavery, "You don't have to be a slave any longer; there is a freedom train and we will help you catch it."

There are still so many people who are waiting for the freedom train. They are just inches away from being captured by addiction, violence, and victimization.

The underground railroad, yesterday and today, works because of faith and resistance. Faith and resistance are the fuels that power the train of freedom and transformation.

Young folks, middle-aged folks, and old folks addicted to Crack or mired in misery need to know that they can be free. The freedom train passes by where each of us lives. We all can catch it. There is room on that train for me and for you. There is a seat reserved for each of us.

Black, red, yellow, brown, and white folks, street folks, hustlers, and those who secure themselves behind their money—all need to catch a new train.

As a people and as a society we've been going in the wrong direction for too long. We've believed that the differences and the social problems that divide us are unsolvable. We have waited too long for a savior to come from afar. We are the ones we have been waiting for. It is up to us to break free and extend a hand to others who long to be free themselves.

Today I say to you, *go down and catch the freedom train for yourself. Then reach out your hand to your brothers and sisters and bring them on into freedom, too.*

I remember when I used to ride the train with my brothers when I was a kid. One time my mother gave my brothers and me a brown bag full of chicken and biscuits. We were going to ride seventy-five miles or so across Texas.

The conductors lead us to the Colored car and pulled the curtain. As the curtain hid us from the view of the white folks in the other cars, my brothers and I started laughing. The conductor and all those white folks couldn't figure out why we were laughing; they probably thought we were crazy. But we laughed because we knew that we were free. That curtain had not closed off our lives. That curtain did not take away our choice to be who we were. That curtain did not take away our humanity; it only tried to hide it, to beat us down.

But the likeness of God, the Spirit born deep inside us, could not be shut out. We knew that curtain would be pulled back one of these days. Someday things would be different.

Decades later we still have much to do to pull back that curtain for ourselves and for our brothers and sisters. I still have a long way to go as a recovering person. Glide has a long way to travel, too. You and yours probably do too.

As for me, I'm going to keep on moving.

Join me and the New Generation—we are already on board and traveling toward our freedom. The train of freedom and recovery chugs on daily. Claim your place on this train.

The freedom train is passing by you. Catch it.

Then listen. Listen carefully. Those on the train are singing. Can you hear the voices of the New Generation? They are singing and shouting with unchained abandoned.

Lift your voice; raise your fist.

You sing, too.

There's no hidin' place down here.
There's no hidin' place down here.
Oh, I went to the rock to hide my face.
The rock cried out, "No hidin' place."
There's no hidin' place down here.

▲　▲　▲

Glide's Facts on Crack[*]

The Psychological Symptoms of Crack Use

When you smoke Crack, certain things will happen to your brain, your emotions, your spirit, and your behavior. The more you use, the more messed up you will get. *This is a natural fact.*

Whether it's your first hit or your thousandth hit, at least two of the following will happen to you within one hour.

1. You will get very high. You will feel indescribably good (euphoria).
2. You will start twitching or making nervous moves (psychomotor agitation).
3. You will think you are the baddest person on earth, capable of doing damn near anything (grandiosity).
4. You will run your mouth and talk shit (loquacity).
5. You will have your highbeams on. You will be overly alert. You will be watching everybody and everything (hypervigilance).

If you start taking larger doses or if you start using over an extended period of time, there is a real chance you will suffer cocaine psychosis. In other words, *you can go crazy.* If you slide into cocaine psychosis, some or all of the following things will happen to you.

1. You will not know the difference between what is real and what is in your mind (break with reality).
2. You will become fearful and suspicious of everyone, including those closest to you. You will think that everyone is out to take you off (paranoia).
3. You will start feeling anxious and nervous just about all the time (agitation).
4. You will have a chip on your shoulder, you will talk and act like you want to kick everybody's ass—all the way from your loved ones to the police (belligerence).
5. You will start seeing things (visual hallucinations).

---

[*]This information is excerpted from Glide's Facts on Crack brochure. Copyright © 1991 by Glide Memorial Church. Used by permission.

6. You will start hearing things, especially human voices talking to you or about you (auditory hallucinations).
7. You will start tasting things that aren't there, especially the rock itself (gustatory hallucinations).
8. You will start feeling things that aren't there, like the sensation of bugs crawling on your skin (tactile hallucination).
9. You will start carrying and using weapons.
10. You will not be able to stand light (photophobia). You will stay up and out all night. When the sun rises you will slink inside. The "Dracula Syndrome."

Crack will make you forget about your need for sleep, food, water, and sex. You will forget about your mama, you daddy, your man, your woman, your kids. The only thing that will matter is your next hit.

Once you have smoked up all your money and the Crack has run out, you will slip into the Post-Cocaine State. These are things that can happen.

1. You will sink into deep depression.
2. You will be nervous and agitated just about all the time.
3. You may try to fight the depression by using one or more downers like alcohol, Quaaludes, or heroin. Many Crackheads also become addicted to whatever they take to fight post-cocaine depression.
4. You may continue to "hear voices" and have other hallucinations up to one month after your last hit.
5. To yourself and others you will minimize your actual use. You will say you've done two 10's when you've really done five.
6. You will run a game on yourself and others by saying that you can control your use. *Don't believe it.*
7. You will lose your sense of self-esteem. You will think you're worthless.

The Physical Effects of Using Crack

If you smoke Crack, certain things will happen to your body *no matter who you are*.

1. Your heart rate will increase.
2. Your blood pressure will increase.
3. Your breathing rate will increase.
4. Your body temperature will increase.
5. Your blood vessels will be squeezed smaller, making your heart work harder and faster.
6. You will lose your appetite; you will become a skeleton.
7. You will lose sleep.
8. The electrical signals from your brain to your body—especially your heart and your lungs—will be affected. You can become paralyzed.
9. You may have loss of hair.

10. Your teeth may dissolve or decay.
11. Your complexion can change (skin gets darker).
12. You may experience blurred vision and memory loss.
13. Long-term smoking can cause your lungs to collapse.
14. You are wide open for seizures, heart attacks, and psychosis.

If you smoke Crack, you are taking a chance on any of the following things happening to you.

1. Chest pains and straight-up heart attack.
2. Irregular heart beat—your heart may stop altogether.
3. Brain seizures.
4. Ruptured blood vessels in your brain, causing a stroke.
5. Because Crack cocaine is an anesthetic (a painkiller) it can hide pain and discomfort that is supposed to warn you that something is wrong with your body. You may not even be able to feel what is happening to you.

If you are a woman and smoke the pipe, any one of these things can mess you up.

1. Your menstrual cycle can be completely disrupted. Your periods may stop. Or you may have excessive bleeding or clotting.
2. You may have loss of breast fullness (Crack depletes the body of fluids).
3. Usual premenstrual symptoms such as headaches, dizziness, sleeplessness, body aches, irritability are extremely intensified, even if you don't have a period.
4. You may lose or have painful urinary functions.

If you are pregnant and smoke Crack, here are things that could happen to you and your baby.

1. If you smoke during the early stages of pregnancy, you have a higher risk of miscarriage or of your baby being born dead.
2. If you smoke during the later stages of pregnancy, you have a higher risk of premature labor and premature delivery.
3. Your baby could have a stroke while still inside you.
4. Your baby could have a heart attack after being born.
5. Your baby could have deformed kidneys and sex organs, and will have a higher risk of brain seizures and crib death.
6. If you use the rock and nurse your baby, you can pass your Crack habit on to your baby.
7. Smoking Crack can cause massive hemorrhaging and death to you and your baby.

This section has been compiled through the research and life experience of WOMEN ON THE MOVE, a women's prevention, intervention, and recovery program of Glide Church. WOMEN ON THE MOVE works with women of all ages addicted to Crack.

▲ ▲ ▲

Glide's Facts on AIDS*

It's Education Time

2 out of every 5 people with AIDS are people of color.
1 out of every 2 women with AIDS is black.
4 out of every 5 kids with AIDS are black or Latino.

AIDS is a disease caused by a virus called **HIV.** HIV breaks down your immune system—that part of your body that protects you from getting sick. When your immune system isn't working well, you can get many diseases.
Here's how you can get AIDS.

1. Having vaginal or anal sex without a condom (rubber).
2. Shooting drugs with someone else's needles.
3. Swallowing someone's semen (cum) or having it in your mouth.
4. Using someone else's sex toys internally.
5. Swallowing fluid from the vagina.
6. A pregnant woman can give it to her baby.
7. There's a small chance with a blood transfusion.

Here's how you can't get AIDS.

1. Everyday contact with people with AIDS.
2. Swimming in a pool with someone with AIDS.
3. Mosquito or other insect bites.
4. Shaking hands, hugging, being in a crowded elevator.
5. Contact with saliva, tears, sweat, urine, or feces.
6. Kissing.
7. Donating blood.
8. Eating food handled by a person with AIDS.
9. From a toilet seat.

---

*Information excerpted from Glide's Facts on AIDS brochure. Copyright © 1991 by Glide Memorial Church. Used by permission.